7960
8158

o/s

£10.00

A PEOPLE'S CONSCIENCE

STRATHEARN GORDON

and

T. G. B. COCKS

A
PEOPLE'S
CONSCIENCE

With a frontispiece after
EUGÈNE LAMI

CONSTABLE & CO LTD
LONDON W·C·2

LONDON
PUBLISHED BY
Constable and Company Ltd
10—12 ORANGE STREET W.C.2

·

INDIA AND PAKISTAN
Orient Longmans Ltd
BOMBAY   CALCUTTA   MADRAS

·

CANADA
Longmans, Green and Company
TORONTO

·

SOUTH *and* EAST AFRICA
Longmans, Green and Company Ltd
CAPETOWN   NAIROBI

First published 1952

MADE AND PRINTED IN GREAT BRITAIN BY
WILLIAM CLOWES AND SONS, LIMITED, LONDON AND BECCLES

CONTENTS

A NOTE ON THE FRONTISPIECE

THE frontispiece to this volume is reproduced from an album of twenty-eight lithographs, after drawings by Eugène Lami and Henri Monnier, entitled *Voyage en Angleterre* and published in 1829. The Paris imprint was Didot Frères, and the London imprint Colnaghi. Each plate in this beautiful and much sought-after album is accompanied by a paragraph of text, and the following is an extract from the text attached to plate 19 : *Rentrée des Watchmen*. It is interesting how closely Lami's comment, written in the mid-eighteen-twenties, approximates to the description of the old police presented in Chapter III of *A People's Conscience*.

'As dawn breaks the watchmen from each quarter of the town crawl home after their all-night vigil over the safety of London. They are for the most part ailing old men, armed only with a pole or a walking-stick. Such effectiveness as they possess derives from their numbers and from a vague sense of their legal authority.

'At the slightest alarm each man can summon his nearest colleague by sounding a rattle; but normally their only duty is to cry the hour every twenty minutes, as though they were clocks walking in the silent darkness.

'Already these watchmen are figures of the past. They will never again be seen save in comedies of manners and old-style plays and novels. A new police force, modelled on the police of Paris, has been created; and these sad old men in their grey coats, with their dark lanterns and rattles, have passed like phantoms into the shadows of a vanished London.'

I

THE COMMITTEE MEET

Go further, Gurney, and thy wondrous Toil,
Shall print the Sigh, and imitate the Smile.
ERASMUS DARWIN

TO BE a witness before Parliament is a rare and intimidating experience. In the course of this century only two such men have stood at the bar of the House of Commons, and they, as well as the whole concourse who stared at them, were obviously aware that their answers were being given at the bar of history. In the committee rooms the experience is uncommon enough to be almost as disturbing and, inevitably, more prolonged. The witness may be called on to answer not one but some fifteen investigators, among them perhaps the greatest lawyers and statesmen of the day. To that extent the process is more arduous than in a court of law. As a rule, too, the witness has no previous guidance, no counsel to object and to intervene on his behalf, no indication of the line he ought to take. As he speaks, the witness can see that every word of his answer is being recorded. His evidence will be retained for ever in the archives and libraries of the State. It is not too much to claim that by their patent honesty—or dishonesty—witnesses before Committees of Parliament have influenced the course of history. In spite of the tremendous significance of such occasions, the witnesses called may be neither learned nor fluent. They are not even subject to those strangely

assorted disqualifications which apply to members themselves. Evidence has at times been sought from minors and
peers, bankrupts and aliens, felons and even lunatics. The
voices of some of those who underwent the ordeal of
examination by committees of the House of Commons are
heard again in this book. For most of them their testimony
is the only memorial which now remains, but, as will appear
from the accounts which follow, they did not always speak
in vain.

Much of the work of Parliament is unknown to, though
not secret from, the nation outside. To a certain extent the
actual debates in the Chamber are known. A fraction of the
population hears them from the public gallery. Others read
them in the Official Report or in ruthlessly abridged form in
the Press. But some of Parliament's most enduring work is
done outside the Chamber, in the great range of committee
rooms upstairs. Most people have but the haziest ideas of
what takes place in these committees. Actually there are,
apart from Committees of the whole House—which, as the
name suggests, imply the entire House of Commons sitting
in their Chamber under a different name—four kinds of
committees. There are large Standing Committees, usually
of forty or more members, whose main business is to consider bills referred to them by the House. At the other end
of the scale are Private Bill Committees, each a court
on its own, composed of only four members carefully
chosen for their impartiality upon the matter at stake, before
whom counsel argue for and against a Private Bill (a measure
for the advantage of some locality, person or body of persons, as distinct from a Public Bill, which is of national
concern).

Intermediate in size are Select Committees upon other
types of bills and Select Committees upon matters of public
interest. It is the last kind of committee which concerns us.
For hundreds of years it has been the practice of the House
of Commons when any subject of interest and importance
seems to merit investigation, and perhaps legislation, and

where evidence should be heard and tested, to delegate the inquiry to a small number of its members—nowadays about fifteen, sometimes fewer, occasionally more. (We are in this volume particularly concerned with the House of Commons, but many valuable Select Committees have been appointed by the House of Lords and the two Houses have often held a combined investigation by means of a joint committee.)

The reason for resorting to the use of committees is purely one of convenience. We have said that even to this day the House of Commons on great occasions summons witnesses to its Bar and there examines them through the mouth of its Speaker, and in older, more leisurely days the practice was frequent, but for inquiries of any length the normal method was a Select Committee. For how many witnesses could do themselves justice in the intimidating presence of the House? And how could 600 members conveniently interrogate them?

But before pursuing our particular branch of committees it may be of interest to glance at the completer picture of the development of parliamentary committees generally. At the outset it is curious to note that originally a 'committee'—like a 'trustee'—was an individual member to whom the matter of inquiry (generally a bill) was entrusted, and only later was the word applied to the body of such members collectively.

Parliamentary committees date back a very long way. The Triers and Examiners of Petitions, first appointed in the reign of Edward I, may be looked upon as the precursors of committees; while the first duty for which committees were regularly appointed seems to have been the drawing up of statutes in satisfaction of petitions to Parliament which the Crown was disposed to allow. A joint committee of Lords and Commons was appointed for this purpose in 1340. In the following year a committee was set up to investigate the accounts showing how the last subsidy had been spent.[1] Soon after the middle of the sixteenth century, when the Journals of the House of Commons begin and with them our detailed knowledge of the proceedings, committees are seen to be regular and indispensable parts of the procedural machinery, with jurisdiction not only to examine bills but to make inquiries and obtain information.

At first committees met outside the House, either in state buildings such as the Star Chamber in Westminster or in legal centres such as the Temple or Lincoln's Inn; but later a special room called 'the Committee Chamber' was set apart at St. Stephen's. In early days, when the House met in the morning, committees generally met in the afternoon, to avoid clashing, whereas the position nowadays is often reversed. Committee procedure soon acquired its main characteristics, such as the freer atmosphere and the right of each member to speak as often as he wished on any question. At first the quorum was half the membership; later specific numbers were fixed. At an early date committees branched into bodies of three to fifteen members, to become the Select Committees which are the subject of this book; and bodies of thirty to forty, sometimes with the addition of whole classes, such as all the 'gentlemen of the long robe'—lawyers—in the House, all its Privy Councillors, all members from North of the Trent, from the Cinque Ports, etc. The larger committees were first formed to consider highly important matters, then definite classes of bills or subjects were referred to them every session, and eventually they became the five historic 'grand' or 'standing' committees on religion, privileges and elections, grievances, trade, and courts of justice, which endured until the nineteenth century. In practice these became Committees of the whole House, since 'all who came' were to 'have voices'. These bodies gradually absorbed almost all the legislative work of the House away from the small Select Committees to whom it had from earliest times been confided. After 1882 such work was divided between true Committees of

1 Most of these facts may be found in Redlich's *The Procedure of the House of Commons.*

the whole House and modern Standing Committees, which today consist of about forty members each and only consider bills and Scottish estimates of expenditure.

Although for our purposes we may disregard all but the smaller type of Select Committee mentioned first above, it is difficult to disentangle their separate history in early days, since some of their powers were first granted to other types of body. In 1640, for instance, the Journal shows the entry: 'Ordered that all committees of the whole House to have power to send for parties' (i.e. witnesses). A strange experiment developed during the Civil War, when Special Committees of the House of Commons, formed from the Puritan majority only, were appointed to carry on the *administrative* government of the country. The experiment has never been repeated.

*

Confining our attention to Select Committees, then, and of those only committees of investigation into special matters of general importance (apart from such matters as privilege and disputed elections), we find that the main developments in the nineteenth century related to size and method of appointment and to the presentation of their work. The normal membership, which had grown to twenty-one, was reduced again to fifteen, and it was laid down that the names of members must be regularly published; that every question asked of a witness should be prefixed by a number and by the name of the member asking it; and that the minutes of proceedings should show the members who attended at each sitting, what proposals were made and by whom, and how each member voted in any division. Such rules are typical of the sensible attitude which the House of Commons takes to its procedure. These particular reforms notably increased the responsibility of members, presented the evidence upon which they based their report in a clearer and more consistent form, and focused public opinion healthily upon their proceedings. Later improvements were the Parliamentary Witnesses Oaths Act of 1871, which enabled committees of the House of Commons to administer oaths to witnesses called before them, and a new standing order passed in 1875 which strengthened the powers of Select Committees by giving them a general authority, if they had the sanction of the House to send for 'persons, papers and records', to make special reports outside their terms of reference if required.

To this historical introduction it is only necessary to add concerning procedure that three simple principles govern the actions of Select (and indeed of all) Committees. First, that no committee has any powers save those which are delegated to it by the House, and if it wishes to take some action which is not inherently within the powers of all committees, such as to meet at some place outside the Houses of Parliament, or on a day when the House is not sitting, or to report its evidence day by day, then it must first obtain the leave of the House to do any of these things. Secondly, once appointed, the committee is free to pursue its own course without interference, and its proceedings may not be discussed even in the House before it has presented its report. Thirdly, the House is in no way bound by the report; it may be accepted, with or without amendment, rejected, or ignored, exactly as the House thinks fit.

Nowadays the pressure upon the time of the House is so great that all Select Committees of the kind we are describing are only appointed by the considered desire or assent of the Government, though often as the result of pressure by the Opposition or by back-bench members. The chairman is generally a member of the Government party. Formerly, however, when the initiative of private members was almost untrammelled, one of these often moved for and secured the appointment of such a committee, of which he was himself elected to the Chair. When legislation may be required to remedy broad public problems the preliminary investigation is still often remitted to Select Committees. Recent examples have been the Select Committee on Capital Punishment in 1929 and on Shop Assistants in 1930. Internal matters, such as the rebuilding of its own Chamber, destroyed by the enemy in 1941, are also considered by committees of the House from time to time. But the work of examining great national problems and preparing them, if necessary, for legislation has been gradually passing, since the early decades of last century, out of the hands of Parliament.

*

Here then, throughout centuries, a most effective probe has lain in the hands of forceful and energetic individuals and groups of members to investigate injustices and to recommend remedies. They have often been stigmatized as 'fishing committees' and their members as busybodies, nosing into other people's business; but it is hard indeed to find one inquiry which has not been aimed at some definite evil, and even if none has been discovered, that fact alone has proved a useful reassurance.

On the whole the work of these committees has been excellently done. Latterly, at any rate, their membership has been chosen with scrupulous fairness. Whatever the number involved it is allotted in proportion to the parties in the House; and so comprehensive are the abilities of the House of Commons as a whole that it is rare indeed for a committee not to contain at least one expert with the highest qualification upon the subject at issue. The House has never been afraid to appoint to these committees persons holding extreme and opposite views upon the matter to be investigated, in order that, in the resulting clash, the truth or a commonsense compromise might emerge. Party policy, on the other hand, though present, is rarely stressed in a Select Committee, as it is in a standing committee, where it must normally be sustained. Once inside the committee room, therefore, partisanship is largely forgotten, the Committee settle down to amicable and effective discussions, and if there is disagreement concerning the terms of the report to be presented to the House, it by no means always follows party lines.

*

Select Committees have been at work since Parliament began, but their heyday can be said to have lain in the years immediately after the first Reform Act, before the Royal Commission was found to be a better instrument in certain spheres. During the next few decades practically the whole political, social and administrative structure of the country was overhauled. By a fortunate coincidence a notable fraction of the upper-middle and upper classes were at that time gifted with high intellectual attainments, a lively social conscience, abounding energy and the political power to secure reform of the terrible evils which afflicted the poor of Britain at that time. Investigation by Select Committee ranked high among their most powerful weapons, and the numerous and extremely important reports of this period have never been surpassed.

It should be explained here that although in the eighteenth century the Select Committee was almost the only machinery available in the field of inquiry, three rivals have since appeared. The first, the Royal Commission, is a body of great antiquity, traced back by one authority to 1386,[1] but dormant for this purpose until, like so many other organs in the body politic, it awoke about the beginning of the nineteenth century and reappeared as a 'Commission of Inquiry'. The distinction between these Royal Commissions and Select Committees is that they are appointed by the executive government (in form by the Crown) instead of by Parliament, although the initiative sometimes comes in the form of an Address from one or both Houses. They are composed of anything between three and over thirty persons, highly qualified by their knowledge or impartiality to investigate the subject at issue, and who are generally unpaid.

[1] Cox, H., *The Institutions of the English Government*, 1863.

Thus, although a Royal Commission often includes members of both Houses of Parliament, it is predominantly composed of persons unconnected at the time with the executive government, and it is able to preserve a political impartiality impossible to an exclusively political body like a Select Committee. The potential recruiting field for Royal Commissions extends far outside Parliament and includes purely technical specialists, retired persons and persons who either have no interest in politics or have not succeeded in being elected.

The other great advantage of a Royal Commission over a Select Committee is that it usually has leisure to work without interruption. Prorogation (the formal ending of a parliamentary session) drops a curtain on the work of a Select Committee, and although it may be reappointed in the following session and given leave to use any evidence already taken, the personnel of Parliament changes and the practical limit of a Select Committee is two sessions; while a Royal Commission frequently sits for years. There is a corresponding disadvantage in these thorough proceedings, however, in that the investigations of a Royal Commission often outlive their topicality; the public grows heartily sick of waiting for a report and forgets the whole subject. On the whole, however, Royal Commissions have become so useful that their scope and functions have gradually been expanded. Some have semi-executive powers, like the Royal Commission on Historical Manuscripts. Others have semi-judicial powers, like the Royal Commission on Awards to Inventors. It is not surprising, then, that such an efficient and flexible instrument (unmatched incidentally outside Britain) for securing impartial expert inquiry has superseded the Select Committee of busy members of Parliament for long and complicated investigations. Some, indeed, have sat for over fifty years, issuing report after report.

Departmental committees ought to be classed next to Royal Commissions among the organs which have during the last century drawn off much work from Select

Committees. They are fact-finding bodies appointed by a Secretary of State or other Minister to investigate any matter within the scope of responsibility of their Departments. They are usually very small, composed of two or three senior civil servants of the Department concerned, and whereas the reports of Royal Commissions are usually made public, in the case of Departmental committees publication remains at the discretion of the Government. Recent examples of notable Departmental committees have been those which reported on the care of children and on flogging.

Select Committees have also been superseded in a much more restricted field. Whenever the conduct and honour of any of its members were involved, but no criminal proceedings were pending, the matter used to be decided by the House itself or by a Select Committee (which had power to hear sworn testimony). However, when a 'domestic' case arose in 1912 it was unfortunately alleged against the Select Committee which exhaustively examined the matter that it had allowed party feelings to affect its impartiality. The elaborate machinery of a Royal Commission, on the other hand, was not considered suitable for such domestic affairs of the House of Commons. Nor could it, without a special Act of Parliament enabling it to hear evidence on oath, deal with a similar category of cases where, for instance, the conduct of the police is called in question.

To obviate these difficulties, therefore, the Tribunals of Inquiry (Evidence) Act was passed in 1921 to cover both 'domestic' and other cases. Whenever either House of Parliament resolves by means of an Address to the Crown that the Act should be invoked in any definite matter of urgent public importance, a small tribunal may be set up, armed with full powers for the taking of evidence on oath, the production of documents and for compelling the attendance of witnesses, who are, on the other hand, entitled to absolute privilege. The practice where members of Parliament are involved still varies. A tribunal decided the case of a Budget leakage in 1936 and the Belcher case in 1948; in other recent cases Select Committees investigated the conduct of members.

Before entering upon our subject, let us see how the proceedings of these Committees have been so accurately preserved for us across the years. Meetings have sometimes been held in public, sometimes in private; but in either case the reports of the Committees to the House have normally been published with the evidence attached and have become what are known as 'blue books'. But few people have time to do more than glance at a brief résumé of these often cumbrous volumes, or perhaps merely a précis of their conclusions in the Press.

Our knowledge of the proceedings and reports of early Select Committees, let alone of their witnesses and evidence, is haphazard. It depends often upon the chance notes or recollections of a single member. About the middle of the eighteenth century, however, a change began gradually to take place. At that time one Thomas Gurney, who was born in 1705 and died in 1770, the son of a substantial miller, forsook farming for more studious pursuits. He became a clockmaker, and one day at a sale bought an odd lot of books, including a work on Mason's system of shorthand. Brief writing, if not swift writing, had been known to the ancient world from the fourth century B.C., and shorthand continued in use until, early in the eleventh century A.D., it unaccountably faded out of use and lay almost entirely dormant for six centuries. When it revived, at first in the form of cypher, in time for the attempt to reproduce Shakespeare's plays from the stage, its development was hindered by inefficiency, but it gradually gained credit, largely by reporting state trials, not verbatim, but sufficiently to interest the public. It was during this period of slow progress that Mason's book fell into Thomas Gurney's hands. He made himself proficient, came to London to practise in the courts and in Parliament, and was appointed official shorthand writer at the Old Bailey.

Shorthand was just coming into use for official purposes and it was the first appointment of its kind in the world. The pay for this rare and invaluable work was extremely poor, and Gurney continued at his clockmaking until his death.

Although Mason's system, called 'La Plume Volante', was the best of its period, it was too complex to succeed. Thomas Gurney simplified it and published the amended plan under the name of 'Brachygraphy', which, as carried on by his successors, went into eighteen editions. His son Joseph succeeded him both in the law courts and in Parliament, where he saw the method gradually accepted. The Gurneys had many competitors. Twenty-five systems had been published before Thomas produced his book; but whereas many attempted to gain the public's confidence by theoretical arguments about the formation of alphabetical signs, the combination of consonants, the use of 'position' and dots, etc., the Gurneys relied on results. By strenuous practice year after year they made themselves superb shorthand writers. In the early years imagination was needed as well as assiduity. The Gurneys constantly improved their system.[1] The prevalent distrust of shorthand in legal circles and among the public was gradually overcome, principally by experience of the increasingly full and accurate reports of famous trials, at that time unreported by the Press. The Gurneys distanced their competitors in the volume and accuracy of their work. Among their copious publications they reported the trials of the Duchess of Kingston, Lord George Gordon, Warren Hastings, Tom Paine and Horne Tooke; and established the custom of giving verbatim speeches and the uncondensed evidence in the form of question and answer. The sensational evidence titillated the public taste and these publications increased the Gurneys' reputation and the demand for their professional services.

[1] For further details see W. H. Gurney Salter: *A History of the Gurney System of Shorthand*, 1924.

In 1786 Joseph Gurney was engaged to report some Slave Trade inquiries for private parties at the Bar of the House of Lords. He was also engaged by the Managers of the House of Commons to report the proceedings at the trial of Warren Hastings, and with but few exceptions he personally took the report at every one of the 145 sittings during the whole of the protracted trial between 1787 and 1794. Most of his shorthand note is still preserved and perfectly legible. Contemporary observers considered that Sheridan and Burke spoke too rapidly for any shorthand writer to keep pace with them, but Joseph Gurney produced reports which were fully approved. At one point a dispute arose as to whether Burke had accused Sir Elijah Impey of murder and thus exceeded his instructions. Gurney was called to the Bar of the Commons and required to read Burke's exact words. As a result the House passed a resolution of censure upon Burke. It was the first public acknowledgement that action by a court of law or similar body could be based upon the verbal accuracy of shorthand, a practice so familiar today.

In 1791 the House of Commons first used note-takers in a private bill committee, and in the same year Joseph Gurney reported the proceedings in six election committees. In 1802 an Act was passed (based on evidence given by Joseph's son, William Brodie Gurney) authorizing the use of shorthand instead of longhand in all election committees; and after a Select Committee had testified to the great public convenience and economy resulting from its use, the system was applied generally to other committees. In 1806, to avoid the confusion resulting from the employment of different writers, W. B. Gurney was singled out from his rivals and told by the Speaker to consider himself the Shorthand Writer to the House of Commons; and on 18th May, 1813, after seven years of assiduous duty, he was formally appointed to the office for both Houses of Parliament.

The strain of some of the long sittings of early days must have been intense. During the inquiry into the Walcheren expedition fiasco in 1810 in the House itself, W. B. Gurney attended at the Bar. To quote from W. Gurney Salter:

> The House more than once sat all night, and W. B. Gurney took notes all the time. 'One morning about two o'clock,' he says, 'Sir William Emerson gave a long description of the fortifications of Flushing. I dropped asleep, and lost myself completely. I was awoke by being called upon to read the last answer. I said to the witness: 'I am afraid I have lost the last part of your answer. Will you watch it as I proceed?' I read on, and at the end came four lines as well written as the rest, but of which I had no recollection. He said, 'That is the whole.' How I had taken it when asleep I cannot conceive.

Thus the Gurneys consolidated their almost unique position in the world of shorthand. Without influential or official connections or any kind of political influence, one member after another of the family gained and held a gruelling job in face of all competition by merit and intense hard work alone. Before the invention of typewriters the labour was enormous:

> Each member of the staff wrote for three or four hours, and often during the whole sitting of a committee. Every half-hour their books were taken from them to their shorthand readers who dictated from them to longhand writers. These readers had not heard the proceedings, and often did not even know whether the subject would be a Railway Bill or a discussion on Finance, etc., till they opened the note-book; yet they dictated from one part of the notes to a longhand writer on their right hand about a dozen words at a time, and from another part of the notes to another writer on their left. In this way from 2,000 to 2,400 words per hour were transcribed, and the whole was revised by the shorthand writer who took the notes, before the report was sent to the printer.

From near the beginning of the nineteenth century the reports of Select Committees are available, suddenly improved upon all that went before, superbly printed and all arranged in the form of plain question and answer. They show to great advantage beside the execrably small cramped type of contemporary newspapers, even of *The Times*. The process of recording the proceedings of Select Committees is still expertly carried out. Nothing is easier or more natural than for members of a committee intent upon their subject to forget the difficulties of the notetaker sitting silently opposite the witness. When it is remembered that he must recognize and record interjections even from members sitting behind his back; that he must miss no single word of the evidence, upon however abstruse or technical a matter; that he takes the note often for hours together, and must then dictate or supervise the transcription so that the whole may be in the committee's hand in printed form next morning, the work is sufficiently remarkable. But when there is sharp cross-firing, or, as occasionally happens, members in the excitement of the proceedings leave their places at the table to examine maps or exhibits, break up into groups to continue discussing in separate corners—and still an apparently connected and complete report (almost to 'every sigh and smile') appears next morning, then the virtuosity of the achievement is indeed outstanding.

*

It is the purpose of this book, then, to exhibit the interest and importance of this small part of the work of Parliament, predominantly but not exclusively at one period. A few only of the hundreds of these Select Committees can be examined, and two principles have been followed in their selection. First, to choose a representative selection of subjects. There have been a number of investigations of resounding fame, such as that into the South Sea Bubble in 1721 (which made seven reports and resulted in the resignation of the Prime Minister, the expulsion of the Chancellor of the Exchequer from the House of Commons and the suspected suicide of the Joint Postmaster General); or that into the Jameson Raid in 1896–1897; or into the

the Marconi share scandal in 1912–1913. But an attempt has been made to include some of the more celebrated inquiries and some of the lesser ones whose results have nevertheless often proved substantial. Secondly, to adduce no evidence, unless otherwise stated, which is not extracted directly from the proceedings of the Select Committees in question. It would have been easy to expand and embroider the results, especially in the light of later knowledge, by the addition of collateral evidence from sources which were not examined by the Committee. But that would have exceeded the intention, which is to show how much Select Committees have by themselves achieved. When considering their achievement it must be borne in mind that the same subject has usually been repeatedly re-examined at different periods. Reform comes by slow stages, meeting disappointment all the way, and the cases chosen here do not always even form the most important links in the chains of inquiry forged by Select Committees through the years. If these investigations seem unduly concerned with sad, gruesome or unpleasant subjects, the answer is that that is inherent in their purpose: a people's conscience is troubled by evil, not good deeds.

II

THE CASE OF THE NAKED MEN

One driv'n by strong benevolence of soul,
Shall fly, like Oglethorpe, from pole to pole.
POPE (*Imit. of Horace*, Ep. ii)

IN THE year 1722 a handsome, high-principled and well-connected young man of twenty-five named James Edward Oglethorpe was elected to Parliament for the borough of Haslemere. It was a precocious age and he had already held a commission in the British army since the age of fourteen, and then served with distinction as aide-de-camp to Prince Eugène in the campaign against the Turks and the capture of Belgrade in 1717.

Soon after entering Parliament an architect friend of Oglethorpe named Castell, born to a considerable estate, unfortunately fell into debt, was committed to the Fleet Prison, forced against his will into a house where the small-pox was raging, and perished miserably, leaving a numerous young family in destitution. It was in the heart of Sir Robert Walpole's twenty-year-long administration, a brutal and rapacious generation of uncontrolled money-making. The South Sea Bubble had recently burst. Speculation was still rampant. The nation's laws were those of a commercial community, weighted on the side of the creditors. Debtors were expected to pay up or to take the consequences. As in all ages, the vast majority of the population, including members of Parliament, accepted contemporary conditions without protest or even query; but Oglethorpe belonged to that choice band of which every British Parliament mercifully contains at least a handful, who do query and do protest.

On 25th February, 1729, Oglethorpe stood up in the House of Commons and moved for a Select Committee 'to inquire into the state of the gaols of this kingdom, and report the same, with their opinion thereupon, to the House'. He was the spokesman for other public-spirited members, who had also heard of misconduct in the gaols. The House agreed and appointed a large committee including many of its best-known personalities, such as the Chancellor of the Exchequer, the Master of the Rolls, Sir John Astley, Mr. Pulteney, Mr. Pelham, Mr. Dodding-ton, General Wade, Mr. Harley, Sir William Yonge and Mr. Wyndham. They were ordered to meet that very afternoon at five of the clock in the Speaker's chamber, and were granted the fullest powers to send for witnesses and records and to meet whenever and wherever they wished.

Within two days the Committee were at work in the Fleet Prison, off Farringdon Street, and day after day they returned there, examining the officials and prisoners and investigating the premises. They found that the Fleet was a very ancient prison, formerly used for the victims of the Court of Star Chamber and more recently for debtors and contempts of court. The office of warden was created an hereditary freehold by letters patent of Charles II to Sir Jeremy Whichcot and his heirs, in consideration of his rebuilding the prison. But the office fell into unsatisfactory hands and was finally bought for the sum of £5,000 by a certain John Huggins, who, growing old and tired, had disposed of it only the previous August to Dougal Cuthbert and Thomas Bambridge, the reigning warden. Both Hug-gins and Bambridge appeared before the Committee. Ogle-thorpe and his companions also visited the Marshalsea Prison in Southwark and the King's Bench Prison near St. George's Fields, and although they made separate reports on each to the House of Commons, much of the evidence was of necessity repetitive, while certain aspects of prison conditions were only investigated at one or other of the gaols. In order to give as complete a picture as possible, therefore, it will be convenient to make selections from the evidence not as it was chronologically received by the Committee, but as it fits in with the narrative.

The wretched business of farming out the authority was common to all three prisons. At the Marshalsea Sir Philip Meadows, then Knight Marshal of the king's household and therefore in control of the prison, had in 1720 deputed the office to John Darby, gentleman, for life, on condition that he did not sublet it without written consent. The condition was broken; the prison was farmed out to William Acton, butcher, for an annual rent of £400, and, in short, 'to make the profits of the prison arise, to answer the exorbitant rents, no kind of artifice or oppression hath been unpractised.' At the King's Bench Prison the office of 'marshal'[1] was mortgaged and the mortgage subdivided and conveyed to trustees 'of mean circumstances', so that eventually a race of men of straw stood between the actual farmers of misery and any possible legal recourse which their victims might have. Here is a typical specimen of one of these creatures. His name was James Slann and he was footman to one of the mortgagees. Being examined by the Committee he says:

> that he is a nominal trustee for the heirs of Mr. Lenthall. And this examinant being asked, what he means by a nominal trustee, and by whom he was appointed such trustee; he says, he does not know, what a nominal trustee is, nor by whom he was appointed such: and being asked how he knows he is a nominal trustee; he says, he is informed that he is such, but does not know by whom he was so informed.

The Committee were nothing if not thorough in their examination of the prison authorities. The existing marshal

---

1 The more modern terms of keeper and governor have later been used to denote the persons actually in charge of the prison and the prisoners.

of the King's Bench Prison was Richard Mullens, the only tolerably humane governor among the three gaols. He explained how he had applied for the office in 1724, met the mortgagee proprietors at Garraway's coffee-house, and there learnt not only of the huge rent he must pay, but also of some rather surprising additional claims upon him. The annual rent was £800, with a quit-rent annually of £20, and £30 to the chamberlain. But then, before being sworn in, he must also pay a douceur of a hundred guineas to each of the three puisne judges of the court, with suitable gratuities to these needy gentlemen in addition at Christmas. The following conversation then ensued and shows the cynical attitude of the proprietors to their responsibilities.

> The examinant objected to all these demands as too exorbitant, from the impossibility of fairly raising the said sums; to which the said proprietors answered, that if he (Mullens) refused to take the said office on these conditions, many others would gladly accept of this offer; and that the former marshals had made a great deal of money of the said office, and particularly Mr. Machen (his predecessor) and got between 2 and £3,000 by it: this examinant replied, that no person could make such a profit honestly; and if anyone got so much money in the said office, it must be by giving liberty to some of the prisoners: to which the said John and Thomas Martin or one of them answered that he (Mullens) must take his chance for that, for he took the said office with his eyes open.

Against the considerable outgoings Mullens stated that his total annual fees and incomings, to which he was legally entitled, including the sale of profits from his taproom, amounted to only about £350. There remained a gap therefore between these two figures which the gaol governor must endeavour to fill, and if possible to fill to overflowing, by means which the Committee were not slow to discover.

One of the governor's only two legal means of recouping his rent was by fees from the prisoners who were committed

to his custody. For an example of how this system worked
let us return to the Fleet Prison. Here an official table of
fees had been promulgated in 1651. It included sums pay-
able to the warden or governor upon arrival and departure,
to the clerk for making the written entries, to the chaplain,
the chamberlain, the gaoler and the porter, and finally, for a
gallon of wine. The total came to £2 4s. 4d., which would
represent a great deal more today. But when the fees were
being revised by the court of Common Pleas two years previously, in 1727, and Bambridge was ordered to read the
warden's commitment fee, he gave the total sum of
£2 4s. 4d., which the judges accepted as correct, and super-
imposed all the other sums upon it, so that most of them
were paid twice over. Even so, Bambridge was not satisfied;
he ordered the new table of fees (which should have been
publicly displayed in the prison) to be taken down, and
charged what he liked.

The second legal method of raising money was by charg-
ing for various degrees of alleviation from the lowest stan-
dard of accommodation in the prison. Each gaol was usually
divided into a Master's side, where prisoners who com-
manded the means could rent a room or rooms, have his
belongings around him and his meals brought in; and a
common side, where the poorest prisoners were housed
and either brought their own bedding or paid a shilling a
week to the governor for providing it. But by regulation in
the Fleet, for instance, the warden was supposed to furnish
all rooms on the Master's side and to charge a maximum
weekly rent of half a crown to one person only, who should
have the full use of the room. In addition, there were outside the walls of most gaols a number of 'sponging-houses',
often controlled by the governor, where prisoners with
means could be accommodated, if they preferred or if the
gaol were full. Finally, some prisoners were permitted, at
the governor's discretion, to reside outside the prison,
within certain limits and conditions. They had 'the
liberty of the rules' and were supposed to provide a sum in

security for their reappearance. Such were the arrangements
assumed by the law to be in force.

During those spring days of 1729 and 1730 Oglethorpe's
Committee did not spare themselves, but went everywhere
and saw and smelt everything. First to the gloomy Fleet,
where 'the walls are 25 foot high, with pallisadoes on the
top, and in good repair; and no seeming possibility for any
prisoner to escape'.

On the common side are three wards, called the upper
chapel, the lower chapel, and Julius Caesar's, in which 93
persons were confined, who are obliged to lie on the
floor, if they cannot furnish themselves with bedding, or
pay a shilling per week as is provided.[1]
The Lyons' Den and Women's ward, which contain
about 18 persons, are very noisome, and in very ill repair.
There are several rooms in the chapel stairs, for each of
which £5 a year is now paid, but did formerly belong to
the common side, and for which nothing was paid, until
charged by Mr. Huggins at £3 a year each; and on this
floor there are several persons, who are uncertain what
chamber rent they shall be obliged to pay, and are at the
mercy of the warden.

What a burden of anxiety and distress, for those already
hard pressed, that last sentence implies. The tale continues:

In some rooms persons, who are sick of different dis-
tempers, are obliged to lie together, or on the floor: one
in particular, had the small pox, and two women were
ordered to lie with her; and they pay 2s. 10d. each for such
lodging.
The windows of the prison are in very bad repair, to
the great prejudice of the health of the prisoners, though
by a late order of the judges, they ought to have been kept
in good repair by the warden.

---

[1] These extracts are printed as they appear in Cobbett's *Parliamentary History of
England*, Vol. VIII, except that unimportant omissions are not indicated and trifling
alterations have been made for the sake of clarity.

When they came to the Marshalsea the Committee gave figures which enable us to judge exactly what the over-crowding amounted to:

In the common side are now confined upwards of 330 prisoners, most of them in the utmost necessity. Most of the wards are excessively crowded, thirty, forty, nay fifty persons having been locked up in some of them, not six-teen foot square. All last year there were sometimes forty and never less than thirty-two persons locked up in George's ward every night, which is a room of sixteen by fourteen feet, and about eight feet high: the surface of the room is not sufficient to contain that number, when laid down; so that one half are hung up in hammocks, while the others lie on the floor under them. The air is so wasted by the number of persons who breathe in that narrow compass, that it is not sufficient to keep them from stifling, several having in the heat of summer perished for want of air. Every night, at eight of the clock in the win-ter, and nine in the summer, the prisoners are locked up in their respective wards, and from those hours, until eight of the clock in the morning in the winter, and five in the summer, they cannot, upon any occasion, come out, so that they are forced to ease nature within the room, the stench of which is noisome beyond expression.

Who were these unfortunate people and how did they come to this pass? Speaking of the Court of Record of the King's Palace of Westminster, which was one of the courts which fed the Marshalsea, the committee point out that many of the prisoners were so poor as to have been com-mitted for a debt of one shilling only. Proceedings were even taken for *one penny*, and carried on till the costs amounted to over 40*s*., when the debtor was thrown into prison. Nor was such a prisoner ever likely to regain his freedom, for even if the creditor relented the debtor was detained for the gaoler's fees and costs of suit, infinitely greater than the original trifling sum which he had been unable to find. The committee went on to describe the subsequent fate of these unfortunates, and in so doing painted perhaps the saddest picture of the whole inquiry:

The crowding of prisoners together is one great occasion of the gaol distemper; and though the unhappy men should escape infection, or overcome it, yet, if they have not relief from their friends, famine destroys them: all the support such poor wretches have to subsist on is an accidental allowance of pease, given once a week by a gentleman, who conceals his name, and about 30 pounds of beef, provided by the voluntary contribution of the judge and officers of the Marshalsea, on Monday, Wednesday and Friday; which is divided into very small portions of about an ounce and a half, distributed with one fourth part of an halfpenny loaf. Each of the sick is first served with one of those portions, and those that remain are divided amongst the wards; but the numbers of the people in them are so great, that it comes to the turn of each man but about once in fourteen days, and of each woman (they being fewer) once in a week.

When the miserable wretch hath worn out the charity of his friends, and consumed the money which he hath raised upon his clothes and bedding, and hath eaten his last allowance of provisions, he usually in a few days grows weak for want of food, with the symptoms of a hectic fever; and, when he is no longer able to stand, if he can raise 3d. to pay the fee of the common nurse of the prison, he obtains the liberty of being carried into the sick ward, and lingers on for about a month or two, by the assistance of the above-mentioned prison portion, and then dies.

As they filed slowly round the prison the Committee now came face to face with bare and stark starvation. We cannot know how many of them were amazed or horrified to find such conditions in the very centre of a civilized state, but they made some attempt at alleviation.

We saw in the Women's Sick Ward many miserable objects lying, without beds, on the floor, perishing with extreme want. And in the Men's Sick Ward yet much worse: for along the side of the walls of that ward boards were laid upon trestles, like a dresser in a kitchen; and under them, between those trestles, were laid on the floor one tier of sick men, and upon the dresser another tier, and over them hung a third tier in hammocks.

On the giving food to these poor wretches (though it was done with the utmost caution, they being only allowed at first the smallest quantities, and that of liquid nourishment) one died: the vessels of his stomach were so disordered and contracted for want of use that they were totally incapable of performing their office, and the unhappy creature perished about the time of digestion. Upon his body a coroner's inquest sat (a thing which though required by law to be always done hath for many years been scandalously omitted in this gaol) and the jury found that he died of want.

Those who were not so far gone, on proper nourishment given them, recovered, so that not above nine have died since the 25th of March last, the day the committee first met there, though, before, a day seldom passed without a death, and upon the advancing of the spring, not less than eight or ten usually died every 24 hours.

At this point the Committee uncovered a particularly mean and despicable practice: though indeed they had no need to wield their probe with any skill, for every corner they turned, every door they opened revealed some fearful scandal. Inevitably, thoughtful and compassionate people had from time to time left charities for the benefit of the prisoners. At the Marshalsea, for instance, Sir Thomas Gresham had provided £10 a year, and every county in England gave £1 a year for what was known as 'exhibition money'; in addition there were many other sums of which the committee had not time to obtain full proof. The prisoners elected a 'constable' from each ward and a 'steward' over the whole, with a seal, which was the only proper discharge for the persons paying the charities and was supposed to ensure that the money reached the right

3

hands. In 1722 the prisoners had chosen a certain Matthew Pugh to be their steward, who was a shrewd man and discovered not only that the gaol officials had got hold of the seal, made a duplicate, and were diverting the funds, but that there were many other concealed charities owing to the inmates. He got things on a better footing by securing a new chest with seven locks which was bolted to the wall in one of the wards. A new seal was also made, marked 'Marshalsea Prison, 1725' and kept in the box. Each constable kept one key and himself the seventh, and, since all were required to be assembled before any receipt could be sealed, the amount of any money received was publicly known and divided. But these arrangements were not pleasing to the marshal and his servants. They complained to the judge of the Palace court that Pugh was 'a very turbulent fellow': he was warned off the prison; the marshal got his own clerk chosen steward; the constables refused to hand over their keys; the chest was therefore broken open and carried off; and the charities were soon flowing in their old channels.

As dishonourable as the rest, the present keeper, William Acton, admitted that he had taken on himself the duties of steward, but had no list of charities, kept no accounts and could show no vouchers from the prisoners. It was extracted from him, however, that over a period of a year he had received more than £115 of such moneys; and the committee sadly remarked that the charities were sufficient for the maintenance of the prisoners, and that even if the £115 had been expended on bread alone, many who had died would have lived.

Let us return now to the prisoners with better connections or sharper wits, those who, unfortunately for themselves, were more interesting from the gaoler's point of view. The first stage of extortion was usually detention (unlawful if against the victim's will) in a sponging-house. The committee found, for example, that Bambridge had often had prisoners carried from the prison gates to such a house, owned by him and rented of him by Corbett, his tipstaff:

who hath there kept them at exorbitant charges, and forced them to call for more liquor than they were inclined to, and to spend more than they were able to afford; and for the more effectually making them stretch their poor remains of credit, and to squeeze out of them the charity of their friends, each prisoner is better or worse treated, according to his expenses, some being allowed a handsome room and bed to themselves, some stowed in garrets three in one bed, and some put in irons.

When they can no longer bear the misery and expense of a sponging-house, before they can obtain the privilege of being admitted into the prison, they are obliged to comply with such exorbitant fees, as the said Bambridge thinks fit to demand; which, if they do not, they are sure under various pretences to be turned down to the common side, if not put in irons and dungeons.

The sponging-house formed the perfect example of the vicious circle, the landlord constantly raising his rent and the tenant as often increasing the pressure of the screw on the inmates. The rent of Mary Whitwood, for example:

has from £32 per annum been increased to £60, and a certain number of prisoners stipulated to be made a prey of, to enable her to pay so great a rent; and that she, to procure the benefit of having such a number of prisoners sent to her house, hath over and above the increased rent, been obliged to make a present to the said Bambridge of 40 guineas, and also of a toy (as it is called) being the model of a Chinese ship made of amber set in silver, for which fourscore broad pieces had been offered her.

Having at last by fee and bribe purchased the privilege of entering the gaol on the Master's side a prisoner immediately encountered demands for 'garnish money' or forced levies for drink at profiteering prices decreed by the gaoler:

and if the unhappy wretch (which is the general case) hath not money to pay, the prisoners strip him in a riotous manner which, in their cant phrase, they call letting the black dog walk.

The accommodation even for these paying prisoners was little better than on the common side. In the Oake room of the Marshalsea for instance:

> nine men are laid in three beds, and each man pays 2s. 6d. per week; so that room singly produces £1 2s. 6d. per week.

The committee saw a prisoner who kept his bed with a fistula, and two other persons obliged to lie with him in the same bed, though each paid 2s. 6d. per week; yet they even submitted to such rent and usage rather than be turned down to the common side.

It is not surprising that such conditions bred vice as well as misery; nor is it suggested that among the honest and unfortunate there were not multitudes of flagrant rogues, game to assist in any devilment. The scandal of the Fleet marriages[1] is a story on its own. But a fruitful source of revenue to gaol governors was the conniving at escapes. It flourished at all three prisons, but seems to have been something of a speciality under the Huggins regime at the Fleet. The committee found that Thomas Perrin, for instance, owing £40,000 to the Crown, and Joseph Vains, debtor for £10,000, had both thus escaped. Sometimes prisoners who had the 'liberty of the rules' and possessed a certain type of business acumen were used by the warden as decoys to trade on the Continent, and having established a connection and drawn off large profits, were eventually pursued by foreign merchants for their dues and found of course to be insolvent debtors. As might be expected, Bambridge proved an apt pupil and the Committee found:

> That the said Thomas Bambridge, who for some years acted as deputy warden of the Fleet, and is now actually warden of that prison, hath himself been aiding and assisting in an escape; that he caused a private door to be made through the walls of the prison, out of the yard where the dogs are, the key of which door was kept by himself; and he with his own hands opened the door and let out Boyce

---

[1] Whereby bogus or disreputable clergy turned a dishonest penny by linking undesirables in wedlock.

the smuggler, charged at the king's suit with upwards of £30,000. . . .

And many other instances.

On the other hand there were voluntary prisoners, idle fellows who preferred gaol life with all its carrion pickings to their liberty. They were maintained by the porters at the lodges in riot and every kind of indulgence, on condition of acting as their spies, decoys and messengers. These were the rascals who impersonated deserving debtors, whose release some charitable person would occasionally send to the prison to procure by discharging their obligations; or who carried begging boxes through the streets to collect for the poorest prisoners, and then stole the proceeds. There was also the case of an unfortunate ex-prisoner, Thomas Hogg, properly discharged by court order, who, happening to stop at the prison gate some nine months earlier to give charity to the prisoners, was seized by one of Bambridge's officials, forced into Corbett's sponging-house and had been detained there ever since without the least cause or legal authority.

The Committee sent for the prison records of the Fleet, with results which by this time they must have expected. Most of the books were of suspiciously recent date. But certain facts did emerge:

1. That no list existed of those having the 'liberty of the rules'.
2. That *382* of such persons had in one year paid to the warden the gigantic sum of *£2,828* 17s. *4d.*
3. That *119* persons had suddenly been discharged since the appointment of the committee, and that 52 remained to go out, many of whom had been due for release at varying dates *since 1718*.

It was evident that the governors of the debtors' prisons had been accustomed to extort money from their victims by every form of fraud and artifice. But of recent years even more sinister methods had been introduced, at least in the Fleet and the Marshalsea. Violence and torture had made

their appearance, in the former under Huggins, and Bambridge had quickened the process. It seems that immediately
upon being appointed warden he had deliberately instituted
a reign of terror. A watchhouse was built and muskets with
bayonets served out to his bully watchmen in place of the
pikes and halberts which had always hitherto proved sufficient. He had dungeons built and claimed unlimited authority to inflict arbitrary punishments, including the application
of torturing irons.

The Committee found, after the strictest inquiry, that no
debtors in the Fleet had ever been put in irons before Huggins' wardenship, nor dungeons required to preserve the
quiet and safety of the gaol. Drunken and disorderly
prisoners had always been punished by the stocks; and those
who attempted to escape, by being placed on a tub at the
gate and so put to shame, or locked in their own rooms.
Moreover, dungeons were illegal, since, when the matter
was brought before the Lord Chief Justice of the Common
Pleas, he had told Huggins he might raise his walls higher,
but that there should be no prison within a prison. Let us
take a few instances only of how the Committee found this
injunction had been respected.

Jacob Mendes Solas, a Portuguese, was one day seized,
fettered and cast into the dungeon or Strong Room on
the master's side. This place is a vault, like those in which
the dead are interred, and wherein the bodies of persons
dying in the prison are usually deposited till the coroner's
inquest hath passed upon them. It has no chimney, nor
fireplace, nor any light but what comes over the door, or
through a hole about eight inches square. It is neither
paved nor boarded, and the rough bricks appear both on
the sides and top, being neither wainscoted nor plastered.
What adds to the dampness and stench of the place is its
being over the common shore, and adjoining to the sink
and dunghill, where all the nastiness of the prison is cast.
In this miserable place the poor wretch was kept by Bambridge manacled and shackled for near two months. The
committee themselves saw an instance of the deep impres-

sion his sufferings had made upon him; for on his sur-
mising from something said that Bambridge was to return
again as warden of the Fleet, he fainted, and the blood
started out of his mouth and nose.

Captain John Mackpheadris, a considerable trader, refused to pay Bambridge an extravagant rent for a room.
After subjecting him to many other cruelties Bambridge
put irons upon his legs which were too little, so that in
forcing them on his legs were like to have been broken,
and the torture was impossible to be endured. He was
dragged away to the dungeon, where he lay without a
bed, loaded with irons so close riveted that they morti-
fied his legs. After long application his irons were changed
and a surgeon directed to dress his legs; but his lameness
is not, nor ever can be, cured. He was kept in this miserable condition for three weeks, by which his sight is
greatly prejudiced, and in danger of being lost. The
prisoner, upon this usage, petitioned the judges; and after
several meetings and a full hearing, they reprimanded Mr.
Huggins and Bambridge, and declared that a gaoler
could not answer the ironing of a man before he was
found guilty of a crime: but [here we get a sad glimpse at
the technicalities of contemporary legal practice], it being
out of term, they could not give the prisoner any relief
or satisfaction.

At the Marshalsea, Acton, the former butcher, whose dishonesty has already been reviewed, was not behindhand in
cruelty, and of him the Committee reported:

Some prisoners who had attempted to escape were
called into the lodge by Acton one by one. One of them
was seen to go in perfectly well, and when he came out
again he was in the greatest disorder. His thumbs were
much swollen and very sore, and he declared that the
keeper, in order to extort from him a confession, had
screwed certain instruments of iron upon his thumbs, so
close that they had forced the blood out of them with
exquisite pain. After this he was carried into the strong
room, where, besides the other irons, they fixed on his
neck and hands an iron instrument called a collar, like a

pair of tongs: and he, being a large, lusty man, when they screwed the said instrument close, his eyes were ready to start out of his head, the blood gushed out of his ears and nose, he foamed at the mouth, the slaver ran down, and he made several motions to speak but could not.

Thomas Bliss, a carpenter, who had also attempted to escape, was one afternoon standing quietly in the yard with his irons on, when some of Acton's men called him into the lodge where Acton was then drinking and merry, with company. In about half an hour Bliss came out again crying; and gave an account that when he was in the lodge, they, for their diversion (as they called it) fixed on his head an iron engine or instrument (which appears to be an iron skull cap) which was screwed so close that it forced the blood out of his ears and nose. And he further declared that his thumbs were at the same time put into a pair of thumb-screws, which were screwed so tight that the blood started out of them. And from that time he continued disordered till the day of his death. He was let out of prison without paying his debt. The miserable wretch was put into St. Thomas' Hospital for help, but died very soon.

For our final piece of evidence, symbolizing all the horror and misery of a debtors' prison, we must return to the Fleet. It is the case of Mr. Arne, an upholder (undertaker) who was suddenly seized without reason given and flung into the new-built dungeon. Let the Committee continue the story:

the dungeon was so damp that the drops hung upon the walls and was very nauseous and unwholesome. In this place was this unfortunate man locked up, and never once permitted to go out; but, by an accident on a Sunday, the door being opened, he ran into the parlour, adjoining to the chapel, during the time of divine service. He had then no covering upon his body but the feathers of a bed (which bed was thrown in to him by a prisoner) into which he crept, to defend himself from the cold; and the feathers stuck and were clotted upon him by his own excrements and the dirt, which covered his skin. He was immediately seized and carried back into the dungeon, where, through the cold and restraint and for want of food, he lost his senses, languished and perished. Notwithstanding the miserable condition of this man and the applications which were made to Mr. Huggins, the then warden, who saw this miserable object lying naked in the dungeon and unable to speak, but lifting up his eyes to Mr. Huggins, the said Huggins had no compassion on him, but caused the door to be close locked upon him.

Throughout the two parliamentary sessions during which their inquiry continued the Committee acted with the greatest promptitude and energy. They started operations at the Fleet, as we have seen, on 27th February, 1729, and almost immediately clashed with Bambridge, whose attitude throughout was one of astonishing effrontery. One of the first prisoners they came upon was Sir William Rich, a baronet, detained for debt, and loaded with heavy chains, which they ordered to be taken off. As soon as they had left, Bambridge, hearing that Sir William had testified damagingly against him, ordered the chains to be replaced; upon which the Committee got him committed by the House of Commons for this contempt to the custody of the Serjeant at Arms.

By 20th March the Committee could restrain themselves no longer. Oglethorpe stood up in his place and (as was customary in those more leisurely days) read an interim report verbatim to the House, and then, by means of a number of resolutions, whose wordiness somewhat detracts from their effect when read today, brought every parliamentary weapon within their power to bear against the miscreants:

Resolved: That Thomas Bambridge, the acting warden of the prison of the Fleet, . . . hath been guilty of the most notorious breaches of his trust, great extortions, and the highest crimes and misdemeanours . . . and hath arbitrarily and unlawfully loaded with irons, put into dungeons, and destroyed prisoners for debt under his charge, treating them in the most barbarous and cruel manner, in high violation and contempt of the laws of this kingdom.

The House agreed *nemine contradicente*, and they agreed to similar resolutions indicting Huggins and the other accomplices, and to a Humble Address to the king praying for prosecutions by the Attorney General, upon which the accused were committed to Newgate gaol. As final shots Oglethorpe moved for leave to bring in bills disabling Bambridge from ever holding office in the Fleet again and for the better control of the prison. All was agreed to by the House.

On 14th May, the last day of the session, the Committee just squeezed in their second report, dealing mainly with the Marshalsea. They were experiencing a foretaste of the life of a modern member of Parliament, struggling simultaneously to follow the business of the House and to attend long hours in the Committee. They were also manifestly suffering from the painful and shocking nature of their work. The report concluded with the resolutions censuring Darby and Acton and the scandal of the charities. By the 11th May in the following year the Committee concluded its labours with a final report on the King's Bench prison. They found, as we have said, that Mullens, the marshal, was a helpful and satisfactory witness, and entitled to favour rather than blame, and their resolutions were concerned with the better administration of the prison, with eliminating the men of straw and stopping the gratuities of the judges and their underlings.

It is often said that Oglethorpe's Committee achieved little or nothing; that the prisons relapsed into their accustomed filth and squalor until John Howard's celebrated visitations and exposures forty years later. But that appraisement would be grossly unfair. The worst cruelties were certainly suppressed, and regulations were introduced for the Fleet in 1729 which dealt categorically with each separate abuse which had come to the notice of the Committee. Some of the immediate consequences of the inquiry were, however, disappointing. Bambridge, who was by profession an attorney, was tried for the murder of Robert Castell, Oglethorpe's original friend, but was twice acquitted. He was later prosecuted in several actions by Huggins and spent some time in the Fleet himself. It is said that twenty years later he committed suicide. Huggins contrived, after his stay in Newgate, to live in credit to the age of ninety. But at least the investigation showed that a committee of the House of Commons could fearlessly enter places and expose evils of which even the judiciary, who should have been most concerned, were ignorant or indifferent. Certainly the reports achieved some good by administering a shock to the thinking public; but the public, and even the mass of the House of Commons, were as yet too insensitive to demand any thoroughgoing reforms of the prison system.

In the person of Oglethorpe the results of the inquiry were enormous. As a direct consequence of his experiences he obtained permission to found a colony in America for English paupers and foreign religious refugees. The venture became the great work of his life and the colony became Georgia, named after George II, who gave it every encouragement. Oglethorpe met countless unexpected difficulties, became a successful general, and died, full of years and honours and maintaining to the last his wide interests and deep moral convictions which earned him Pope's admiring couplet.

For us in the twentieth century this Select Committee has a double interest. It may serve to remind us that not long ago little Belsens were suffered to exist in the heart of London; and that the modern scrupulous control of accounts and conduct in public institutions, which seems sometimes so exaggerated, is nevertheless essential. Moreover, those interested in parliamentary history have here a fascinating link with the past: for the drama of those tragic revelations has been preserved for us for ever by an unusual incident. One of the members of the Committee, Sir Archibald Grant of Monnymusk, Baronet, knight of the shire for Aberdeen, had commissioned a young man, James Hogarth, as yet almost unknown as a painter, to sketch the Committee as they worked in the dark and sordid Fleet. Lurking by a pillar, Hogarth produced the famous painting of which one version is in the National Portrait Gallery. Although all the figures are known to be genuine portraits it is surprising that but a few have as yet been thoroughly identified. Of these Oglethorpe sits severe and dignified at the left with his hand upon some instrument of torture of which Huggins holds the other end. It is also known to be the egregious Bambridge who stands on the extreme left, probably justifying himself with shameless audacity. Of the members grouped round the table, grim and stern of mien, the prominent person in the foreground is said to be Sir William Wyndham, with Sir Andrew Fountaine on the chairman's left hand and Lord Percival behind him. The miserable, filthy and half-naked prisoner crouching in the foreground, apparently demonstrating the 'tongs', focuses attention upon the terrible nature of the inquiry. Hogarth gave a sketch in oils of the same scene to Horace Walpole, whose enthusiasm expressed itself as follows:

. . . On the other hand is the inhuman jailer. It is the very figure which Salvator Rosa would have drawn for Iago in the moment of detection. Villainy, fear and conscience are mixed in yellow and livid upon his countenance; his lips are contracted by tremor, his face advances as eager to lie, his legs step back as thinking to make his escape, one hand is thrust forward into his bosom, the fingers of the other are catching uncertainly at his buttonholes. If this was a portrait, it is the most striking that ever was drawn: if it was not, still finer.

III

THE CASE OF
THE DANGEROUS SUBJECTS

'I have always been of the opinion that a police officer is a dangerous subject to the community.'—Evidence before a Select Committee by John Townshend, 1816.

IN RECENT years public opinion in the United States has been shocked by the findings of inquiries into the administration of criminal justice. Links between the bench and the criminal, with the police acting as unscrupulous intermediaries, have been hinted at. Innocent persons were found in some cases to have been subjected to the will of gangsters, with police aiding the criminal, not the victim. There were tales, often proved true, of police extracting confessions by violence; of police suppressing evidence which would have helped to convict; and of police taking bribes from proprietors of gambling saloons or from procurers and prostitutes. In a word, it was found that crime was paying large dividends and that among the ordinary shareholders were police, lawyers, district attorneys and, worst of all, some of those who occupied the seat of justice itself.

Reading of such happenings, it was natural for the British public to feel both complacent and comfortable. These things that happened in America could be accounted for by the fact that it was a new country; that undesirables

from Eastern Europe formed a large part of the criminal
population; and that the normal sense of justice which is
part of the heritage of every Englishman was largely absent
from public life. From these reflections, it is only a short
step to the claim of the innate British superiority; but such a
claim would rest on false foundations. Fundamentally the
public life of a country willing to examine its own weak-
nesses may be in a healthier state than that of a country
which dare not undertake a basic review of its system. In
England the system of public order was once as bad as any-
where in the world, yet fifty years of anxious parliamentary
inquiry were needed before a Parliament was found brave
enough, in the great age of reform, to sweep away the whole
existing system of police and law enforcement and to re-
place traditional corruption with a new structure.

In the year 1829 an Act of Parliament swept away every
vestige of the old order of law enforcement in London and
founded in its place the Metropolitan Police—the body
which has since won the enduring admiration of the city
and country that gave it birth, and fame throughout the
world. It is impossible to read the heart-searching inquiries
and reports of the Select Committees of the House of Commons without realizing what a tremendous risk the new
enterprise entailed. The plan was drafted in haste and
despair by a Select Committee in 1828, after a review of
fifty years of exhaustive but ineffectual seekings after some
milder remedy which would preserve the best of the existing
order and only chip away the rotten wood of London's
police. But by 1828 it was realized that every branch of the
tree was decayed. Parliament acted, and though afraid of the
consequences, it brought to an end the supremacy of those
'dangerous subjects' the old police.

*

There is an impression, which perhaps originated with
the designers of Victorian Christmas cards, that old London
consisted of many jolly taverns, outside each of which an

amiable beadle or watchman, armed with a staff and a yellow lantern, called the hours of the night. It is true that there were taverns, but the atmosphere was depraved rather than jolly, and the London beadle, in spite of his archaic name, was often as great an enemy of society as the criminal he was engaged to hunt. To put the old policeman in perspective, it may be appropriate to begin with a disconcerting fact given to the Select Committee of the House of Commons which inquired into the state of the police in 1828. That Committee found that within a few years certain banks had paid sums amounting to over £200,000—today the equivalent of perhaps £1,000,000—to 'fences' (or receivers of stolen goods) as a bonus for getting property returned to its rightful owner. In one case, for example, the 'fence' had paid the thieves £200 for the property and then charged the original owners £2,800 for its return. Some of the old stagers among the police at Bow Street were admitted by Sir Richard Birnie, their head, to have been 'go-betweens' in these lucrative transactions. On one occasion when a 'fence' had been arrested, the prosecution was suddenly withdrawn and the property subsequently restored 'for a sum not ascertained by the Committee'. Under pretence of helping the owner to regain his stolen goods, some at least of the police had a double share, taking their commission from both parties to the transaction. It was an arrangement which obviously depended for its success on a safe haul by the original thief; the bigger the haul, the bigger the sum necessary to procure restitution. Where cash was stolen, a dividend of approximately 20 per cent. was demanded from the unfortunate bank. Blackstone, explaining the system as it existed a hundred years earlier, wrote: 'This was a contrivance carried to a great length of villainy in the beginning of the reign of George I; the confederates of the felons thus disposing of stolen goods, at a cheap rate, to the owners themselves and thereby stifling all further inquiry.'

Among those who connived in the system, which was in fact illegal and punishable by hanging, were certain police court magistrates and solicitors 'of that class whose practice lies chiefly in the defence of culprits, and commonly denominated "thieves' attorneys".' Here was a good solid kind of corruption of the cleaner sort, where the medium for dealings was golden coin. There were more exotic forms of vice in which the police were rather more than agents; they played principal rôles.

As the metropolis grew, crime grew; already at the beginning of the nineteenth century the inhabitants of London numbered close on a million, and for many years Parliament had been wringing its hands over the increase of robberies and the imperfections of the officers of the law. In 1772 a Select Committee, appointed by the House of Commons to inquire into the question of burglaries and robberies in London and Westminster, reported that the 'mode of watching the town' was defective. The Committee found that even within the limited confines of Westminster itself every parish was under a separate commission. The commissioners for each parish appointed beats for the watchmen without conferring together—'which leaves the frontiers of each parish in a confused state'. Where one side of a street lay in one parish and the other side in another parish, the watchmen of one side were disinclined to proffer any help to persons on the other side. A witness from Soho was asked (at a later parliamentary inquiry in 1817):

> Do the watchmen in your parish consider it their duty to assist the watchmen in an adjoining parish?—No, they do not; it is a difficulty which frequently occurs. So that if any disturbance occurs in the same street, if out of his parish, the watchman would not think it his duty to interfere?—No, he would not; perhaps he would stand and look on.
>
> Of course he would assist in felonious cases, or in a breach of the peace?—Under those circumstances perhaps he might; but he would not consider it his duty under his appointment; some would be anxious to shrink from it.

Twenty-one years passed without any improvement; and in 1793, another Select Committee sat and reported the somewhat obvious finding 'that the present mode of watching, and pay of the watchmen, is very irregular and various, and ought to be put under proper regulations'. Still nothing was done; and in 1812 a wave of atrocious murders again drew attention to the subject. 'A general alarm, inducing great temporary exertions and precautions, pervaded the metropolis'.[1]

A Select Committee reported to the House of Commons in the same year, 1812, that, except in the city of London, the mode of watching was 'generally bad', and the men employed, both in number and ability, were wholly inefficient for the purpose. In 1816, 1817, 1818 and 1822 the question of police and crime occupied the prolonged attention of a series of Select Committees, who approached the problem from every point of the compass. They all reached the same conclusion—that the system was ineffectual. Not until 1828, however, did a Committee find the courage to recommend radical change, with the institution of a single new police force for the whole metropolis, leaving only the City of London with a separate force. Before the point was reached at which so great a reform could command the support of public opinion, the world had to learn, largely from the evidence given before the Select Committee of 1817, the evil nature of the force which then served the capital.

The old police were startlingly few in number. A patchwork quilt of historical anomaly and empirical creation covered the various districts of London. In no two districts were the wages or the numbers, the duties or the hours, identical. The strongest permanent force, the police of the City of London, consisted of forty-five men under orders of the two City marshals. There was a police establishment of eight men at Bow Street, and, under the superintendence of the chief magistrate there, the foot patrol and the horse patrol. From eight to twelve policemen were attached to each

[1] H.C. 533, p. 23 (1828).

of the seven other London magistrates' courts, such as Great Marlborough Street, Union Hall and Thames police-court.

The Bow Street foot patrol was a comparatively recent innovation. Five men patrolled at will in each of sixteen districts in the metropolis. The horse patrol was established in 1805 to deal with highway robberies up to a distance of twenty miles out on the great roads leading into the capital. Its members were required to have served with credit in a cavalry regiment.

Small though the numbers of the principal police establishments were on paper, they were even less in practice. In March 1822 the eight policemen of the Bow Street establishment were disposed as follows:

John Townshend and John Sayers, who attended King George IV when he was out of town, were at Brighton with him. William Salmon and George Ruthven had just returned from a trip to the Continent, where they had been sent in pursuit of a couple of city clerks who had absconded with their employers' property. Daniel Bishop was away hunting criminals in the provinces. Samuel Taunton was at Maidstone assizes. John Vickery was ill at his native Odiham in Hampshire: 'he has never been well since he was very ill-used some time ago and nearly murdered'. The last of the eight officers, James Smith, was at Baldock in Hertfordshire; but as the clerk to the Bow Street police-court explained in evidence, any of the eight were ready to devote their time to London crimes when they were not called out of town to attend to offences committed in the country.

Besides these police, who were chiefly engaged in criminal investigation, each ward in the city or parish outside the city appointed a certain number of beadles, constables, watchmen and street keepers. This heterogeneous bunch of parish officers was responsible for public order, prevention of nuisances, apprehension of criminals and, above all, for the maintenance of a nightly watch. Crime, like other 'deeds of darkness', took place mainly at night.

The beadle was elected annually by the inhabitants, and paid an average of £50 a year. His business was to bully out of the inhabitants the rate necessary to pay for the watch-men, and then to set the nightly watch. The office of con-stable was also one to which candidates were elected by the populace, and there were usually several constables for each parish. A constable had in theory to attend the watch-house throughout the night; but the office had the disadvantage of being unpaid and more often than not the elected constable found a substitute to take over the more arduous side of this honorary position for a few shillings a week. The watchmen were, in theory, the active fellows on the beat: these were the men who actually fought the robbers and snatched the thieves. In some parishes they were not re-cruited above the age of forty, but in others, there were men going on for seventy, and deaf. Paid according to the length of their watch during the night, they began at sun-down and went home at dawn.

The streetkeeper, as a rule only one for each parish, was the only official regularly on duty during the day. His prin-cipal function was to remove obstructions, such as market stalls which obstructed the footpath. That the moral as well as the professional standing of watchmen was not high may be gathered from the typical examination of Samuel Roberts, head of the nightly watch in Bloomsbury. This officer's evidence to the Select Committee of 1817 was pretty evenly divided between denouncing crime which was out of con-trol and defending his friend Cummins, whose enterprise was barely within the law:

To what police office do you report?—Marlborough Street; we have reported several publicans, for harbouring watchmen in the night.

Have many persons been robbed in Russell Street to your knowledge recently?—Yes; there were two boys to come up to-day for robbing a lady of her bundle; one trod on the heel of the lady, and she turned to look at him, and another snatched her bundle containing a crimson velvet pelisse and a gown, and bonnet and some feathers; but Mr. Cummins detected those boys.

Is that Mr. Cummins the husband of the lady who keeps some houses of which the Committee have heard?—Yes, he is.

But still he suffers his wife to keep those houses?—I cannot speak of that; the houses of Mr. Cummins are not conducted in general as houses of that sort are; they are generally very secure; there is no robbery in them, I understand.

They are supposed to contain much accommodation?—Yes, no doubt of it.

From one hundred to one hundred and fifty beds?—I cannot speak to the number.

Are they weekly or nightly lodgers?—Nightly, I believe. Or hourly?—Yes, some of them, I apprehend.

Did you ever hear that eighteen pence to two shillings per hour was the price?—I do not know.

Have you reason to believe that persons of both sexes go to Cummins's houses?—I have reason to believe that.

And that they continue there for a less time than the night?—I have reason to believe so, certainly.

Are there many robberies in High Street?—There have been many.

By what description of persons?—By boys principally; there was one on Saturday night; a lady was robbed by a boy who ran down by the brewhouse into the Rookery, as we call it; it is impossible to catch them there; and at the end of the Hampshire Hog-yard, in Broad-street, there have been several robberies.

Are there any brothels frequented by very young persons in your parish?—Yes, several.

Where are they?—There is one situated in Charles-street, Drury-lane, and in Parker-street, Drury-lane; and in George-street, late called Dyott-street, there are a great number of them.

Of what age are those young persons?—Some not above eleven or twelve years of age; I have seen girls of that age.

And frequented by many of that age?—Yes, many; five or six in a room.

Are you acquainted with a woman of the name of Harland, in Buckeridge-street, who keeps a house of that description?—I am not acquainted with her, I have heard of her.

Mrs. Philips? No.—Mrs. Mahoney? Yes.—Mrs. Rusher? Yes.—Mrs. Fleming? Yes.

They all keep houses of that description?—Yes.

Mrs. Linnett, in Dyott-street? Yes.—And the great Mrs. Cummins? Yes.

Mrs. Cummins keeps her carriage, does not she?—No; she only keeps a spring cart.

Has she a country house?—She has a house at Camden Town.

A respectable house, and well furnished?—Yes.

Is she a person reputed to be possessed of considerable property?—Yes, she is.

Do you know of any houses in your parish which receive stolen property?—There are two or three houses in Short's-gardens that do, I have not the least doubt; one instance happened last Tuesday, when we were going from this Committee; we were going down Short's-gardens, and we met two boys we well knew, one of the name of Cruikshanks and another of the name of Parsons; I catched hold of Cruikshanks and I felt a pair of women's shoes buttoned under his coat; I took him in custody and took him to the watch-house, and told him 'If you will tell me where you were going to sell those shoes, I will forgive you;' and he told me he was going to a certain house which he mentioned, and that quite convinced me they were receivers of that kind of property.

The equipment of the watchmen under the control of such a leader as Roberts was as unsatisfactory as their method of patrol. Their greatcoats were by no means uniform. Their lanterns were not dark lanterns, but shone out brightly, and so announced the watchmen's approach. In loud voices they called the hour so that nobody could fail to know their whereabouts; but to make the criminal's

work even easier the watch had fixed rounds for its pic-
turesque perambulations. Pay was irregular and in any case
very small.

A typical example of local police strength is provided
by the busy and populous district of Hatton Garden,
centre of London's jewellery and diamond trade. The
parish appointed their beadle annually, and paid him
£26 a year. He had to attend the churches as well as
performing all parochial police duties. Under him were
five constables and five head boroughs, or assistant constables, all unpaid, who were supposed to attend the
watch house on alternate nights, while by day one streetkeeper, paid at the princely rate of £5 a year, had the duty
of preventing nuisances in the streets and 'taking up
disorderly persons'.

At night, when the jewellers retired to rest over their
shops, and their assistants, as often as not, reposed under
the counters, the two night beadles, one of whom was paid
£30 and one £10 per annum, sent out their force of thirteen
watchmen, who were paid from ten to twelve shillings a
week according to the time of year. Apart from a chance
incursion by the Bow-street patrol there was nothing else
between the robber and his victim: and by crossing the
parish boundary to the south a thief would be able to make
his escape into the separately administered parish of St.
Mary le Strand, where there was no night beadle and only
four watchmen. A few parishes valued lives and property
more highly; and paid out of rates for the maintenance of
forty, fifty and in rare cases, eighty or ninety watchmen.
From these parishes, witnesses came to Parliament to say
that they were well satisfied with the policing of their particular district. But the very efficiency of such parishes was
a danger to their less alert neighbours, since these received an overflow of thieves who had been driven out
of parishes where the state of vigilance was higher. The
parish of Chelsea, for example, where the watchmen were
few and futile, was 'very much exposed'; and as the

Chelsea watchmen were only paid according to results, their remuneration was proportionately low.

> Last winter [said a witness before the Select Committee of 1828] there were five or six houses robbed in Park Place, going down to Battersea bridge. There was one of these old watchmen who collected the wages weekly; the old man told me his wage had once been as high as 25*s*. a week, and now he collects 7*s*. but he has not bread, and cannot afford to do this duty. The people have withdrawn their subscriptions in consequence of the number of robberies; he is unfit for the duty.
>
> That is the general state of the parishes around that part?—Yes.

The practice of paying the police a negligible wage did not prove a true economy. If a man's wages are inadequate, he will as often as not find a way of bringing them up to a tolerable level.

So it was with the police. In the reign of Queen Anne an Act had been passed for the worthy purpose of encouraging the discovery and apprehension of housebreakers; and the considerable sum of forty pounds was promised upon the conviction of every burglar or housebreaker. Other Acts promised similar reward for the conviction of forgers of counterfeit coin and of sheep-stealers. While the offenders found guilty of these crimes took their stand on the gallows —at that time the prescribed penalty for such offences—the fortunate policeman who apprehended them was entitled to claim a decent sum as recompense for his trouble. Not unnaturally, the sums paid out by way of encouragement were regarded by the sensitive as tainted with blood: but it did not prevent the old police and watchmen from collecting the reward for seizing their human game. The amount paid out in rewards rose from £7,770 in 1798 to £18,000 in 1815. The weight of evidence offered to Parliament by magistrates and even by some of the police themselves was that the system was dangerous.

'It has the tendency, and in some cases has produced the practice, of inducing persons to forswear themselves for the lucre of reward,' said the Committee of 1817. They reported the terrible conclusion that: 'Sometimes the innocent have forfeited their lives, from the cupidity of those who swore them away, to obtain the money which was to be paid on conviction of the accused.' In other cases, humane juries refused to convict, because they felt the police witnesses were speaking with their minds on the reward rather than on the truth. The system also meant that the police had an interest in winking at small crime in the hope that the tyro would one day commit a crime which was serious enough to bear a cash reward.

In the words of the Committee:

There can be no doubt that offenders have been suffered to be trained on in their career of crime from the first offence which made them amenable to law, though not yet objects of profit, till step by step, they have been led to the commission of offences, for which on their conviction, the parliamentary reward could be obtained.

Apart from the big rewards, some of the parishes offered the police the chance of making a few shillings out of vagrants. The Committee of 1817 referred to the practice described by Mr. Barnley, the beadle of Hatton Garden and Ely Rents. This witness stated that in his parish ten shillings was paid for the apprehension of a vagrant. He had often seen police giving a penny or twopence to the poor and then bringing them in to the police station at Hatton Garden and swearing that they found them begging, when in fact they never begged at all. The pauper got seven days in the house of correction and the policeman got his reward. The practice was so general that the expression 'getting an easy ten shillings' was coined to describe it.

Throughout the reports of the Select Committees of the House of Commons which examined the state of the police, there is one constant cry—the denunciation of 'flash houses'. With unconscious humour, the Select Committee of 1817

defined them as 'those places of low resort, which for their
superior infamy are called flash houses'. The evidence given
in 1817 by Mr. William Crauford, secretary to a society for
combating juvenile delinquency, showed how the con-
nivance of the police sustained the influence of these
finishing schools of crime. The boys who were there corrupted grew to be highly skilled in theft, while the girls were
acquiring the sister art of prostitution.

I apprehend that the greater part of juvenile depredators occasionally cohabit with girls of their own age.
This early association of the sexes prevails, I fear to an
alarming extent. We have had reason to believe that there
were houses exclusively for the reception of boys and
girls. It is stated, that there were several in St. Giles's, and
that at one house four hundred beds are made up every
night; a boy who was in the habit of visiting this house
confessed that he had slept there upwards of thirty times
with girls of his own age, and he particularly named five;
this boy was fourteen years of age, the girls were to be
met with at the flash-houses to which he resorted.

The money obtained for accomplishing those purposes
was obtained by thieving?—Certainly; when boys are in
prison they are frequently visited by those girls; they obtain
admittance as relatives; there is a boy now in Cold Bath
Fields, who, when he was visited by a girl, desired her to
continue the lodging in which they had lived, for the
three months during which he was to be confined.

How old was the boy?—Fourteen.

What age was the girl?—About the same age.

Stating that fully 1,000 persons under twenty had been
convicted in a year, Crauford also drew a sympathetic picture of the young criminals who were the particular prey of
the police:

The condition of the greater number of juvenile
depredators is calculated to excite pity rather than severe
censure. It is very easy to blame these poor children, and
to ascribe their misconduct to an innate propensity to

vice; but I much question whether any human being, circumstanced as many of them are, can reasonably be expected to act otherwise; numbers are brought up to thieve as a trade, and are driven into the streets every morning, and dare not return but with plunder; others are orphans, or completely abandoned by their parents; they subsist by begging or pilfering, and at night they often sleep under the sheds in the streets and in the market places.

Once convicted, and after serving a term of imprisonment, the boys had little chance to 'go straight', because, as the witness explained, there was no way to keep alive except by renewed theft. When detected in minor pilfering they were committed to prison, often severely flogged, and then turned loose without a shilling in their pockets and more hardened in character than before.

They declare their readiness to shun their former connections, and to abandon their vicious pursuits: but how are they to subsist? Without friends or character, who will give them employment? Without temporary aid, where can they procure food? I am convinced that many are driven to renew their depredations by their necessities. I know of several instances in which this has been the case, and thus some boys are no sooner discharged from prison than they are again brought in, for in reality a prison is their only home. There is a lad now in Newgate, who has been convicted four different times, at short intervals; when discharged he resorted to a flash-house, where his companions relieved him, upon condition that he should renew his depredations.

William Crauford's censure of the police was reinforced by the report of a committee of his society which in 1816 inquired into the alarming increase in juvenile crime in the metropolis. The report showed that the modern catch-phrase 'crime does not pay' would have been untrue in the case of the old London police.

The punishment of death was at this time prescribed for

upwards of two hundred offences, but though the police were able to claim the cash rewards there was a chance that extreme youth would save many of their victims from the ultimate penalty. A few examples of the types of young thief with which the police had to deal and from whose convictions they drew profitable rewards may be given:

A.B. aged thirteen years. His parents are living; he was but for a short time at school; his father was frequently intoxicated, and on these occasions the son generally left home, and associated with bad characters, who introduced him to houses of ill fame, where they gambled till they had lost or spent all their money. This boy had been five years in the commission of crime; and been imprisoned for three separate offences; sentence of death has been twice passed on him.

C.D. aged ten years. He was committed to prison in the month of April 1815, having been sentenced to seven years imprisonment for picking pockets. His mother only is living, but he does not know where she resides; he has a very good capacity, but cannot read. When first visited he discovered much anxiety about his situation, but every favourable impression was effaced shortly after his confinement in prison.

E.F. aged eight years. His mother only is living, and she is a very immoral character. This boy has been in the habit of stealing for upwards of two years. In Coventgarden Market there is a party of between thirty and forty boys, who sleep every night under the sheds and baskets. These pitiable objects when they arise in the morning have no other means of procuring subsistence but by the commission of crime; this child was one of the number; and it appears that he has been brought up to the several police offices upon eighteen separate charges. He has been twice confined in the House of Correction, and three times in Bridewell; he is very ignorant, but of a good capacity.

G.H. aged fifteen years. During the time that he should have been receiving instruction at school his parents suffered him to range the public streets; he there mixed promiscuously with boys of bad character; he entered into their schemes, and continued in connexion with them until he had committed a capital offence, for which he was tried and received sentence of death. Thus situated he attracted the attention of the committee; intercession was made for him; his life was spared, and he is now in a situation where he is receiving the benefit of instruction whilst he is training up in habits of industry.

Q.R. aged twelve years. He has had no education: has a mother who encourages the vices of her son, and subsists by his depredations. She turns him into the street every morning, and chastises him severely when he returns in the evening without some article of value.

The vested interest in crime, which too many of the police possessed, demanded that prostitution should be encouraged on the widest scale. Evidence before the House of Commons Committee of 1817 showed that too often the watchman drew a nightly retainer from the prostitute who walked the same beat as himself.

The practice of watchmen receiving money from prostitutes to allow them to parade the streets is a matter of common notoriety.

As the prostitutes far outnumbered the watchmen, the total of the retainers was heavy. The higher police disdained the offerings of the humble prostitute; they made huge profits from the intelligent exploitation of disorderly houses.

James Wade, a constable in Westminster, one of a chorus of witnesses, expressed the position with frankness:

Do you not believe that there is a practice prevailing in the metropolis, of the watchmen levying contributions on the unfortunate women walking in their district, either in the shape of money or spirits?—Yes, both, nightly; and they will endeavour to take their parts frequently, to plunder persons, or will take their part when the woman cannot succeed in obtaining money from a person that she may have laid hold of; each of them has her proper beat, the same as the watchmen themselves have, and each watchman knows those who have given to him.

In 1816 the proud Corporation of the City of London was driven to petition Parliament to do something to reduce the number of disorderly women who frequented the streets. Appropriately, the petition was referred to the Select Committee who were currently inquiring into the state of the police of the metropolis.

From Dandson Coates, a private investigator, the Committee learned of brothels and prostitutes in several parishes. The figures afford their own comment on the efficiency of the police:

Returns from three parishes, which appear to have been most accurately made, give 360 brothels and 2,000 prostitutes, out of 9,925 houses and 59,050 inhabitants. . . .

The details are as follows: in Saint Botolph without Aldgate 60 brothels, 300 prostitutes, 961 houses, and 5,265 inhabitants; in Saint Leonard's, Shoreditch, 100 brothels, 700 prostitutes, 7,282 houses, and 48,930 inhabitants; and in Saint Paul's, Shadwell, 200 brothels, 1,000 prostitutes, 1,682 houses, and 9,855 inhabitants. This account of the number of houses and inhabitants with which the number of brothels and prostitutes is compared, is from the census of 1811.

The same witness had diligently questioned over a hundred prostitutes, and even discovered their ages:

Were the persons whom you examined, young or middle-aged?—Their ages varied from 14 years to 54, the largest proportion appearing to be of the ages from 18 to 22. From their own account, their ages were as follows: one of 14 years; one of 16; one of 17; 11 of 18; 12 of 19; 10 of 20; 13 of 22; six of 23; one of 24; three of 25; 10 of 26; nine of 27; four of 28; six of 29; seven of 30; five of 32; two of 33; five of 35; three of 36; and one of 54, making a total of 111; and out of 85 of these individuals, it appears they had been in a state of prostitution from a period of two months to 20 years. The largest proportion of them state from two to three years.

Can you give the Committee any information as to the extent of the mortality among that description of persons? —It would appear, from the period of their continuance upon the town, being generally not more than two or three years, that the mortality must be very great in that class of persons.[1]

The assiduous Dandson Coates was assisted by the vestry clerk of the parish of St. Paul, Shadwell, who supplied a detailed picture of his own district:

What is the state of your parish, with respect to the appearance of prostitutes in the streets, and their manners and conduct there?—The prostitutes residing in this parish are of the very lowest description; their manners and conduct disgusting in the extreme; they not only infest the public streets nightly for the vile purpose of prostitution, but are to be seen there all hours in the day, enticing the unwary, and using the most obscene and profane language, to the great annoyance and injury of the inhabitants and passengers. The greatest encouragement is given to these abandoned and profligate women, through the accommodation which is afforded them by several licensed victuallers, who suffer them to use their houses as a constant resort, and which houses are principally supported by such miserable objects.

What is the state of your parish, with respect to the number of houses of ill fame, or suspected to be such?— The limits of this parish are very confined; and, comparing it with the extent of the adjoining parishes, the number of houses of ill fame therein is considered very great, it having been ascertained upon a recent survey, *made expressly for the purpose*, by the parish officers and trustees, that there are upwards of two hundred.

What number of prostitutes do you suppose reside within

[1] 1817, Evidence, p. 459.

your parish, distinguishing, as far as possible, the number in brothels, and the number that reside at their own lodgings? Upon the survey before-mentioned, it was also ascertained that the number of prostitutes living in such houses of ill fame is about six hundred, but the number residing in their private lodgings cannot accurately be known, although it is certain that there are very many of this description; and it may most painfully be presumed, that the whole number is very little short of one thousand, or nearly one-tenth of the population of the parish.

Have you any reason to suppose that prostitutes remain on the town through inability to get their living in an honest employment; and, if so, what proportion of them? —It is probable there may be some who remain on the town through inability to get their living in an honest employment; but it is considered, from their early habits of vice, by far the greater part of the prostitutes living in this parish continue their miserable practice from a depraved inclination, aided by the constant excitement of the procuresses, who, receiving the whole of the wretched produce of their prostitution, are necessarily active to prevent the possibility of their reformation; for which purpose they attend them in their nightly and daily walks, especially watching those most recently initiated into their baneful course, and keeping them continually in a state of inebriety, if not in a state of absolute intoxication. The state of slavery in which those unhappy females are held is beyond description or belief; they have not anything they can call their own, but appear to be entirely abandoned, in body and in mind, to the service and advantage of the persons with whom they reside, and from whose trammels it is impossible they can escape.

Can you suggest any mode of providing for or giving employment to prostitutes, who may be desirous of quitting their present iniquitous and destructive course of life?—From the present distressed state of the country, and the general stagnation of trade, which has thrown so many honest industrious persons out of employ, no mode can be suggested by the officers of this parish, for giving employment to the unhappy objects of this inquiry.

The statement went on to show that one of the organizers of vice had been successfully convicted; but that even in this instance it was a case of *reculer pour mieux sauter*.

While it was true that public pressure forced the police to take occasional action against brothels, the ingenious officers of the law found a means of turning an extraordinarily dishonest penny out of the machinery of justice itself. The churchwardens and overseers of the parish of Saint George's, Southwark, managed several times to indict one or more of the two or three hundred brothels with which the area was infested.

Joseph Meymott, a churchwarden, described how particular houses, where very gross complaints existed, had been indicted: but the parties had seldom been convicted. When such attempts were not frustrated by defects in the indictment the police themselves took a hand.

I remember an instance which occurred within a year or two, in which a great deal of cruelty had been used towards some of the females in the house. We got two of the young girls whom we took into the workhouse, and there we kept them, for the purpose of taking care of them, as well as to produce them as evidence against the house itself; we made all the inquiry we could of those girls, and we found that the woman of the house, not the man, but the wife, was almost the entire agent in the business; indeed they informed us that the man had frequently complained of keeping such girls at all in the house. We therefore thought it right to indict the woman, for the law allows any party to be indicted for such a nuisance, either man, woman or servant. We indicted the woman, and had her brought to trial at the Sessions; when upon cross-examination, the counsel for the defendant drew out from one of the girls one solitary expression, that the man, though he had constantly remonstrated with his wife for keeping such girls, had once said to her, if these girls are to go out, it is time they were dressed and gone out of the house; upon which the indictment was immediately quashed, because it was said, it ought to have been brought against the man; so much for the difficulty. But though we feel this evil, we are now feeling a much greater; the parish officers recently (within this month) heard that ten or twelve houses in our parish were indicted for being disorderly houses; about a fortnight previous to that, two or three persons living in a place called Baron's-buildings, called upon me as churchwarden, stating that their neighbourhood was notoriously bad, and requesting that the parish would indict the houses as disorderly. I told them that the parish would be very glad to do so, but for the difficulty of procuring evidence, and the immense expense attending these indictments, together with the uncertainty of success. They said, it does not signify, the parish should and must indict them.[1]

The magistrates, bewildered by the sudden admission of so much guilt, called on the ten defendants to enter into recognizances to abate the nuisance, and then discharged the apparently penitent brothel keepers. The sequel was a demand on the unfortunate parish for an immense reward in respect of the convictions. A claim was put in under an Act of George II's reign for punishing persons keeping disorderly houses:

> Sir, As the agents of John Clarke and Thomas Hunt, two of the inhabitants of Saint George the Martyr, in the county of Surrey, residing in Baron's buildings, in the parish aforesaid, (and being duly authorized by them in writing under their hands) I do hereby demand of you, as overseer of the above-mentioned parish, the following sums for the prosecution and conviction, by the said John Clarke and Thomas Hunt, of the under-mentioned defendants, for keeping disorderly houses, pursuant to the statute in that case made and provided. The sum of £40 for the conviction of John Small and Elizabeth Small: The sum of £20 for the conviction of Sarah Scott: The

---

[1] 1817, Evidence, p. 465.

sum of £20 for the conviction of William Beazley: The
sum of £40 for the conviction of John Bray and his wife:
The sum of £40 for the conviction of Christopher Leach
and Louisa Leach; and the sum of £40 for the conviction
of Thomas Roberts and Harriet Roberts. Total, £200.

Dated this 1st day of May 1817.
20, Great Suffolk-street, Borough.

James H. Burden.

The signatory, Burden, was 'one of those harpies' who
hung around the police court: but the man behind the whole
scheme was one Reeves, the chief clerk at the police office.
The suspicion of the parish authorities that they had been
tricked by the police soon became a certainty. The good
churchwardens described what happened when they came to
the magistrates' court to settle the question of rewards
demanded by the impudent Burden:

In consequence of this letter we made an appointment
to meet him. He then produced what he called an account
of the constables' expenses: the magistrates asked him,
whether those were all the expenses (amounting somewhere to about twenty or thirty pounds) with which he
meant to charge the parish. He said, 'Oh! no; there are a
great many other expenses, but the magistrates have
nothing to do with those.' Mr. Serjeant Sellon, the pre-
siding magistrate, said he thought the parish officers
would be doing wrong to pay anything till they knew the
utmost amount of the expenses; and he put off the settling
of the expenses till next Friday, requiring in the meantime,
that Mr. Burden should make out a regular bill of his
charges; in consequence of which he has sent two bills,
the one for one set of houses, and the other for another;
one amounting to £121 19s. and the other to £70 13s. 4d.
making together £192 12s. 4d.; but they were accompanied by a note, stating, that to this sum would be
added the costs of attendance on Mr. Russell the vestry
clerk and the magistrates, and letters, &c. since the
convictions.

The accounts handed in by Burden proved that his reputation for extortion was well deserved:

	£	s.	d.
The costs of the prosecution v. Small and wife	17	2	6
The like costs against Sarah Scott	17	2	6
The like against Beasley and wife	17	2	6
The like against Roberts and wife	17	2	6
The like v. Leach and wife	17	2	6
The like v. Bray and wife	17	2	6
	102	15	–
The constables' expenses in the above six prosecutions	11	4	–
By expenses on occasion of the loss of time of 12 witnesses	8	–	–
	121	19	–

To which sum of £121 19s. will be added, the costs of attendances on Mr. Russell and the magistrates, and letters, &c., since the convictions.

	£	s.	d.
The cost of prosecution against Powell and wife	15	15	10
The like costs against Anderson and wife	15	15	10
The like against Watts	15	15	10
The like against Davis and wife	15	15	10
By the constables expenses in the above four prosecutions	5	10	–
Expenses for the loss of time of witnesses	2	–	–
	70	13	4

£121 19 –
70 13 4
———————
192 12 4

To which sum of £70 13s. 4d. will be added the costs of attendances, as above, since the convictions.

The evidence went on to show that the whole proceeding had been devised by the police, with Burden as their agent, to enrich themselves at the expense of the unhappy parish, without inflicting any great hardship on their allies of the brothels.

Liquor played a great part in sustaining the uproar of the streets in the early years of the nineteenth century; in view of the evidence of their other scabrous activities it was scarcely surprising to find that the police were hand in glove with the worst sort of publican. A witness described the Brown Bear Inn in Southwark as being

> an intolerable nuisance for some years past, in consequence of a man having a private house adjoining, where he keeps a bear, and has dog-fighting and every thing of that horrible description. I have applied to the magistrates many times to refuse the licence to the house adjoining, as being the focus where the refuse of London meet, I believe, twice a week, and characters of the very worst description assemble there. The howlings of the dogs are the most hideous one can conceive. At last this house was empty. I soon applied to the magistrates in session, and stated to them that the house was empty, and to request that they would pause before they licensed it again; for it was so great a nuisance, that it really was insufferable.

A new licensee appeared who was recommended by the police: but he was soon found to be a very bad character:

> I then felt that I had no other remedy but to watch the conduct of the man. The very first Sunday following I went to the house, during the time of divine service, with some other gentlemen; we found it full of people of an improper description, such as bear-baiters, dog-fighters, and such like. I had the man called up to Union Hall (the local police court); there I was confronted by a constable of the name of Holmes, who came to give this man a very good character. He said that he knew him to be a very good man; that he was a very excellent man; but that,

unfortunately, he had had a man drinking there whom he
could not turn out of his house. The consequence was,
the man was ordered to pay ten shillings.[1]

A great weight of evidence from all over London showed
that the beadles whose duty it was to report on the state of
public houses gave false reports, while accepting bribes
from publicans or brewers. The vestry clerk of Soho square,
a practising solicitor, was asked:

Have you ever heard that it has been customary for the
beadles to get the licences from the licensing clerk, and to
receive a small perquisite when he takes them round to
the publican?—It is the constant practice.

Is it a part of the duty of beadles to visit public houses?
—We consider it to be so; we make them make a report
upon their oaths of any disorders which they may have
discovered.

Do you believe that that is done according to the terms
of their instructions?—I do not, and have frequently
said so, because I have often received information from
other sources that the houses have been disorderly, and
exactly contrary to the beadles' account, and they have
been severely reprimanded.

Since the police were ineffective and either corrupt or in-
dolent in the exercise of their powers, private societies made
some pathetic attempts to enforce the existing law 'against
the more open and daring violations of public decency'.
The Guardian Society tried, in a practical way, to give employment and relief to destitute women of the town. In
addition to general law enforcement, the Society for the
Suppression of Vice instituted a vigorous series of prosecutions against the vendors of licentious books, prints, drawings and toys. Their rapid success in this field shows how
much might have been achieved by an uncorrupted police.
To their surprise the Society found that young ladies in
respectable boarding schools were among the most ardent

[1] 1817, Evidence, p. 470.

purchasers of indecent merchandise. The agents in the well-organized traffic in obscene books and prints amounted to at least six hundred.

It was discovered that the principal vent for their commodities were schools, and those chiefly for females, into which they would contrive to introduce these articles by means of servants. Women were also employed as agents in this trade, who would gain admission into schools for females, under the pretence of purchasing cast-off clothes from servants. It also appeared that opulent tradesmen, of fair reputations, were concerned in the same trade, who obtained large importations from the continent in return for the works of native artists. Many of the keepers of ballad stalls were also implicated in these transactions, and several booksellers were known to be in the habit of supplying country orders of the same kind.

Having obtained undoubted evidence of the practices, the Society immediately sent cautionary letters to almost all the schools for female education in and about the metropolis, and to the head masters of the different public schools. They afterwards prosecuted two itinerant dealers to conviction, and have continued, up to the present time, to watch the trade with a vigilant eye, until, by successive prosecutions, they have reduced it to a state of comparative insignificance.

In giving this evidence, the secretary to the Society also gave the reason why the police were not interested in prosecuting. There was no profitable reward to make their trouble financially worth while.

When these offences were first brought to light by the Society, magistrates have expressed their astonishment at the extent of the evil, of the great prevalence of which they before had no conception.

It seems strange that the Society should come to the knowledge of offences so little known to the police; how is this to be accounted for?—Because it is one of those offences, for the detection of which there are no rewards.

At the end of one more instance of the indifference of the police to any duties which did not lead to personal profit, there came a lighter touch.

The secretary to the Society was describing snuff boxes, decorated with obscene engravings and pictures, 'some of them very highly finished', which found their unauthorised way into ladies' boarding schools—those 'wholesome seminaries of female education'. Abruptly he was interrupted by a member of the Committee: 'How do the Society dispose of the obscene articles which come into their possession?' The witness's answer did not encourage further curiosity:

> They are always destroyed in the presence of two members of the committee, except a few specimens, which are preserved as evidence of the convictions which have from time to time been obtained by the Society. These specimens are kept in a tin box secured by three different locks, one of the keys of which is kept by the treasurer, one by a member of the committee, and one by the secretary, so that the box can at no time be opened but with the concurrence of these three persons.[1]

Some of the magistrates were in league with the brewers to prevent the closing down of flash houses. Wherever the magistrates had a concealed interest in keeping these places of lurid gaiety going, then they were kept open in spite of all protests, with the police loyally abetting corrupt masters.

> The most disorderly and licentious conduct of the houses [as the Committee explained] does not ensure the loss of licence; but if at last, from the notorious infamy of the parties complained against, the Magistrates are compelled to interfere, the least possible punishment is inflicted, the tenant is shifted, a real or fraudulent transfer is made, and a new landlord takes possession, to follow the old practices in the same house, with aggravated misconduct; the maxim is 'the house being brick and mortar, cannot be guilty of any moral crime' and the old system is revived with the same profit as before.

[1] 1817, Evidence, p. 484.

The police offered a specious and impudent excuse for their own constant attendance in the flash houses, of which many eye-witnesses gave seamy descriptions:

> It is the practice of police officers to associate in those houses with thieves and other bad characters; they sit down with them, and form part of their company. They go there for their prey, as gentlemen to their preserves for game. . . .

It was not a game preserve which impressed the Select Committee of 1817, particularly after they heard Mr. Fletcher's story of a flash house in Shadwell, and how he struggled vainly, without help from the police, to close it down.

The worst of the flash houses were found by Mr. Fletcher to be the Paviors Arms, the Duke of York, and the White Hart. Describing the Paviors Arms, Mr. Fletcher said:

> I have seen the front of the Paviors Arms so much surrounded with the lowest class of prostitutes and lascars as to impede the path; repeatedly during the last three months I have gone inside and found it filled with the same description of persons, drinking, half naked, and both men and women sitting in indecent and improper postures, and using very dreadful language.

Remonstrated with by Fletcher, the landlord merely offered abuse, probably because he knew that there were higher powers who would protect him. Undeterred, Fletcher, with some of his colleagues in the parish, took up the matter in court. The magistrates, who appeared themselves to have some concealed interest in maintaining the houses, treated Fletcher's request to have the Paviors Arms closed in a contemptuous manner. He nevertheless proceeded to describe the setting in which the White Hart and the Duke of York invited custom.

> He said that those houses were situated in the High-street and nearly next door to each other; that each had a communication by a back door, with a cross street and

passage, filled with houses of ill fame; that both the Duke of York and the White Hart were fitted up for the reception of large parties; that in each there was a long back room, with two rows of benches and tables at the sides, and a large open space down the middle; that upon every occasion when he and his colleagues had gone in, and indeed during the whole of every day, and great part of the night, these rooms were continually filled with prostitutes and sailors; that music was provided by the landlord, and that a succession of parties were continually dancing and drinking.

The magistrates continued to affect a sceptical attitude. They demanded some more serious evidence of abuses. One of them, Mr. Robson, spoke up for the houses concerned, making the worn plea that youth must have its fling:

Dancing among sailors and their girls could not be considered as an evil: that such men must have recreation, and it was better that the women should be in the houses than in the streets; that he could see nothing in all that had been advanced, and he affected to treat the complaint with levity. Upon which Mr. Fletcher proceeded to state, that it was impossible for any man with proper feelings, to witness such scenes and contemplate their consequences without horror; and although he wishes to have been spared the pain of particularizing, and expected to have experienced different treatment, yet as he found it necessary to be explicit, he should not shrink from the task, nor hesitate to declare what was awfully true, that from one to three hundred women of the town were constantly assembled in these rooms, which were the high exchange of prostitution, where every indecency and obscenity were carried to the greatest pitch; that the procuresses and their girls walked the streets in open day, to the annoyance and terror of the inhabitants; that they decoyed men and boys into these houses, where they were plied with liquor, and assailed with women and music; that the floor was constantly occupied by their dancing in the most libidinous manner; that amidst these scenes of riot and debauchery, the bargain was made with the procuresses, and the price of prostitution paid, while the immediate communication with the brothel afforded an easy transition to complete the ruin of those who had been so unfortunately betrayed. Mr. Fletcher further stated, that he believed Henneky, the landlord and reputed proprietor of the Duke of York, had himself purchased the lease of the brothels behind his house, lately belonging to Wolff Cohen, whom the parish had at a great expense prosecuted to conviction, and who had stood in the pillory for keeping them. These and many more such facts were corroborated by the testimony of the other parish officers; and the magistrates were most solemnly conjured as men, as fathers, and as the guardians of public morals, to interpose their authority to remove such scenes of infamy, for the sake of the daughters, the female servants, and the apprentices of the neighbourhood.[1]

In the face of Fletcher's powerful indictment, the magistrates were at length compelled to agree to withdraw the licences; but following some manœuvres by the brewers, new licences were almost immediately granted by the same magistrates to the same three houses, enabling them 'to vie as before in the triumph of impudence and vice'.

Exulting in the defeat of Fletcher and the parish authorities, 'the landlords came down home, increased the number of their musicians; filled their houses with guests, and spent the night in riot and debauchery', at the same time swearing to do an injury to any of Fletcher's friends who might interfere with their pursuits in future. Assured of magisterial support, the guilty publicans joined with the landlords in publishing a florid letter of thanks to the bench for being permitted to carry on with their malpractices:

Even in a case of error, the fairest face of justice beams with a pitying smile towards mercy. May you live long, gentlemen, to enjoy the pleasures arising from a benevolent and virtuous impulse; and afford to others like us,

[1] 1817. Evidence, p. 133.

that pleasure which can be only felt, the pleasurable sensations of a grateful heart.

The letter, signed by the gratified sinners, was addressed to a bench which appeared as partial as the police to the maintenance of flash houses.

*

It is easy to appreciate, in retrospect, that the old system of law enforcement was bad and that the evidence against many of the police was strong enough to justify the decision of Parliament to bring them all under a new and sterner discipline. But it is only fair to give some impression of the hardships with which a good policeman, surrounded by so much disorder and laxity, was faced. John Smith, special constable and beadle of the parish of St. Giles, showed in his evidence before the Committee of 1817 how arduous it was to patrol the streets in days when unemployment and a mean poor law combined to engender an atmosphere of crime. His description of a constable's life in those unreformed days explains why many found it easier to acquiesce in crime rather than to fight it:

What is your district?—Round part of High-street, part of Great Russell-street and what we call the Back Settlements, down the right hand side of George-street, including Buckridge-street, Church-street, Church-lane, Bainbridge-street, Carrier-street and Lawrence-street.

Amongst the lowest descriptions of inhabitants of St. Giles's parish?—Entirely so.

What are the principal evils existing in that district, with regard to the police?—A very great multiplication of crimes, the resort of thieves in particular, as well as great drunkenness.

In what state are the public-houses in that district?— Generally speaking, they keep very correct hours in my division; whenever I find any who exceed the bounds prescribed to them, I always report them to the watch committee; they appear before our gentlemen the first

Monday in the month, and they are told, if they suffer a thing of the kind, they will be suspended.

At what hour do they shut at night?—Eleven o'clock.

At what time do they open in the morning?—Some of them, I am sorry to say, at four in the morning.

Are those in markets or in the immediate vicinity of markets?—Oh dear no, there is no market there; it is in George-street principally.

What is the object of their opening so early in the morning?—I cannot account for it, but from a view of their taking a great deal of money from the Irish people. The Irish are a description of people, that if they are in labour and they come home on the Saturday night with their wages, those wages are spent on the Saturday night or the Sunday morning; and then they shuffle on the rest of the week with their herring and potatoes, or whatever it may be. There are cook-shops and coffee-houses kept open during all the night till the publicans open in the morning.

Have you seen much of the bad effects of dram-drinking in St. Giles's?—Not so much latterly: I have, in times past, and recently, some of it; and I am convinced that after they have been to our Board to get relief, the first thing they do is to go into a gin-shop; and I have picked some of them up drunk at six o'clock, after they have been relieved at the Parish Board.

Then a great proportion of the money given at the Parish Board, is spent in that way?—Yes; I should think three parts out of four is spent in that way.

Are the low Irish almost driven to madness by the drinking of spirituous liquors?—Yes, it is not so prevalent now; they are not so bad in their conduct as they were eight or nine months ago.

Did you see much of the bad effects of dram-drinking a few months ago?—Yes; I have seen them fighting one with another till they have run down with blood, and I have been obliged to interfere to prevent further mischief.

Have you frequently observed quarrels between

husbands and their wives in consequence of their drinking?—I have.

Have you received many charges in consequence?—Yes, I have, many. There was one that alarmed me very much at the moment. A watchman came down to the watch-house; I was up that night; he said, 'Mr. Smith, for God's sake, will you come up with me; there is murder, I believe, in the Bear and Ragged Staff-yard, in Drury-lane.' There had been a sad disturbance, so much so, that the man had absolutely beat one or two patrols and two of the watchmen, and one of them was severely hurt in attempting to go up into his room. The watchman said, 'What shall we do? I will go into the room first, if he sees your hat he will know what you are come for;' he went to the door, the man got hold of the poker, he said, 'I come as a friend; I come to take your part, understanding you have been used very ill.' The man became more cool and put the poker down, and I came in at the moment to his assistance and secured him; that poor woman, from his being in that mad state of drunkenness, was cut dreadfully; I thought she would have died; her hair was all a mass of blood, and her clothes covered with blood.

Do the women often come to the watch-house to complain of their husbands?—Frequently; but I am sorry to say they do not appear the next day to substantiate the charge, after they have suffered themselves to be beaten about in that inhuman manner; they never will appear before the magistrates to substantiate their charge if they can help it.

Do you find the men or the women the worst when they are in liquor?—The women I have found to be so.

Are there any coffee shops in St. Giles's?—Yes, there are several.

Are they considered as nuisances by the parish officers? —The greatest nuisance in the parish, in my opinion.

In what respect?—From being the receptacles of bad women and thieves of the worst description, in fact, bad characters of every description.

Do you think them worse than the public-houses?—

There is no comparison in my opinion between the two, with the exception of one or two.

Are not those coffee-shops places where many poor persons get their coffee or saloop for breakfast?—There is one at the corner of the Bull Yard, which used to be the Black Dog public-house, which used to have bad company, but the man has got rid of them; he shuts up at eleven o'clock at night, and opens at six or five in the morning on market mornings, but others continue open all night.

Then it is the abuse which you complain of in those establishments?—Yes; I have been afraid of going into them without some of the parish officers.

Have you prosecuted any of them as disorderly houses? —I have, one, and the man has absconded.

Are there any cook-shops which are open also during the night?—Yes; there is very little distinction between them, they are receptacles for thieves and prostitutes.

How are children of both sexes brought up in St. Giles's?—In a very shocking manner; a great many of them seem to be left to do as they please.

Are the boys brought up to be thieves, and the girls as prostitutes?—Yes; they appear to be very much so.

Is the number increasing?—Very much so.

Do you not think that that arises from the distress of the times preventing the parents providing for their children, and their turning them out to prey upon the public in consequence?—No, I think not; because in many more respectable parts of St. Giles's parish they are more distressed than they are there, for if we go to examine their apartments, there is the greatest apparent misery, only a bed of straw perhaps, and I know those persons can spend four or five shillings a day; and as to speaking of those young lads or men, I am of opinion they never will work if they can get any thing to steal, and while they associate with girls of the town, who if they find money will find them in drink; they sit and smoke all day long, and if at night they run short of money and the girl has none, they will turn out to commit depredations; there is St. Giles's Pound which has become very lately dangerous, even in the day-time; as I came from Mr. Parton's office, at two o'clock in the afternoon, one of Mr. Meux's clerks called me and said 'Mr. Smith, I want you;' a young lad was standing with him. I said, 'What is the matter?' Mr. William said, 'this lad has been robbed of some lady's half-boots.' I said, 'what! so early in the day as this?' He said, 'yes, and they have done it in a very daring manner; they drove him into the yard, and put his hat over his eyes; they struck him two or three times first, and he could not tell which it was that got the boots away.'

Has Great Russell-street, Bloomsbury, become the resort of young thieves lately?—Yes, particularly the corner of George-street.

Have many robberies been committed lately in consequence?—Not so much lately, because Mr. Furzman and myself and others are out very early in the evening; there was an instance in Caroline-street, last Saturday at two o'clock in the afternoon: there was a young lad made a snatch at a bonnet, and tore the bonnet and got it away, and one of Mr. Dancer's lodgers helped in rescuing the lad and he was not secured; this lodger, Hannah Ragin, had been to our parish last Wednesday, it was out of her day, and she had got the sum of eighteen-pence given to her.

Is she a prostitute?—Yes; she came back and met with another woman, and she says, 'here, this is what I have got from my bloody parish; come, never mind, we will see if we cannot melt some of it down;' and they went into a gin-shop; she did not immediately observe me, I waited till she came out, she was full of abuse respecting the parish; I have found out since that this woman rents a front parlour at Mr. Dancer's, No. 2, next door to where this man was taken in New-street, St. Giles's. A young poor unfortunate creature between thirteen and fourteen years of age, applied for relief at our Board last Saturday; she was asked 'where do you live?'—'at Mr. Dancer's.' Mr. Earle, the clerk of the Board said, 'you are injured.'— She denied that stoutly; she said that she did not want to come into the work-house, particularly if they would allow her some relief out.

It became the duty of the rest of my fellow servants as well as myself, to make inquiry who she was; and I found there were several of these poor unfortunate girls who inhabit this house; some of them rent a room together, but this Hannah Ragin has got the front parlour, and she said to these girls, 'you may as well let me have some of the money, as I rent the room,' and she has the common practice of these unfortunate creatures walking into her room with men, and she walks out during the time they are there, and then returns.

Have you known any washerwomen robbed of the bundles in the street going home with their clothes?—Yes.

Is that a common practice?—One instance occurred within this fortnight; but fortunately the woman had got the bundle too tight in her hand; I do not know whether he did not pull her down; and there was a case of two young persons whom I saw go up Russell-street today, who were charged with robbing a very genteel young woman of a velvet pelisse and other things.

Was she a milliner?—I do not know.

What was the age of the eldest?—The eldest of them was not fourteen.

Those thieves generally attack milliners, and ladies with reticules?—They do; the day after the stealing the half-boots, to the best of my recollection it was not past three o'clock, if so much, a lady and gentleman were going past Mr. Meux's brewhouse, and the boys were pushing one another about to obstruct the passengers, and one of them snatched the lady's reticule and ran up Bainbridge-street with it; the gentleman followed and cried out 'stop thief;' but he was told by some of the inhabitants, that they thought it would be unsafe for him to go any further.

Do you apprehend it would be safe for any person to pursue a thief in the interior of St. Giles's?—Not unless he is an officer.

Would it be extremely difficult to find out a thief in those places?—Indeed there is very great difficulty, even in the officers themselves doing it.

Are the houses numbered?—There are three or four of the same number in the same street.

And a number of courts and alleys?—Yes.

So connected together as to afford facilities of escape? —Very much so.

Children of eight or ten years of age learn to drink spirits from being allowed to beg in the streets?—They do; and I have known their mothers to get so much money from those children sweeping the causeways that they have not been sober for a week together.

From your knowledge of the state of the poor in St. Giles's, do you apprehend that a very large sum is obtained from the parish under false pretences?—I have not the least doubt of it; in the subscription, one of the gentlemen asked me, 'Smith, on your division, if there are any deserving persons you can find, I will distribute some of the relief to them; I had much rather give them double relief, if I knew them to be deserving:' I made inquiry, and could not find above one that I considered a deserving person in that division.

Do you recollect any other flash-houses than those you have mentioned, which are not public-houses?—Yes, Mrs. Mahoney's; I further beg to state, that that person that was tried at the Old Bailey Sessions for the murder of Morris Welch, the watchman; that house was No. 5, George-street. I apprehended her after the Coroner's Inquest, and she was tried for the offence at the Old Bailey, but acquitted principally through the evidence of a little child that was in possession of the fact, though she had acknowledged to Mr. Parton, the vestry clerk, that had she seen her cut the rope off his neck, she would not acknowledge it in court.

How long was this ago?—Last September sessions; from that time Mr. Cummins has turned them all out; there is another private house, No. 4, Church-street, St. Giles's, and there used to be sixteen pick-pockets inhabit that house but they have lately been thinned; some of them have been tried at the Old Bailey and transported, and some imprisoned. From the information I have received, I have not much doubt; that the woman who keeps this house is the person who receives principally the stolen property.

It is my firm belief, that this house is the house, and she the person who in a great measure receives the stolen goods from robberies such as those committed at the Pound; I have not a doubt I shall be able to bring her to justice in the course of time.

There is another circumstance I would beg to mention, which is, that there is a cook-shop in George-street, which was the house where Hickey lived, who was apprehended for a highway robbery; he broke away from Newgate, and has not since been apprehended; and a few days after he broke prison, I was coming down George-street, they were cleaning the house out and whitewashing it, and the man was cleaning out the privy; he pulled up something, he did not know what it was, he called me and shewed it me, and it proved to be a pair of fetters, which I have by me now; it was thought by me, as well as the landlord of the house, as Hickey had lived there, and was taken from there, that he had returned there, and that his irons must have been knocked off there.

Do you know whether there are many houses in St. Giles's for the reception of stolen goods? I have not been able to ascertain it, though I have strong suspicions of the fact, and those houses in particular that I have enumerated.

When a thief escapes into St. Giles's with property, is it not very difficult to detect him with the property upon him?—It is in many cases; my reason for saying that is, that there is a number of loose girls about, who are always ready, in case a man has committed a depredation, to render all the assistance they can to help his escape; and there is a certain character, a jew, who has been seen about there just at break of day; I have no doubt that he conveys away the principal part of the property; that has been my idea for some time.[1]

Such was the problem of law enforcement as seen by John Smith, one of the better sort among old-time beadles, but

---

[1] 1817, Evidence, pp. 149–156, 168.

bigoted and ineffectual by police standards of today. Yet
when some foreign visitor admires the general incorrup-
tibility and efficiency of London's present system of law
enforcement, it is almost a denial of history if he contents
himself with the time-worn reflection 'Your policemen are
wonderful.' Formerly, as Parliament found by diligent
inquiry, the police were not wonderful; and they might
never have become so of their own volition. Gratitude and
admiration ought really to be directed towards that Parliament which, in 1829, by a measure of drastic reform, brought
into being the metropolitan police system as it is today. It
might be argued that in any case standards would have risen
with the passing years. But conditions which are fundamentally bad do not inevitably improve with the passage of
time or the increase in the general level of civilization. Time
in itself is not an agent of reform. Other cities in other
equally civilized countries are not so fortunate in their police
as London is today, because they have not enjoyed the
benefit of the parliamentary method of searching inquiry
followed by legislative remedy. Defending some policemen's predilection for beating a suspect in order to obtain a
confession, an American judge has observed, 'There's a lot
of law at the end of a night-stick.' If there is more law in this
country, it is perhaps due to the fact that Parliament has
been even more vigilant in controlling the police than the
police in controlling crime.

IV

THE CASE OF THE
CLIMBING BOYS

Some few odd lads that you remember not.
(THE TEMPEST, Act V, scene 1.)

IN 1817 the chimneys of Britain were swept, not by a brush pushed up on sticks, but with a brush carried up the chimney by little boys. Everyone knew that; and in addition master chimney sweepers knew that by an Act of Parliament children younger than eight years must not be used. It was that soft-hearted old bachelor philanthropist Jonas Hanway (who incidentally introduced the umbrella) who was at the bottom of an Act to that effect, which was passed, after his death, in 1788. The Act had originally contained other provisions to protect these 'climbing boys' from the 'various complicated miseries' to which they were liable; but these provisions had been thrown out by the House of Lords.

On 5th June, 1817, however, a petition numerously signed was presented to the House of Commons against any employment of boys to sweep chimneys. A Select Committee was immediately appointed to examine the matter, and ordered to meet next day in the Speaker's chamber to begin proceedings. It was composed of twenty-one members, the usual number at that date, of whom five were to form a quorum. They chose as their chairman the Honourable Henry Grey Bennet, member for Shrewsbury, second son of the 4th Earl of Tankerville, and one of the small band of sincere social reformers who had been known since the beginning of the century as Radicals. He was a genuine and sympathetic man, somewhat boisterous and somewhat emotional, who was excellently described by his friend Creevey, the well-known diarist, in a single sentence as 'most amiable, occasionally most *boring*, but at all times most upright and honourable.' His aristocratic and privileged circumstances never prevented him from battling incessantly to better the condition of those of his countrymen who were downtrodden and miserable.

The first witness examined by the committee was William Tooke, secretary and treasurer of a society formed fourteen years previously, in 1803, to procure the abolition of chimney sweeping by climbing boys. He testified that:

> The total number of master chimney sweepers (in London) might be estimated at 200, who had among them 500 apprentices; that not above 20 of those masters were reputable tradesmen in easy circumstances, who appeared generally to conform to the provisions of the Act; and which 20 had upon the average from 4 to 5 apprentices each. We found about 90 of an inferior class of master chimney sweepers who averaged 3 apprentices each, and who were extremely negligent of the health, morals and education of those apprentices; and about 90, the remainder of the 200 masters, were a class of chimney sweepers recently journeymen (qualified day-labourers working for another) who took up the trade because they had no other resource; they picked up boys as they could, who lodged with themselves in huts, sheds, and cellars, in the outskirts of the town, occasionally wandering into the villages round, where they slept on soot bags, and lived in the grossest filth.

The chairman then asked Mr. Tooke:

> Can you give the committee any information with respect to the ages of the climbing boys?—The apprentices

of the respectable part of the trade we found to be generally that prescribed by the Act, namely from 8 to 14; but even among the most respectable it was the constant practice to borrow the younger boys from one another, for the purpose of sweeping what were called the narrow flues. Of the apprentices of the other classes of the trade it was found impracticable to obtain accurate accounts of the ages, but they had the youngest children, and who, in many instances, it was ascertained were much below the prescribed age: thus, the youngest and most delicate children were in the service of the worst class of masters.

Did you ever know of any cases in which a child so employed was not older than 4, 5 or 6 years?—I have known one instance of a child under six years, and you will have evidence before you from other persons of children under five.

Have you heard that it has been the common practice for parents to sell their children for three, four or five guineas?—In many instances.

Do you know whether it has been the custom for parents to employ their own children as chimney sweepers? —They do; and consider themselves entitled so to do, without their being apprentices, owing to an ambiguity in the Act; and they do not consider themselves bound by the Act as to the age of a child who is not apprenticed.

Have you ever heard of cases in which children, even younger than those that have been mentioned, have been so employed by their parents?—Chimney sweepers have told me themselves that they were sent up chimneys by their parents at five years of age.

Mr. Tooke's further evidence presented a very miserable view of the life of a chimney sweep. He explained that in the first place it was a depressed trade, since there were one-third more master sweepers than were required; and since the boys were maintained out of the master's profits, where these were small the children were bound to suffer. They were worse fed than other apprentices, and recognized everywhere by their emaciated appearance and knock knees. All but the best masters, who sent their boys to Sunday school as enjoined by the Act, neglected their education entirely, so that of the 500 London boy sweeps not more than twenty could write their names and the vast majority could not read. The witness dropped sinister references to certain dangers and complaints to which they were prone. Moreover, the despised nature of their employment during the very early hours of the day, their filthy clothes and notorious bad habits tended to cut them off from the rest of society. By about sixteen, or whenever they became too big to climb, they were often virtually unemployable, and drifted ever deeper into vice and crime.

The Society had endeavoured to protect the boys by sponsoring a bill to appoint guardians for them, who should secure that all master sweeps must be registered, and that the boys should be assured of an apprenticeship to the age of twenty-one unless with the guardians' consent they were bound to another trade at sixteen. This bill also was unfortunately rejected by the House of Lords, and the Society concentrated their efforts upon promoting mechanical sweeping as an effective alternative. Let us see first, however, how far subsequent witnesses corroborated Mr. Tooke's sad story.

John Cook, the only master sweep who honestly tried (according to Tooke) to use a machine in preference to boys, had started work between six and seven years of age. Parents, he said, habitually sold their children for £2 or £3 and understated their ages:

> Do you give more for children that are delicately formed, and who therefore are better calculated for ascending small chimneys?—The smaller they are the master generally likes them the better, because they are generally more serviceable to them.
>
> So that a small boy bears a better price than a full grown boy?—Yes, if he is strong enough to do the duty, and is a hearty looking boy of his age.
>
> Is it not the practice of some masters to advertise themselves as being in possession of small boys for the purpose

of ascending flues?—Almost every one has got it in their bills, that they keep small boys for register stoves, and such like as that; I do not recollect ever seeing it in the newspapers, but they do it in their bills.

How do you ascertain the age of the boy when he is offered to you as an apprentice; do you take the parents' word for it?—The parents will often say that he is older than what he is.

Are you in the habit of getting any other evidence of their ages than the parents' own words?—No.

Do you ever get a certificate of their age, or is it the practice of other masters to get one?—No, I cannot say I ever heard of it.

Do you not know that the Act of Parliament required it?—I do not know that it does.

Then you think it never is attended to?—I think that it is never attended to, that is, the certificate.

The witness emphasized the extreme of difference between the treatment of children by humane and by cruel masters, and all which follows must be read in the light of that consideration.

Are the boys ever washed?—Yes, I wash mine regularly; but some of the lower class are not washed for six months.[1]

Do they receive any education?—Many do not.

Is it a general practice to attend divine worship?— Great numbers are neither washed nor attend on the Sunday.

Are not climbing boys subject to sores and bruises, and wounds and burns on their thighs and knees, in consequence of ascending chimneys?—Yes, because learning very fresh boys makes their knees and elbows very sore, but when they have properly learnt their trade these parts get very hard, and they very seldom get sore again unless they meet with an accident; sometimes they get burnt by chimneys partly on fire.

The committee understand, by use, that the extremities

[1] The Journal of the House of Commons for 1 May, 1788, quotes cases of no washing for four or five years; not perhaps an acute misery to boys.

of the elbows and of the knees become as hard as the heel of the foot of a person who walks without shoes?—Yes, it does.

What time does it take before those parts get cartilaginous?—Six months.

Do you find many boys show great repugnance to go up at first?—Yes, most of them do.

And if they resist and reject, in what way do you force them up?—By telling them we must take them back again to their father and mother, and give them up again; and their parents are generally people who cannot maintain them.

So that they are afraid of going back to their parents for fear of being starved?—Yes; they go through a deal of hardship before they come to our trade.

Do you use any more violent means?—Sometimes a rod. When I was an apprentice, journeymen often used to keep a cat, made of rope, hard at each end and as thick as your thumb, in their pocket to flog the boys; and I think it is sometimes used now.

Have you ever known a journeyman ill-use any of the children?—Yes, for very little faults they will frequently kick them and smack them about; the boys are more afraid of them than of their masters.

You said that the elbows and knees of the boys, when they first begin the business, become very sore, and afterwards get callous; are those boys employed in sweeping chimneys during the soreness of those parts?—It depends upon the sort of master they have got; you must keep them a little at it, or they will never learn their business, even during the sores.

Is the skin broke generally?—Yes, it is.

Other witnesses described different methods of persuasion. George Reveley, Esq., explained how he came to belong to the Society:

I will relate a circumstance which settled my opinion in this matter. A young boy was brought to my house to sweep the copper chimney, which runs nearly perpendicular to the top of the house, and is about a brick and a half in width, and pretty nearly square, so that its dimensions may be easily ascertained; there was a hole made in the side for the boy to go up, and the boy was repeatedly driven in at the hole, but the mortar and soot fell in such great lumps upon his head, and with such force, that if he had not had a cap upon his head it would have been broken. Upon seeing the boy writhing in order to get into the chimney, and being satisfied he could not conveniently get up, although the man who was his master, being without feeling, seemed to say it was mere idleness in the boy, and that he would force the boy up, I would not suffer it, and the chimney was not swept.

John Fisher, another master sweep, was asked:

Have you known many instances in which masters have ill-treated their children to force them up chimneys?— Many masters are very severe with them.

What methods do they use to make them go up?—I have seen them make them strip themselves naked, and threaten to beat them; I have been obliged myself to go up a chimney naked, but I do not like to see my children do so.

Benjamin Meggott Foster, Esq., a member of the Climbing Boys Committee, stated:

One mode of teaching children to climb which I understand to be common, though I will not say universal, is to send a greater boy up the chimney after the lesser one, who has a pin in his hand, and if the little boy does not climb properly he sticks it in his feet.

Do you happen to know this of your own personal knowledge?—I have heard of it as a practice, and when I was at Norwich I made particular inquiry upon that subject. In the whole city of Norwich I could find only nine climbing boys, two of whom I questioned on many particulars; one was with respect to the manner in which they are taught to climb; they both agreed in that particular, that a larger boy was sent up behind them to prick their feet, if they did not climb properly. I purposely avoided mentioning about pricking them with pins, but asked them how they did it; they said that they thrust the pins into the soles of their feet. A third instance occurred at Walthamstow; a man told me that some he knew had been taught in the same way; I believe it to be common, but I cannot state any more instances from authority. One part of the sufferings of the children is in what is called clearing chimneys, that is, going up to clear out the rubbish which the workmen, from the slovenly mode of proceeding, often let fall into the chimney; when they are built at the outside, the mortar and little chips of brick fall in, and the clearing of these out is, as I am informed, a very painful operation; it cuts their feet, and lacerates other parts of the body. Another cruelty is, by driving them up with lighted straw or hay.

Did you ever know of that fact?—A man at Walthamstow, of the name of Hedbury, related a circumstance to me, which happened some years ago; the lad was ordered to sweep a chimney at Wandsworth when he was an apprentice, he came down after endeavouring to ascend, and this occurred several times before he gave up the point, at last the journeyman took some straw or hay, and lighted it under him to drive him up; when he endeavoured to get up the last time, he found there was a bar across the chimney, which he could not pass, he was obliged in consequence to come down, and the journeyman beat him so cruelly, to use his own expression, that he could not stand for a fortnight. Another circumstance, which has not been mentioned to the Committee, is that there are several little girls employed; there are two of the name of Morgan at Windsor, daughters of the chimney sweeper, who is employed to sweep the chimneys of the Castle; another instance at Uxbridge and at Brighton and at Whitechapel (which was some years ago) and at Headley near Barnet, and Witham in Essex, and elsewhere.

The Committee received authoritative medical and surgical testimony from Mr. Richard Wright, a surgeon who had worked at Guy's and St. Bartholomew's hospitals. He handed in the following tragic statement[1]:

1 Slightly curtailed.

Dear Sir,

Agreeably to your request relative to the diseases, accidents, etc. incidental to chimney sweepers, I take the present opportunity of enumerating a few of their complaints, as far as my practice has afforded me an opportunity of observing . . . I shall begin with deformity:

I am well persuaded that the deformity of the spine, legs, arms, etc., of chimney sweepers generally if not wholly proceeds from the circumstance of their being obliged not only to go up chimneys at an age when their bones are in a soft and growing state, but likewise by that of being compelled by their too merciless masters and mistresses to carry bags of soot (and those very frequently for a great length of distance and time) by far too heavy for their tender years and limbs: such circumstances I have unfortunately too often been an eye-witness to.

(Later evidence showed that a child of eight or nine would sometimes have to carry the wet sweeping-cloth weighing up to 30 lb. and a bushel or so of soot in a sack as well.)

The knees and ankle-joints mostly become deformed, in the first instance, from the position they are obliged to put them in, in order to support themselves, not only while climbing up the chimney, but more particularly so in that of coming down, when they rest solely on the lower extremities, the arms being used for scraping and sweeping down the soot in the mean time: this, in addition to that of carrying heavy loads, confirms the complaint.

Cancer is another and a most formidable disease, which chimney sweepers in particular are liable to, especially that of the scrotum; from which circumstance, it is called 'the chimney sweeper's cancer'. In general they are apt to let them go too far before they apply for relief, because they dread so much the knife, in consequence of foolish persons telling them it is so formidable an operation and that they will die under it.

They are very subject to burns, from their being forced up chimneys while on fire, or soon after they have been on fire and while overheated: and however they may cry out, their inhuman masters pay not the least attention, but compel them, too often, with horrid imprecations, to proceed.

Stunted growth, in this unfortunate race of the community, is attributed in a great measure to their being brought into the business at a very early age, so early even as five years. And I have heard of instances of children of four years and a half being compelled to go up narrow chimneys.

Cough and Asthma.—Chimney sweepers are, from their being out at all hours and in all weathers, very liable to cough and inflammation of the chest; and which are generally increased by the wretchedness of their habitations, as they too frequently have to sleep in a shed exposed to the different changes of the weather, their only bed a soot bag, and another to cover them, independent of their tattered garments.

Short life is very common among them, frequently from their being exposed to colds, coughs, and from the poor miserable and half-starved manner in which they generally live, as many of them are not allowed anything to eat, except what they obtain through the generosity of the inhabitants whose chimneys they sweep, and in many cases they come off very scantily, so that in order to procure they take every opportunity of purloining any article which may be worth their while, if it should come in their way; and which, when they take it home to their master or mistress (for they seldom know how otherwise to dispose of it) they are rewarded perhaps with some cold and broken victuals, or a little money to procure some. This is another calamity, as it initiates them at early life in acts of depredation, a disposition which increases with their years, and for which several unfortunate creatures have paid the forfeit with their lives.

Accidents they are very liable to from several causes, and among the rest, that of getting fixed in a chimney so as not to be capable of extricating themselves; and there are several instances wherein part of a chimney has been obliged to be taken down before the unhappy sufferer could be relieved.

Clothing.—The clothing of these poor creatures is in general very wretched; not that they require good clothes. but it is essentially necessary for their health and comfort that their clothes should be entire and not a bundle of rags half stitched together, and half torn to pieces.

Diet.—In cases where the masters or mistresses provide the food for their apprentices, it is in general not only of the coarsest sort, but what is worse, mostly of the poorest and stalest meat they can get, and at the most inferior price, which lays a foundation for scurvy, general debility, loss of limbs, and often consumption, by weakening the organs of life.

Time.—I think it very prejudicial to the health of the poor creatures, to be sent out all hours of the night and morning without regard to weather, as it subjects them to most violent colds, etc., and they are exposed to this for no other reason than because it is customary for them to come early, as if a chimney could not be much better swept in the day than during the night, or that part of the morning when it is necessary to have a light in the room, the chimney of which is to be swept, as is constantly the case during the winter months, when the sweep comes long before day-light.

Should the foregoing ideas be worthy your attention, I shall feel myself exceedingly happy in having penned them, and remain.

> Dear Sir,
> Yours, most respectfully,
> (Signed) Richard Wright.

389, Rotherhithe,
July, 16, 1816.

Let us fill out these tragic paragraphs with some supporting evidence. First, concerning deformity, John Cook was asked:

Does not the custom of sending those little boys up the chimneys produce crooked, deformed limbs, and stunt the growth of the children?—I do not know about the growth; I think it may sometimes, because now they have their chimneys sometimes built round, and as they climb

up them they are obliged to be as a corkscrew, and this
will turn the cap of their knees; this I know has often been
the case.

In general, are they not more stunted and deformed
than any other class of children in any other trade?—Yes;
but there are a great many deformed a little before they
come to it, though certainly working at the trade so young
deforms them more.

John Fisher had limped into the room for his examination
and was asked:

Are you at all lame yourself?—No; but I am 'knapped-
kneed' with carrying heavy loads when I was an
apprentice.

In general are persons employed in your trade either
stunted or knock-kneed by carrying heavy loads during
their childhood?—It is owing to their masters a great
deal; and when they climb a great deal it makes them
weak.

And John Harding, another in the long procession of
chimney-sweeper witnesses, some of whom had swept that
morning, completed the picture:

Would you not say, in general, that people who are
employed in that trade are stunted in their growth, and
are apt to have deformed limbs?—Yes, I should think so;
for one seldom sees chimney sweepers, who have been
regularly apprenticed, grow to the same height as other
people; they are almost always deformed or lame. There
was an instance of that near the London Tavern yesterday;
a lad was resting himself against the pump there, who
could scarcely carry the cloth; his knees were bent almost
double.

What was his age?—He was a stout lad; he had been in
the business many years.

Can you inform the Committee, what is the weight
that you have known imposed on the back of a child?—
It depends upon who is with them; the journeyman sometimes will put upon the little boy a heavy sack, but sometimes he will carry it himself.

Can you speak to the greatest weight that you have ever known?—I have known from twenty to thirty pounds.

At eight or nine years?—O yes, a boy always carries the cloth.

Do they ever carry any soot in the bag as well?—Yes, very frequently; he must when he is sent by himself, and the sack and all.

Do you think twenty pounds to be the weight of the cloth alone, when it gets wet?—Yes.

Do they carry a bag too?—O yes, frequently; they frequently give them a bag too.

And sometimes they have soot in the bag also?—Yes, they have.

Have you known many cases of boys not being washed for months together?—I have know many instances.

Did you ever hear of a boy that had not been washed for three months?—O yes; I recollect when I was an apprentice I was never cleaned from holiday to holiday, that is, from Easter to Whitsuntide, and so on; but there are more laws now than there used to be formerly.

Harding added a distressing footnote to one of Surgeon Wright's paragraphs:

Have you known many cases of cancer?—O yes, a great many; it is scarce one in five but who have it.

Is it in the face?—No, it is in the private parts generally; there are many who have undergone the operation for it.

In general there is a great unwillingness to undergo the operation?—Yes; because it is either kill or cure.

Did you ever know any person in your trade die of that complaint, who refused to undergo the operation?—O yes.

Surprising facts came to the Committee's ears. Many of the climbing boys were illegitimate or parish children, and most came from or were enticed out of the poorest homes. But not all. Mr. George Reveley is cited again:

That boy who was sold for £8 8s. od. was also really a fact: I heard it in the neighbourhood of Beverley.

To what story do you allude?—It is printed in our Report; it is the case of the boy who was sold for £8 8s. od.

Was he a stolen child?—Yes, he was a stolen child. I wish to state to the Committee that case in particular, because it comes home to the better sort of persons in higher life. It seems that the child, upon being asked various questions it appeared that he was taken away: the child was questioned how he came into that situation; he said all that he could recollect was (as I heard it told at that time) that he and his sister, with another brother, were together somewhere, but he could not tell where; but not being able to run so well as the other two, he was caught by a woman and carried away and was sold, and came afterwards into the hands of this chimney sweeper. The Society's Report describes the case more fully:

About or in the month of August 1804 a chimney sweeper at Burlington (or Bridlington) in Yorkshire bought a little boy for the sum of eight guineas of a beggar woman; this child, who appeared to be about four years of age, was employed to sweep a chimney in that town; he was taken up it by an elder boy, who left him there, when, as might reasonably be expected, he fell down; by which accident he bruised his legs terribly against the grate; his air and manner appeared so different from those of the children who are usually employed for that purpose, that the Miss Stricklands of Boynton, hearing of the child, went to see him; they were much interested with him, and so persuaded that he had been stolen that they took him home with them, (the chimney sweeper being glad to part with him). Soon after he got to Boynton, the seat of Sir George Strickland, a plate with something to eat was brought him; on seeing a silver fork he was quite delighted, and said, 'Papa had such forks as those.' He also said the carpet in the drawing-room was like papa's: the housekeeper showed him a silver watch, he asked what sort it was—'Papa's was a gold watch;' he then pressed the handle and said, 'Papa's watch rings, why does not yours?' Sir George Strickland, on being told this circumstance, showed him a gold repeater, the

7

little boy pressed the spring, and when it struck, he jumped about the room, saying, 'Papa's watch rings so.' At night, when he was going to bed, he said he could not go to bed until he had said his prayers; he then repeated the Lord's Prayer, almost perfectly. The account he gives of himself is, that he was gathering flowers in his Mamma's garden, and that the woman who sold him, came in and asked him if he liked riding? He said 'Yes;' and she told him he should ride with her. She put him on a horse, after which they got into a vessel, and the sails were put up, 'and away we went.' He had no recollection of his name, or where he lived, and was too young to think his father could have any other name than that of papa. He started whenever he heard a servant in the family at Boynton called George, and looked as if he expected to see somebody he knew; on inquiry, he said he had an uncle George, whom he loved dearly. He says his Mamma is dead; and it is thought his father may be abroad. From many things he says, he seems to have lived chiefly with an uncle and aunt, whom he invariably says, were called Mr. and Mrs. Flembrough. From various circumstances, it is thought impossible he should be the child of the woman who sold him, his manners being very civilized, quite those of a child well educated; his dialect is good, and that of the south of England. This little boy, when first discovered, was conjectured to be about four years old; and is described as having beautiful black eyes and eye-lashes, a high nose, and a delicate soft skin.

Mr. Reveley was asked about the child's fate:

Was he afterwards restored to his family?—He was not.
Was he advertised?—Yes; but some lady took the child and educated him.

The poignant evidence includes sworn testimony and the reports of coroners' inquests upon the young victims of the calling. There are cases of boys suffocated:

. . . John Carney, chimney sweeper, upon his corporal oath, saith, Has known the deceased, Robert Tinson, for two years past: that on Wednesday last about the hour of six in the morning, witness and the deceased were going about in their business . . . that at the house of Mr. Buck, No. 13, Cumberland Street, the boy was employed in sweeping the library chimney, and, knowing it to be a troublesome chimney, two boys went up at the same time; the little boy went out at the top of the chimney, the deceased was in the slanting part, and was as the witness supposed, overpowered by the soot and suffocated . . . a bricklayer was got and the chimney was broke into, where the boy was found, his head surrounded on all sides by the soot; he was suffocated and dead; a surgeon was sent for and all assistance was rendered him, but without effect; he was nearly an hour and a half in the chimney.

The X mark of John Carney.

Boys dead from exposure:

On Friday morning, 12th February, 1808, a climbing apprentice to Holland, in East-street, Lambeth, was sent at three in the morning to sweep some chimneys at Norwood; the snow was so deep and the cold so extreme that a watchman used this remarkable expression, 'that he would not have sent even a dog out;' the boy having swept two chimneys was returning home in company with another, but at length found the cold so excessive that he could go no further; after some little time he was taken to the Half Moon public house at Dulwich, and died in the course of an hour. . . . A coroner's inquest was held on the body, and a verdict was returned—Died from the inclemency of the weather.

Boys cruelly beaten:

On Friday, 31st May, 1816, William Moles and Sarah his wife were tried at the Old Bailey for the wilful murder of John Hewley, alias Hasely, a boy about six years of age, by cruelly beating him. . . . He was forced up the chimney on the shoulder of a bigger boy, and afterwards violently pulled down again by the leg and dashed upon a marble hearth; his leg was thus broken, and death ensued in a few hours, and on his body and knees were found scars arising from wounds of a much older date.

Boys burnt to death:

On 29th March, 1813, a master sweep called Griggs brought an eight-year old apprentice named Thomas Pitt to sweep a small chimney in the brewhouse of Messrs. Calvert and Co. in Upper Thames Street. A fire had been burning for hours and the narrow flue must have been almost red hot, but no sooner had Griggs extinguished the fire than he put the boy in from the top of the chimney. Soon becoming alarmed he called to him to come up, only to receive the answer 'I cannot come up, master; I must die here.' The alarm was given, a bricklayer got the boy out and a surgeon was called:

On inspecting the body various burns appeared; the fleshy part of the legs, and a great part of the feet were injured; the elbows and knees seemed burnt to the bone, from which it must be evident that the unhappy sufferer made some attempts to return as soon as the horrors of his situation became apparent. The Jury returned the following special verdict: That the master set the deceased, an infant of about eight years, to clean the said chimney for him; that deceased accordingly got into and descended the said chimney, and by the heat thereof, a fire having just been in the grate thereof, the deceased was burned and hurt in divers parts of his body; and also by the foulness and unwholesomeness of the air in the said chimney, the deceased was suffocated; of which said burning, hurts, and suffocation, the deceased then and there died, and so the jurors upon their oath say that he died in the manner aforesaid, and by misfortune came to his death.

There is but a single touch of light relief, if such it can be called, among these terrible stories. It described how a boy climbed into a chimney-pot on a roof to clean it. It fell with him into a stone court and was smashed to pieces. Fortunately he was not hurt, and crawled out 'like a bird out of an egg'.

John Fisher was interrogated as to the later history of the boys:

What becomes of those boys who get too large to go up chimneys?—They get into a roving way, and go about from one master to another, and they often come to no good end at last. They get one with another and learn bad habits from one another; they never will stop long in any one place.

What becomes of them at last?—They frequently go into the country and get various places; perhaps they stop a month at each; some try to get masters themselves, and some will get into bad company, which very often happens.

Do they turn thieves?—Yes, they get lazy, they won't work, and people do not like to employ them lest they should take anything out of their houses.

Do you think that the generality of them ever settle in any steady business?—No, they do not.

They generally turn loose characters, then?—Yes, when they get linked with these bad characters, people will not employ them lest they should take anything out of the house.

In order to evade the statutory maximum of six apprentices, master sweeps often employed young boys without apprenticeship as journeymen. The average wage for a journeyman, whether he was ten years old or twenty-five, was the handsome sum of two shillings a week, together with lodging upon a sack of soot in the cellar and scraps of food. A few questions and answers will show the deplorable relations between the journeymen and the boys and will round off our gloomy picture. Thomas Allen was called in and examined:

What trade are you?—A chimney sweeper.

How long have you been in that trade?—Near twenty-two years.

At what age did you begin?—When I was between four and five years of age.

Is it the practice in the trade to hire boys who are not

apprentices?—Yes, frequently, boys of eight or nine years of age, and they allow them so much a week.

What wages are allowed to journeymen chimney sweeps?—Two shillings a week; they give them their victuals, and that is all.

Are the two shillings a week sufficient to find him clothes and other necessaries?—No, certainly not; it is hardly enough to find him with shoe-leather, for they walk over a deal of ground in going about the streets.

In what way then is the journeyman able to live upon those wages?—They get halfpence given them: supposing he is sixteen or twenty years of age, he gets the boys' pence from them and keeps it; and if he happens to get a job for which he receives a shilling, he gets sixpence of that, and his master the other sixpence.

What do you mean by getting the boys' pence?—What the boys get after they have been doing their master's work; they get a penny or so, and the journeyman takes it from them, and 'licks' them if they do not give it up.

Do the journeymen gamble with the boys for this money by playing at chuck-and-toss?—O yes, that is frequently done; even men who are twenty-two and twenty-three years of age will play with the young boys and win their money.

That is, they get half the money from them by force, and the rest by fraud?—Yes.

Are they not driven to this course from the low wages which the masters give them?—Certainly; because they have no other means to get anything for themselves, not even the few necessaries which they may want; for even what they want to wash with they must get themselves.

Perhaps the most cogent evidence of all came from the same witness. He was describing a long, narrow flue at the Goldsmith's Hall, which he had himself swept as a boy. It was nine inches square.

How long is a boy generally in the flue to which you have alluded?—I went in at eight, and came out at two.

What are the smallest flues up which boys are sent?—Seven inches.

Square?—Yes.

The Committee could with difficulty believe it.

Each way?—Yes; that is the smallest we ever send a boy up.

Such is the adaptable intrepidity of some human spirits that there were probably contented and perhaps even happy little London chimney sweeps in 1817, but what must have been the despair and exhaustion of the average child of that age, shut up for six long hours in a flue no wider than a biscuit box, and beset by all the other 'complicated miseries' to which we have listened, including perhaps a brutal master waiting for him below?

A great part of the evidence which the Committee heard was concerned with devices to avoid the use of climbing boys. It all added up to this: that by means of either a brush pushed up on jointed sticks, or a brush pulled down behind a round weight, the vast majority (over 90 per cent.) of the existing flues could be cleaned as efficiently and economically as with boys. The insertion of small iron shutters at critical junction points would achieve the same result in the majority of the remaining flues. It was only in a minute fraction that boys could do what 'machines' could not. There were of course master sweeps prejudiced against all innovation, which at best might require their supervision, instead of a life of ease at the expense of their little slaves. These delighted in showing how much confusion and dirt they could produce in a household with a demonstration of the new machine, so as to have it banished for ever. There were also servants who bad-worded it for fear of losing some secret bribe or perquisite, as Mr. Smart, inventor of one such machine, constantly found:

You said that servants were opposed to the use of the machine, being influenced by the sweeps?—Yes.

Do you know what arguments the sweeps used with the servants to influence them?—The first winter I went out with this machine, I went to Mr. Burke's in Token-house Yard, who was a friend of mine, with a man to sweep the

chimneys, and after waiting above an hour in a cold morning, the housekeeper came down quite in a rage, that we
should presume to ring the bell or knock at the door, and
when we got admittance, she swore she wished the
machine and the inventor at the devil; she did not know
me. We swept all the chimneys, and when we had done,
I asked her what objection she had to it now; she said, a
very serious one, that if there was a thing by which a servant could get any emolument, some damned invention
was sure to take it away from them, for that she received
perquisites.

From whom did she receive these perquisites?—The
master sweep.

Do you imagine the master sweep would give perquisites, if they used the machine?—I do not know; she
said her master allowed her half-a-crown for the kitchen,
and one shilling for every other flue.

Would not chimneys be likely to be done as cheap by
the brush as by the climbing boys?—Yes.

Then although she was influenced by such corrupt
motives, might she not have expected to make a prey of
her master on the one system as well as on the other?—
Knowing I was an acquaintance of her master's she could
not, that might make a difference in my case.

But the truth was plain enough. The Committee therefore
resolved at the conclusion of their report to the House of
Commons that their Chairman should move for leave to
bring in a bill to prevent the further use of climbing boys in
the sweeping of chimneys. The way was hard. Bennet's first
bill perished with the session for want of time. His next
passed the Commons in 1818; but the Lords saw no reason
for speed. They in their turn appointed a Select Committee
who in their turn advised further delay until the Surveyor-
General could in his turn report on the practicability of
superseding climbing boys. Meanwhile, the bill dropped.
When the Surveyor-General's report was received it was
found, not unnaturally, to echo the original conclusions of
Bennet's Committee. It stated that 990 out of every 1,000

flues could be swept with a 'machine' or with ball and brush. In the case of the remaining 1 per cent. of especially complicated flues, the doors which ought to be inserted at the angles as a minimum protection for the boys would themselves immediately allow of sweeping by machine. Unfortunately, the Surveyor-General himself added an ambiguous sentence in his covering report, quite at variance with his expert's evidence, to the effect that the total abolition of climbing boys was not yet practicable.[1]

A few days after the report Bennet returned to the charge with a third bill. He pointed out that the difficult flues were only found in the large houses of rich men, who could easily afford the necessary alterations, and that the arguments for the bill were really unanswerable. It passed in spite of light-hearted opposition in the Commons: but in the Lords it encountered equally frivolous but more effective resistance. Since it is interesting to watch just how the forces of reaction so frequently triumphed at this period, let us glance down into their Lordships' Chamber when the question was being debated, on 15th March, 1819, for going into Committee on the bill. Only three peers seem to have spoken, two in favour of the bill, and the third, who had much the greatest effect, against. The following extracts admirably convey the tone of the Earl of Lauderdale's remarks:

The merits of the present bill might, perhaps, be illustrated by a story which he would take the liberty of telling their lordships, though he was himself the subject of it. The physician who attended him in his late illness, had prescribed large doses of calomel, so much indeed, that he thought it necessary to ask him the reason of such prescriptions. 'O!' (said the physician) 'I can easily prove to you the advantage of my practice. The calomel is like the climbing boys, it finds its way into every corner and cranny of the frame, and sweeps every deleterious particle clean out; whereas the other sorts of medicines resemble the machines, and accordingly do the business very imperfectly. They do not follow all angles and turnings, but

[1] See J. L. and B. Hammond, *The Town Labourer, 1760-1832*, pp. 187-191.

pass over many important parts untouched, and leave heaps of matter, which afterwards kindle into mischief.' (Loud laughter). If this story had any effect in explaining the policy of the measure, he might relate another, which perhaps would serve to render its humanity more intelligible. In some parts of Ireland it had been the practice, instead of employing climbing boys, to tie a rope round the neck of a goose, and thus drag the bird up the chimney, which was cleaned by the fluttering of its wings. This practice so much interested the feelings of many persons, that for the sake of protecting the goose they seemed ready to give up all humanity towards other animals. A man in a country village having one day, according to the old custom, availed himself of the aid of a goose, was accused by his neighbour of inhumanity. In answer to the remonstrances of his accuser, he observed that he must have his chimney swept. 'Yes,' (replied the humane friend of the goose) 'to be sure you must sweep your chimney; but you cruel baist you, why don't you take two ducks, they will do the job as well?' (Laughing).

The zealots for this bill had in their blind eagerness to relieve a partial suffering, as completely forgotten the general interests of society, as had the poor Irishman disregard for the ducks in his anxiety to save the goose. He certainly should be happy to see the use of climbing boys totally abolished; but if a Machine can be invented to sweep chimneys, that invention could not be promoted by this Bill. He must, therefore, oppose it altogether.

Fifty-seven peers voted in the division, twenty for committing the bill, thirty-seven against; Lord Lauderdale's speech carried the day.

For the last time, in May, 1819, Bennet lowered his sights and brought in a fourth bill, no longer to abolish sweeping by boys but only to improve their conditions. Again it passed the Commons; again the Lords voted it out. Bennet had shot his bolt; it remained for others to carry on the struggle. In 1834 an Act at last prohibited the apprenticeship of boys under ten years of age, and even they must be willing. Six years later another Act forbade anyone under twenty-one years from climbing chimneys. Unfortunately these laws were not everywhere enforced and young boys continued to be used and to suffer fatal accidents. It was left to Lord Shaftesbury to try again and again to protect the grimy little victims, and he was not finally successful until his Chimney Sweepers Bill of 1875 secured the effective control of master sweeps by means of licences—the very method originally suggested by Mr. Tooke's Society. By this time climbing boys were unknown in London and many of the large towns in Britain, but Lord Shaftesbury's harrowing speech in moving the second reading of his bill reviewed the situation elsewhere. He quoted evidence from the report of a Royal Commission in 1864 describing the training still used at that date. Mr. Ruff, a master sweep of Nottingham, testified:

No one knows the cruelty a boy has to undergo in learning. The flesh must be hardened. This must be done by rubbing it, chiefly on the elbows and knees, with the strongest brine, close by a hot fire. You must stand over them with a cane, or coax them by a promise of a half-penny if they will stand a few more rubs. At first they will come back from their work streaming with blood, and the knees looking as if the caps had been pulled off. Then they must be rubbed with brine again.

'It is remembering the cruelty which I have suffered,' remarked another master sweep, 'which makes me so strong against boys being employed. I have the marks of it on my body now, and I believe the biggest part of the sweeps in the town have the same. That (showing a deep scar across the bottom of the calf of the leg) was made by a blow from my master with an ash-plant—i.e., a young ash tree that is supple and will not break—when I was six years old; it was cut to the bone, which had to be scraped to heal the wound. I have marks of nailed boots, etc., on other parts.

The Official Report records Lord Shaftesbury's peroration:

He had shown that for more than 100 years that horrible system had been known to the public; that no one

could in honesty plead ignorance of it; that it had occupied the attention of individuals and of Parliament, who
had endeavoured at various times and in various ways
to restrict and suppress it. But the effect had only been
partial. He had shown the long succession of disgusting
and unsurpassed physical and moral cruelties which had
been inflicted and which were still being inflicted on
children of the tenderest years. He had shown that the
law had been inoperative in many places—nay, had been
wilfully and systematically disobeyed through the hostility
of the magistrates, both unpaid and stipendiary, through
the indifference of the public, and the obstinacy, reckless-
ness or parsimony of corporations and private gentlemen.
. . . Surely they would now . . . emphatically declare
that their laws were passed to be obeyed, and not to be
systematically broken; that their beneficent statutes
should not be set aside by high or low, rich or poor. . . .

The speech had a great effect and the climbing boys were
rescued at last. Meanwhile Bennet, who had struggled so
hard to befriend them, had died in 1836. It is lamentable
that he should appear to have achieved so little. But at any
rate he did his duty as a member and vindicated the House
of Commons. Like so many other reformers, he carried the
torch aloft for a stage in the race and handed it on to eventual victory. If public opinion chose to ignore or to tolerate
the scandal of climbing boys for thirty-five years after the
perfectly adequate Act of 1840 had been passed, that cannot
be laid at the door of Parliament. Some years ago an exasperated Minister was stung by incessant ecclesiastical admoni-
tions into protesting with words to this effect: 'the short-
comings of politicians are under perpetual review by the
Church; surely we are occasionally entitled to retort, "Well,
then, let the Church give us better men and women to work
upon!" ' There was much justice in his plea.

V

THE CASE OF THE WHITE HOUSE
AT BETHNAL GREEN

'The body labours in this unhappy predicament until it is destroyed . . .'
—Evidence before a Select Committee on Madhouses by Sir Henry
Halford, 1816.

THE COACHMAN must have grumbled to himself
when the horses were ordered. The record shows that
darkness had already fallen on that February night in
1827 when Lord Robert Seymour's coach set out from
his splendid house in Portland Place, in the centre of
fashionable London, for a drive eastward towards open
country.

First they would have passed the narrow markets of the
city—Leather Lane, Hatton Garden, Poultry; then past the
Bank in Threadneedle Street, the strong heart from which
the gold veins of England were fed. From there the horses
followed the streets leading eastward from the Mansion
House till they stumbled into muddy tracks past ill-lit hovels
and out into the dark fields of Cambridge Heath.

Standing boldly on the green at Bethnal in the parish of
Stepney was the imposing block of buildings which was the
destination sought that night by Lord Robert. A couple of
centuries earlier, a city merchant with more wealth than discretion had almost beggared himself by the lavish scale on
which he had laid it out. It was in Queen Elizabeth's reign
that John Kirby had built a summer mansion in which to

entertain his fellow merchants in a nearly regal style; and his friends had mockingly called it Kirby's Castle.

In Charles II's time the diarist Pepys had slipped away from the stricken city to forget the twin scourges of plague and fire in candlelit feastings within its hospitable walls; and he has left us his impression of the magnificence both of the orchard without and the women within.

At the turn of the seventeenth century, Bethnal House, as it was then called, declined. After the death of Pepys' friends, it fell into hands which found that its isolation and size could be shaped to a sinister use. Part of the old Elizabethan mansion remained as the White House, but part was torn away to make room for a sombre, three-storey, eighteenth-century mansion—the Red House.

Such were the buildings before which Lord Robert Seymour's coach drew up. He knew well enough the owner of the Red House, a respected and influential man of property named Thomas Warburton, who held a medical degree; but on this February night Lord Robert had no wish to encounter him. Instead, he crossed the narrow yard beneath the tightly shuttered windows of the old White House and rapped with his cane on the bolted door. When at length it was grudgingly opened, as Lord Robert later told a Select Committee of the House of Commons, he consulted his watch. It was a quarter to eight. The man who then confronted Lord Robert was one Jennings, a sneering, offensive fellow. To his demand for admission, Jennings retorted: 'Surely you would not wish to see females in their beds at this time of night?'

It was an excuse which Seymour did not countenance, because a moment before he knocked he had seen men carrying a coffin through the yard which led him to observe drily that the hour was not unseasonable for some purposes. But the mystery which Jennings sought to conceal was not to be solved that night, or for many nights to come.

In the near distance the waiting coachman heard voices raised in anger; a minute later Lord Robert returned and brusquely ordered him to drive back to London. To the manservant, who had also noticed the coffin-bearers, the succession of events must have been baffling, but these were days in which servants did not demand and were not accorded explanations from their masters. To Seymour, the frustration of what was admittedly an attempt to gain entry by surprise was ominous. For years now he had lived with the memory of Thomas Warburton, a seemingly upright and gentle figure, testifying to the excellence of all that lay behind the darkened windows and barred doors of the White House. For Jennings, he knew, was in Warburton's service and Warburton, owner of the Red House, knew and bore responsibility for all that took place in his demesne. The rambling Elizabethan wing was, in fact, a private mad-house, and within it were confined certain miserable paupers with whom Lord Robert was concerned: as one of the guardians for the wealthy London parish of St. Marylebone, he felt it his duty to satisfy himself that rumours of neglect and ill-treatment were groundless.

The disposal of pauper lunatics was a problem which the local authorities of those days were each expected to solve as best they might. As the population grew, the increase in the number of idiots or insane persons was becoming a dis-quieting question. Many parishes did not yet see the need for distinguishing between the sane and the insane, so far as paupers were concerned. In a few cases, provided they were harmless, they were allowed to roam according to the dim promptings of their clouded minds. One parish compla-cently records that: 'George Lane, a negro, is deranged and at large . . . sleeping in stairs and closes through the town from choice; is sometimes a bishop, and at other times a duke, as the mania operates; quite harmless.'[1]

Less harmless lunatics were confined in a single work-house with the other paupers, though by this date the more enlightened parishes were beginning to put their pauper patients into charitable hospitals or profit-taking private

1 Port Glasgow—8th June, 1816.

madhouses. Apart from the mighty Bedlam, there was in
London but one great charitable foundation wholly devoted
to the care of lunatics—St. Luke's Hospital in Old Street;
but so great was the demand for admission there that the
master had seven hundred applications to fill a single
vacancy. On the other hand, the private madhouses were
eager to admit pauper lunatics. Each was paid for out of
parish rates and there were no troublesome relatives to
inquire into the manner of their upkeep or of their eventual
demise—for there were few in this class who ever recovered,
for reasons which will be seen.

For many years before 1827, however, the public conscience had been stirring. Some of those who in Hogarth's
day had gone to stare and laugh at the crazy folk who were
then prodded into performing, like animals, behind bars,
must have come away protesting. Nearly a hundred years
before Warburton's day, when the White House was kept
by a ruffian named Wright, a poor devil broke out and
escaped across the fields to Mile End. In rags and with
chains still dragging from him, he was found at last by the
parish officers of Aldgate within the city of London, and
mercifully allowed to petition the Lord Mayor, who gave
him his liberty. The man who thus escaped was Alexander
Cruden, author of the Concordance to the Bible. Describing
life in the White House at Bethnal Green in 1737, he told
how he was chained like a galley slave among dozens of
other screaming men and women. Rough-and-ready
methods to subdue resistance were violent purgatives and
profuse bleedings administered by the 'surgeon', and the
dreaded strait waistcoat, laced so tight that resisting patients
turned black with the pressure on their veins.

Several times during the eighteenth century Parliament
had been seriously concerned by such revelations; and in
1774 the last word in ameliorating legislation was agreed to
by both Houses. Commissioners were appointed with the
duty of granting a licence for each asylum; of visiting each
licensed house once a year; of seeing that each private

patient within the house had been duly certified as insane by 'a physician, surgeon or apothecary'; and of inspecting the accommodation of the patients, their food and bedding. This model Act was scrupulously observed; but in 1807 and in 1815, Select Committees of the House of Commons reported adversely on it. It appeared that nothing so well-meaning could have worked worse. First, the Commissioners appointed under the Act could only grant, but never withhold, licences. Secondly, since the term 'apothecary' had no legal definition, everyone could—and many did—adopt this description for the purpose of certifying a patient as insane. Thirdly, the power of inspection was supported only by the feeble weapon of recommendation. The worst asylum keepers were therefore immune from penalty.

The main object for which the Commissioners had been appointed was the protection of private patients. Pauper lunatics were assumed to be already protected and provided for, in a manner appropriate to their station, by the local authorities, who were not, as they are now, under the general control of the central government.

Twelve years before his clash with Jennings, Lord Robert Seymour had sat as Chairman on the Select Committee of the House of Commons which investigated the problem in 1815. In a second capacity, as guardian of the poor of the parish of St. Marylebone, he had offered evidence which helped to illustrate the variation in treatment of poor lunatics by different parishes. The parish of Marylebone sent its paupers to the White House, the apparent excellence of whose administration had attracted two other metropolitan parishes—St. Pancras and St. George's, Hanover Square. The respected proprietor, Thomas Warburton, was thus skimming the profit from three of London's most wealthy parishes.

In 1815 Lord Robert was proud to state that Marylebone was 'in the excellent practice of visiting, by its medical staff, its insane poor every month.' The staff comprised 'an eminent physician, a surgeon and apothecary, who, after their

8

visitation, make to the directors of the Poor a report in writing of the state of every pauper they have seen, as well as of his provisions and bed.'

Seymour also produced a sample report which, in spite of the date, evidently gave himself and the Committee complete satisfaction:

Monthly Report, Bethnal Green. April 1st, 1815.

I have visited the Wards, they were very clean and well ventilated, and the beds turned down to the feet. The provisions were also inspected and found to be proper and of a good quality.

Signed: W. F. Goodger, Apothecary.

So much for an—apparently—good house and conscientious parish officers. Unfortunately, what Lord Robert referred to as 'the humane and tender attention' of Mr. Warburton and his staff was not available everywhere. The Committee over which Seymour presided heard something of what was going on further afield. On 20th December, 1815, the weather in Scotland was extremely severe. During a storm of wind and snow an emissary from the Committee inspected certain private madhouses 'in order to ascertain the care taken of the patients at that rigorous season, when no inspection could be looked for.' It had been rumoured that patients were treated harshly in Mrs. Bourhill's little house in Cottage Lane, Musselburgh, where eleven inmates—or victims—were confined, and the state of one such patient is vividly described:

. . . On opening the door, the room appeared nearly dark, there being an outer shutter closed upon the window, which, though shattered and thereby insufficient to exclude the wind and the snow, in a great measure excluded the light. On causing this shutter to be opened, it appeared that five panes of glass were wanting, and that a quantity of snow had drifted into the room. In a bed without curtains, placed betwixt the window and the door, being within a foot of the former, lay the unfortunate patient chained by the leg, coiled up under two piles of thin blankets. She had under her a single mattress containing so little wool, that the lower part was quite empty; her feet were cold and edematose, and there were chilblains on two of her toes. She could give very little information about herself, but in general complained of ill treatment and must have suffered much from cold during the then rigorous season. It was indeed hardly possible to conceive a human being in a more wretched condition. . . .[1]

It was during the study of evidence presented to this Committee that Lord Robert Seymour and his fellow members found that delay or reluctance in opening up a house to visiting officials almost inevitably betokened an evil establishment where filth and cruelty abounded. As chairman, it was his duty also to question a brother and sister who suggested that Thomas Warburton had unprotestingly witnessed appalling ill-treatment within the narrow walls of the White House. Neither witness was still employed there, and apart from deploring some unnecessary overcrowding, the Committee had no fault to find with Thomas Warburton. Indeed, the chairman himself had kind words for him, and the allegations of the two former keepers were disposed of by a short examination of Mr. Warburton himself, in the course of which he denied, firmly and absolutely, the whole of the unfavourable statement which his former employees had made about him.

The parish of Marylebone, therefore, saw no reason to discontinue sending their pauper lunatics to the White House, and for twelve more years they continued to be placed there. It was a course which Lord Robert Seymour countenanced, and if he, as their most distinguished guardian and chairman of a parliamentary committee of inquiry, approved of the practice, no parish official was going to suggest any alternative.

1 Answers by Sir Wm. Rae, Sheriff Depute of the County of Edinburgh, to the Queries of the Committee of the House of Commons on Madhouses, 26th April, 1816.

All these reflections and memories must have come crowding back into Seymour's mind on the night in 1827 when Jennings refused to admit him. He had only gone down to Bethnal Green at such a late hour in the hope of allaying rumours and suspicions put about by a busybody named Pepys, a fellow guardian who had been repeating unfavourable gossip about the state of the paupers in the White House. Now it seemed, from Jennings' uncompromising refusal to admit him, even after he had declared himself to be an interested party, a magistrate and a member of Parliament, that perhaps after all these years of acquaintanceship he had been deceived in Warburton. Moreover, he would have to admit to his fellow guardians that he had himself been fooled, that true evidence given at an inquiry under his chairmanship had been rejected in favour of false, and that he had been indirectly responsible for twelve years of continuing misery which Marylebone's defenceless paupers had suffered. All this was as yet unproven. At best there were doubts and suspicions to which Warburton might once again be able to offer satisfactory explanations.

*

The secrets of the house kept by Jennings caused continued whisperings in the limited circles concerned with the welfare of the poor, and the case of the White House at Bethnal Green finally reached the ears of certain public-spirited members of Parliament. In the course of the succeeding summer, the House of Commons agreed to the appointment of a Select Committee to inquire into the treatment of Pauper Lunatics in the County of Middlesex. With remarkable speed, the Committee went to work and within a fortnight had made a report which represents an outstanding piece of quasi-criminal investigation, not least remarkable because it was undertaken in days before Sir Robert Peel had instituted the Metropolitan police. In the course of that fortnight, between the 14th and 28th June, 1827, a widely varied assortment of witnesses came and

went through the courtyards of the Old Palace of Westminster, where the Committee met. In a dimly lit room the
Chairman, Robert Gordon, assisted by his fellow members,
questioned over fifty men and women, ranging from dishonest professional men to discharged lunatics of integrity.
The story which emerged from their sometimes truthful,
sometimes lying lips was sordid and painful. Though in
their report the Committee made no adverse comment on
any of the personalities in the case, the skill and persistence
of their questioning was such that no normally astute
reader could be left in doubt whether a witness was an
honest man or a perjured rogue.

The first of the principal witnesses called was Mr. John
Hall, who, like Lord Robert Seymour, was a guardian of
the parish of Marylebone. In a vivid story he explained that
Marylebone had now removed its patients from the house
in question after he and a clergyman colleague had accidentally made the discovery of some hidden and filthy premises
never previously inspected.

Lord Robert Seymour lay ill in his house at Portland
Place, and could not attend the Committee. But that public-
spirited magistrate wrote to the Chairman to claim, perhaps
a little tardily, that for twelve years at least disgraceful
conditions had existed at the institution which Jennings
ran on behalf of Mr. Warburton.

Mr. Garrett Dillon, a surgeon employed by the parish of
St. Pancras, was then called before the Committee. He had
visited the White House for the past six years. In his first
answers he showed clearly that he was not going to speak
in favour of Mr. Warburton.

Will you state, in the first place, your opinion as to the
medical treatment in that establishment with regard to
the cure of the patients?—With regard to the cure of
derangement there is no medical treatment.
Will you have the goodness to state to the Committee
your opinion of the state of the house?—My opinion of the
condition of the White House is that it is unfavourable

to recovery; in fact, that it almost offers every obstacle to recovery that can well be conceived. . . .

Will you state these obstacles?—The principal obstacles are, that there is no observance whatever as to the regulation of diet; the high and the low are allowed the same description of food; in the day-time, persons labouring under every form of insanity are in the same rooms and in the same yards; there is no classification whatever; some of them are chained to seats and some of them are handcuffed; and there are some exceedingly noisy, and others are melancholy and dull, all in the same apartments, and in a yard too small for such a number, where they have not room for exercise or for employment; there is no employment whatever, which I think, as a medical man, would be very useful in curing many forms of insanity.

The doctor ended his evidence by admitting that bad though conditions at the White House were, it had been chosen by the parish as being the best, and that no other private establishment was likely to be better. The parish of St. Pancras supported some 35 to 38 pauper lunatics at Mr. Warburton's, and paid for them nine shillings a week each. In view of the modest costs of living in 1827, this might be considered an ample, even a generous provision. Advertised in *The Times* newspaper in the same month in which the committee of inquiry was sitting were 'cheap unfurnished apartments, to be let in a respectable private house within 1 mile of Charing Cross, first floor consisting of a handsome drawing room and bedroom, a large boarded kitchen and a wash house at 8 shillings a week.'

After the Committee had heard reports on several other visits of inspection, a witness came forward who was able to describe life at the White House from the point of view of a patient: Mr. William Solomon told the Committee, from his own experience, that the patients were treated in a very cruel manner, particularly those patients who were confined in the crib rooms.

Will you describe the manner in which they were

treated?—They were in the habit of treating those men by chaining them down of an evening about an hour previous to dusk, in things called cribs, which are boxes containing straw, and leaving them there till the following morning locked in, without any attendance being paid to them in the course of the night, let whatever would occur; and on the Saturday evenings, they were locked down in the same state, and kept till Monday morning, without being unchained or allowed to get up to relieve themselves in any way whatever.

On the Monday morning what was done?—On the Monday morning, like the other mornings, when they got up, they were many of them in a very filthy state, and I have seen them in the depth of winter, when the snow has been upon the ground, put into a tub of cold water and washed down with a mop. . . . I have seen many men die in that place, I consider, from entire neglect; I will mention the case of one Wheatly, who belonged to St. George's parish; he certainly was a man who was at times very saucy, and frequently gave the keepers offence; this man gave one of the keepers offence, and he was taken into the long room, and he had a pair of handcuffs put on, and was chained, in a manner which is very generally practised there, to the side of the room; another of the patients, who acts as a keeper though he is a patient himself, came into the room, and Wheatly and he got quarrelling while he was in chains in this manner; he beat Wheatly very severely, and in the course of two or three days, Wheatly was still kept chained; he was taken very ill, lost his speech; he remained in that state for some time, and was chained down for the night in one of these cribs; at last he got into a very dangerous state, in fact he was dying, and on Tuesday morning, when Mr. Warburton was expected, he lay on the ground in the hall, and he was spoken to by one of the keepers, of the name of Barnard, and told to get up and not lie there, as his illness was all sham, that was the expression used; he did not pay any attention to him, and he was taken up in the infirmary and he died the following evening.

During the time that you were in Mr. Warburton's

establishment, had you any reason to believe that any effort was made to promote the cure of mental disorders? —Nothing more, I believe, than a very strong medicine administered to the patients that were high; it is a very strong purgative medicine, which acts very forcibly on the poor men, and some of them suffer very dreadfully from it.

Was that given indiscriminately to all?—Only to the high patients.

Which are the high patients?—The high patients are those who are placed in cribs of a night.

Are high patients and wet patients the same?—There are many patients who are subject to fits, and during the time they are under that affliction, they are not sensible of what they do, and as such they are put in those cribs, but there are many of those men that sleep there for weeks and months that never commit any offence.

Have you any reason to believe that that strong medicine has been administered on a Saturday evening to the crib patients, who were afterwards allowed to remain till the Monday morning without being removed?—That medicine is generally administered in a morning.

Have you ever been in the infirmary?—I have been in it once or twice.

Was that in a very bad state?—It was generally in a very dreadful state, till it was visited accidentally, or I should rather say by force, by two gentlemen who came from Marylebone parish one afternoon without giving any notice of their intention; they walked up into the infirmary, and I believe they found it in a very dreadful state, and one of the men belonging to that parish died that afternoon or the following day. Colonel Clitheroe, with one of the gentlemen that had been there the previous day came to visit the infirmary, but previous to that, as early as five o'clock in the morning, this infirmary was whitewashed and cleaned out, new blankets and new coverlids put on the beds, and the place was made to appear comfortable.

When you state that it was in a very dreadful state, will you describe in what state it was?—I cannot describe it farther than the filth; I never was in it above once or twice; but I understood that when those gentlemen went up to it, they were quite affected from the stench that arose from the patients and the filth about the place.

With regard to the general care as to cleanliness, is there any attention paid to the personal cleanliness of the patients?—In the first place, there is no soap allowed in the house in that department; there were at one time very nearly 170 men in that department of the place, and one towel only was allowed, once a week, for their use and accommodation, for the whole number of persons that may happen to be there.

William Solomon went on to describe the barbarous methods of restraint employed on the crib patients. They were chained by both hands and by both legs, and they remained in that state the whole of Sunday, at the mercy of their fellow lunatics.

Was it the custom generally to appoint the convalescent patients to what is called crib-room men, or to have the superintendence of a separate crib-room?—The convalescent patients have the care of the whole of the crib patients; they put them all to bed. The keepers themselves, after they are put to bed, go to see that they are all safe; but they have nothing to do with putting them to bed; and at times they are very violent, and use the poor men extremely ill.

Do you mean, that they do that without the presence of the other keepers?—I do.

Do you speak that of your own knowledge?—I speak from my own knowledge.

How long were you there?—I was there fifteen months, with the exception of three days.

You were discharged in consequence of the interposition of Mr. Dillon?—I was.

Considerable difficulties having been thrown in the way of such discharge?—Very much so.

The Committee then asked him about the food: from the context, it appears that the diet was considered to be 'of a very common description'; though a modern dietician might well commend it.

The bread was very good, and a very good quantity of it; but as to the other part of the diet, I cannot speak in praise of it; the meat was of the commonest description, such as stickings and clods of beef; and they had broth of what they termed the marrow bones, twice a week, which was very common fare; on Wednesdays they had a little boiled rice, and on Fridays a bit of plain pudding for dinner; they had in general water gruel, oatmeal and bread, for breakfast, unless the friends paid something extra for tea and coffee; and they had bread and cheese for supper.

Was it the custom of one patient to sell to another who might have the means of buying?—There were bargains of that description frequently made.

How often did Mr. Warburton himself inspect that part of the establishment with which you are acquainted? —They were in the habit of coming down, either the old gentleman or his son, twice a week, Tuesdays and Fridays.

Then, excepting that visit twice a week, the establishment was entirely under the superintendence of Mr. Jennings?—It was.

How often did Mr. Jennings visit the different departments of the asylum?—He was in the habit of coming in very seldom; he used to come round on a Monday morning to give money to those patients that were allowed a certain sum of money weekly[1]; he might have come in once or twice in the course of a week besides.

Then it was not the custom either of Mr. Warburton or of Mr. Jennings to examine each department of the asylum twice a day?—It was not.

You stated that a strong purgative medicine was administered to the patients; by whose advice was that administered?—I should think it was by the advice of Mr. Dunston, the surgeon of the house.

Was he constantly resident at the place?—No; he came twice a week, always at the same time.

[1] This money, the witness explained, was provided by relatives. Patients used it to buy 'snuff or porter'.

How many regular keepers were there?—In this department there were two for a considerable time after I came in; but I believe when I left there were three.

How many lunatics were there at that time in the establishment?—There were at one time 164, but I believe after that they were reduced, and part of them were sent to the next house.

For the superintendence of those 164 persons there were only two regular keepers?—Yes.

Incidentally, Mr. Solomon threw an interesting light on the difficulty of getting away from the White House, otherwise than in a coffin. It only took one doctor and half an hour's examination to put him in, but had it not been for the good doctor Dillon it is improbable that Solomon would now have been giving testimony as a free and evidently sane man:

In February [he told the Committee] after I was sent in in December, Mr. Warburton used, when he came into the yard, to hold conversation with me, and he asked me what relatives I had; I told him that I had a father and mother (and I am sorry to say they both died while I was in confinement), and that I had a brother; and he requested me to write to my brother, and desire his attendance on the following Tuesday; I did so, and he never came: I remained expecting him every day that Dr. Warburton came, but he never came, and Mr. Warburton told me that he would write to him upon the subject. Since I have been out, I have seen my brother, and he tells me that he never received any communication upon the subject; and it appears to me as if it had been done for the purpose of irritating my mind.

Another crib patient, John Nettle, then gave some details which fully confirmed the evidence of Solomon. Nettle told the Committee that he himself had been confined in the reeking crib-room for seven months. The questions continued:

At what time in the evening were you generally put in

there?—According to the time of the year; we went to bed about three o'clock in the afternoon, and we did not get up till about nine in the morning.

When you were put into one of the cribs were you fastened down?—I had my two hands locked in this way (describing it) and a large iron round my leg.

Were you ever put in there on a Saturday night and kept till Monday morning?—Yes, we were locked down at three o'clock on Saturday night, and there we laid forty-eight hours, and more than that in winter time, fastened in that way, never loose; we could hardly get our meals, indeed we had our victuals brought to us.

Were you not unloosed when your victuals were brought to you?—Certainly not; some men were locked all fours, I had only one leg locked; but some of them had both legs with a large staple fastened to the crib.

But you were confined with both arms?—Yes.

Will you state how your food was administered to you on the Sunday?—The people that were keepers of those crib-rooms were the patients, and there was Mr. Dalmy and Mr. Barnard were keepers over the patients, they used to bring the food to us on the Sunday.

Who fed you?—We fed ourselves as well as we could but nobody fed us; we had a long chain, so that we could get our hand to our mouth; but we never had a knife or fork, or any thing else to use.

While you were confined in those cribs from Saturday night till Monday morning, had you a shirt on?—Not a bit.

You were perfectly naked?—Perfectly naked.

You had only the straw and the rug?—The straw and one blanket only to cover us.

And you were left in that state in your own filth till Monday morning?—Yes.

Ann Gibbons, a woman inmate, was then called. She drew some interesting comparisons between Bedlam and the White House and threw further light on the methods of management of the latter by Mr. and Mrs. Jennings.

How long were you at Mr. Warburton's house at

Bethnal Green?—I was two years and ten months the last time, and I was between nine and ten weeks the first time. I went from Mount-street to Bedlam and from Bedlam to Bethnal Green, and from there I went to my brothers, and then I came back again to Mount-street.

You were the person that gave the information to the parish officers relative to the rooms that they had not discovered?—Yes.

Will you state generally what was the condition of that place?—What I saw was the poor people that were put into the crib; they were made quite naked and put into the crib rooms; they were put to bed about four o'clock on a Saturday evening and they remained in that state till Monday morning about six, chained down.

Can you give the Committee any information as to the infirmary?—If any of the gentlemen belonging to the parishes came, and any of their patients were fastened in this way, they were put into a blanket and carried up stairs into the infirmary and put into one of those comfortable beds till after the gentlemen were gone, and they were brought down again and put into the crib again naked.

Did you ever see the women beat much?—No, I did not; they would take them back into the straw rooms, and after they had confined them they used to beat them, because we have heard the cries and we have heard the blows, but I have not been present to see it.

You never were an assistant keeper yourself?—No, never; they did not like me to be present, because I was apt to notice a good deal, I never had any confinement myself, I never stood in need of any.

Then you do not complain of any ill usage yourself?— No, I was not ill treated myself, but I have seen many others that were.

By convalescent keepers?—Some of them were.

Did you perceive any difference in the treatment which the patients experienced from the regular keepers and that which they received from the convalescent keepers?— The servants themselves, if any of the patients offended them, they used to fasten them down and sometimes use them very ill.

How was it with respect to the convalescent keepers?—They were sometimes in a very bad temper and sometimes they used to beat them.

Then the principal part of the duty must be done by the convalescent patients?—Yes.

Did the regular keepers ever perform those duties which were ordinarily performed by the convalescent patients?—They sometimes beat them, they used to use them very ill.

How many female patients were there?—I am not quite certain, but I think between two and three hundred.

How are the crib patients cleaned?—They were cleaned on the Monday morning after they got out of their straw.

How were they cleaned?—They used to have their clean things put on.

They were not washed in a tub?—No, they were washed in a pail, but not in a tub.

There was nothing wrong in the manner of cleaning the women?—No; I did not see any thing amiss in the way of cleaning them.

Were the women always attended by the female keepers?—No; when there was any female patients that was rather obstreperous, some of the men used to come to assist in confining them.

Were the women naked in the cribs?—Quite naked.

Did it frequently happen that men were called in upon those occasions?—Yes, sometimes it happened two or three times in the course of one week, and sometimes it did not happen more than once in two or three weeks.

Did you prefer the treatment at Bedlam to that at Bethnal Green?—It was very kind indeed at Bedlam.

Can you state any respect in which the treatment at Bedlam differed from that at Bethnal Green?—I never saw any chained and strapped all day at Bedlam, they were up every day.

Were they better cleaned and better dieted?—Yes, much better.

How did you find the diet at Bethnal Green?—It was very indifferent; any person that was quite well in health it might do very well for, but for a person that was sickly it was very indifferent.

What was the diet in Bedlam?—On Sundays we had boiled beef; on Mondays we had a boiled pudding; on Tuesdays we had sometimes baked meat and sometimes boiled; on Wednesdays we had pea-soup; on Thursdays we had meat again; on Fridays we had baked pudding; and on Saturdays we had boiled rice milk.

In what respect do you think the diet at Bedlam is better than that at Bethnal Green?—Every thing we had was of the best; what we had at Bethnal Green was very common, the meat was not good; in short it was so indifferent that I could not eat it.

You mean that it consisted of coarse and bad pieces?—Yes, it was very hard.

Were you ever in any other of those establishments?—No, I never was.

Did the female patients at Mr. Warburton's suffer from cold very much?—I should think so, but I did not hear them complain; I have seen them go quite across the room when the snow has been upon the ground into their back straw rooms naked.

Was the window to the crib-room glazed?—It was a little window, what they call a bird-cage window; there was a kind of shutter that drew backward and forward.

Was there any glass?—Yes, a little kind of bird-cage glass.

Was the same diet given to all patients at Bethnal Green?—It was to all the parish patients; but the privates I believe had something better.

In Bedlam was that the case?—No, any one that was sick was put upon sick diet, such as a bit of fish or a light pudding.

Then in one of those places of confinement attention was paid to diet with reference to the health of the patients, and in the other that was not the case?—Yes.

When the officers of the parish came to see you, did you ever make any complaint?—No, I dare not.

Have you ever known an instance in which an individual making a complaint was treated worse in consequence?—If their friends came to see them, and they
made any complaint, they have been ill-treated when they
came back again.

You know that the keepers were never present when
they asked you as to the treatment?—No, they were
just outside the door; they stood inside the kitchen
door, which is close to the parlour; Mr. and Mrs. Jennings
were always present in the kitchen when they were
there.

*

The Committee had heard the evidence for the prosecution, as it might be called. They now sought to find out
why the parliamentary enactment which since George III's
day had provided for inspections by commissioners to
asylums, had proved ineffective in this case. They therefore
called Dr. John Bright, the secretary of the commissioners,
to give an account of the ordinary system of visits. His
apathetic evidence revealed the complete inadequacy of the
Act (14 Geo. 3, c. 49), providing for inspection of private
asylums, which required them to visit the patients of each
madhouse once a year only, and then only private patients,
the Act not extending to pauper patients, who were not
even entered on their returns.

Other defects of the power vested in the commissioners
included the granting of licences to keepers whatever
offences they may have committed—save that of actually
refusing entry to the commissioners. Again, the Act was
vague in its definition of medical men; there was nothing to
prevent someone calling himself an apothecary and then
certifying a man insane, the certificate being endorsed by
the asylum keeper (also defined as a 'medical person').

Describing the Commissioner's visit to the White House
in April, 1827, one of the forty-eight in and around London,
Dr. Bright said that he found conditions satisfactory; this was
corroborated by another commissioner, whose colourless

evidence only served to illustrate the futility of the existing method of inspection.

An independent medical witness, Sir Anthony Carlisle, who had made a special study of lunacy, gave a downright condemnation of the system with which the complacent commissioners seemed content.

If there should be any establishment, in which there are confined upwards of five hundred patients without any resident medical men, and to which only occasional visits were paid by medical men, you would consider that establishment deficient in its medical appointments?— Quite improper, that would be my judgment of it.

Do you think that those five hundred patients would require much more medical attendance, than any other five hundred persons?—I am of opinion that no insane person is ever in perfect bodily health, their bodily health requires constant attention, and they are more liable to bodily errors than persons who have no mental disease, that is my judgment of them.

Most of the evidence already given about the White House, when put in an entirely general way to this expert, received his adverse comment: his answers may be held to illustrate the most enlightened alienist opinion of the age:

Do you not think it would be of great advantage in those establishments, if a register was to be kept of the process towards cure of each individual, in which the resident medical gentleman was to insert all the circumstances attending each case?—It would be very important to the medical art, to the healing art altogether, if the public were made better acquainted with the history, the progress, and the treatment of insanity; it has been kept a secret, it has been kept close, and in the hands of individuals for a purpose which it is not necessary to mention; in consequence of that there is in the medical profession generally a great want of knowledge of what is done, or what ought to be done, and the history of the case, and the progress towards cure, or the relapses and the causes which may lead to the one or the other are very

9

insufficiently known; they are not diffused in the profession at all, but I think it would be of great importance, and it would lead to the improvement of the treatment of the disease, and certainly to a better understanding of it generally, if such reports and registers were kept and made public from time to time.

As you have stated that variety of diet is very necessary in particular cases, would you not consider variety of medicine very important?—Certainly, there can be no sweeping rule for giving medicine.

Then if it has been stated that the same medicines had been given to all the patients throughout a madhouse, do you not consider that a great error?—I think it a great medical error.

And that it might be productive of very injurious consequences?—Yes, certainly.

In that case are there not many instances of lunacy in which an allowance of 9s. a week would be extremely incompetent to procure the necessary treatment of mind and body?—I think 9s. a week would be quite insufficient.

Have you ever considered that the situation of a Lunatic Asylum is a matter of great importance?—I think in some parts near London they might find places sufficiently healthy: I think when a man is in a state of convalescence he should be removed to a convalescent establishment or to his friends; if there was a public garden twenty miles off, where a man was permitted to work and to tie up seeds and so on, an auxiliary to the main establishment, it would be a most important thing, and probably it would pay itself; I merely take leave to throw out that, particularly a kitchen garden, a market garden.

The resident superintendent at Bethlem hospital, Dr. Edward Wright, showed that most of these precepts were already put into practice at the New Bethlem.

Will you have the goodness to state to the Committee the mode of restraint adopted in that asylum?—The modes we have are only the waistcoat, the belt and gloves, and the hobbles for the feet, a sort of strap going from ankle to ankle, but allowing the individual to walk with about half a pace.

Are you in the habit of using much restraint with regard to the patients?—Very little indeed; the report for the last week was, that seven individuals had been more or less under restraint, none of them constantly.

At this point, a statement was delivered in by Mr. Warburton, strongly defending himself against the charges made against the White House by the majority of the witnesses already called by the Committee.

From the perusal of the evidence (he wrote) I collect that the principal charges against myself and my establishment at the White House, Bethnal Green, are,

That the house is too crowded with patients:

That no medical attention is paid:

No curative process is used:

No classification of patients:

No variation of food, according to the health and state of the patients:

Not sufficient number of keepers:

Inhumanity and neglect of superintendents and keepers towards the patients:

That convalescent patients are *made* to act as keepers:

That maggots were found in the cribs from want of cleanliness.

In asking leave to answer this formidable list of charges, which he himself so aptly summarized, Mr. Warburton drew up an imposing list of witnesses whom he wished to call. This began with the three senior medical commissioners, included the guardians and doctors of the various London parishes which sent patients to the White House, and ended with his own asylum keepers and, audaciously, Lord Robert Seymour himself.

When he appeared in person before the Committee, however, Mr. Warburton's answers were by no means as convincing as his statement.

Ill-treatment, overcrowding, were proved against him in the first few questions.

You state in your paper, 'I have never had a complaint made either by the medical commissioners or by the medical gentlemen of the different parishes'. Do you mean, after the questions that have been put to you by the Committee, upon reflection, to persevere in that statement?—As to the general treatment of the patients, no such complaint had been made, to my recollection; I do not recollect any.

It appears that on the 20th of June, 1817, the commissioners state that the rooms were ill numbered, and that the number of keepers was insufficient; do you remember that complaint having been made?—Upon recollection, I think there was a complaint of that sort.

What steps were taken, in consequence of that; was the number of keepers increased, in consequence of the complaint?—I should think the keepers were increased in proportion to the increase of patients, but I have no recollection of any increase at that particular period.

You have no recollection of that report of the commissioners complaining of an insufficiency of keepers being followed up by an increase?—I have no recollection, but if it was a necessary one, I am sure it would have been.

Do you remember the report of the commissioners on December 5th, 1816, where they state that the paupers were much crowded, and the day rooms close and offensive?—No such report ever came to my knowledge; it might be a minute upon their books, but I have no recollection of any such report coming to my knowledge.

On December the 10th, 1817, there was a visitation of your house, when they stated that the rooms were much too crowded, that they were close and oppressive, that they were not improved since their last visitation, and the secretary was desired to state this to Mr. Warburton?—That I recollect being stated.

Will you have the goodness to say whether, after these circumstances are placed before you, you still persevere in the statement which you delivered in to the Committee, that no complaint had ever been made by the medical commissioners?—Not of the treatment of the patients, or of the crowdedness of the house. If the Committee refer to my statement, they will find that I have admitted that the house was fuller than I wished it to be, but by ill treatment, I meant personal ill treatment.

Do you not consider, that keeping patients in a crowded and offensive room is a want of care and attention to those patients?—Certainly, if such were the case, so as to be found injurious, but it never was.

Were you always present when the commissioners visited your house?—Hardly ever; I never knew when they came, nor did any one.

Then, in case they found fault with any of the proceedings of your house, what was the course generally taken, of making their observations known to you?—I never heard an observation of any ill treatment of the patients beyond what might be supposed to arise out of the house being too full of patients.

Had the commissioners any opportunity, while they were there, of ascertaining the treatment of the patients? —Certainly; I should think so; they inquired of every patient who was capable of giving a rational answer how they were treated; it was a rule with the commissioners to do that.

Do you remember the commissioners, in December 1816, communicating this circumstance; 'That Philip Sturges having reported an instance of rough conduct towards a debilitated patient by her keeper, M. Jones; and Dr. Frank having returned to the pauper women's house for the purpose of inquiring into the facts, and found them to be in some respects correct, the keeper was called in, and pleading provocation for the excuse of her conduct, was admonished and censured thereupon'; have you any recollection of these circumstances having taken place in your house in December 1816?—I have not.

The Committee next proved him capable of unscrupulous price-cutting to draw patients away from rival establishments:

When you usually demanded 9s. a week for pauper lunatics, why did you take patients for a less sum, though you mentioned that they could not be maintained for that sum?—A person of the name of Fox, had been round to almost every parish in the county of Middlesex, and offered to take patients at 8s. a week, finding them in every thing; I refused two of the parishes to keep them under my care at that price, and they were removed; he went to other parishes, and I sent for answer, that I would keep them for nothing sooner than such a man acting in so very unjustifiable a way should obtain possession of the patients.

Then the Committee are to understand that you did take from those parishes patients at 8s. a week?—I did, for the cause I have assigned.

Then do you mean to say, that out of humanity to those people you took them at that price, knowing at the same time that they could not be kept, and kept in every thing, for 8s. a week?—My motive was to prevent a man taking those patients who had made an application in the way he had done.

What number of patients may you have now at 8s. a week?—I cannot exactly recollect the number, there are several parishes.

Have you 100 patients at 8s. a week?—I should think as many nearly, if the question includes both houses; I should say 80, at least.

Do you know a house at Hoxton belonging to Mr. Burroughs?—I have no connection with it; I know there is such a house.

Do you know at what price Mr. Burroughs takes those patients?—I do not.

Did you ever hear it?—Never to my knowledge.

You never heard that he does not take patients for less than 9s. or 9s. 6d.?—Never.

From Mr. Warburton the Committee learned that a doctor visited the White House three times a week. The examination continued:

What is the name of the medical gentleman?—Mr. Dunston.

Is he a regular surgeon or physician?—A regular surgeon.

Is he a relation of yours?—Yes, he married my daughter.

Is he a regularly educated medical man?—Perfectly so.

Where is his usual place of abode, how far from your establishment in Bethnal Green?—In Old Broad-street.

The names of two doctors now appear for the first time; the Committee were later to prove both men a disgrace to their profession.

Do you mean to say that you have no other medical attendance than that of one surgeon every other day?— There are two; one regularly attending and another gentleman, a Mr. Cordell, a very respectable surgeon, who attends perhaps two or three times a week in addition to the other.

What do you mean by regularly attending?—I mean that he frequently comes to the house, he is a friend of Mr. Dunston and attends for Mr. Dunston.

That is to say, when Mr. Dunston does not attend he attends?—He does.

But the regular medical attendance upon which you can count is only Mr. Dunston's upon every other day in the week?—Yes.

Have you any resident apothecary in your establishment with an establishment of pharmacy?—No.

If any one of your patients should be suddenly seized with apoplexy or any other disease, to which of course you know that insane persons are particularly liable, have you any means of procuring him instant relief?—Immediately; there is a surgeon who lives within three or four hundred yards of the house, and whenever any sudden illness takes place, he is sent for immediately.

In case he should not be at home, of course you could not have his assistance; he does not belong to your establishment?—He does not.

Who is that surgeon?—He lives close by Bethnal Green, but I do not recollect his name.

In point of fact, have you ever known that man sent for?—Repeatedly.

But you do not know his name?—I do not; I could learn his name in five minutes.

You say he has been repeatedly sent for?—Not in my presence.

Is Mr. Cordell's attendance in addition to Mr. Dunston's, or when Mr. Dunston happens not to be able to come, does Mr. Cordell come in and take up a case about which he knows nothing?—Mr. Cordell visits for Mr. Dunston in his absence.

And only then?—Frequently when Mr. Dunston is on the spot he comes with him, and on other days by himself, not on the particular days Mr. Dunston attends.

Is Mr. Cordell his partner?—No.

He is a friend only?—A friend.

At what hour in the morning does Mr. Dunston come? About ten o'clock generally.

At what hour does he go away?—He does not stay longer than to examine the patients and to make his observations upon them.

In case he should neglect to come on any one of those days what would arise?—Mr. Cordell would come instead of him.

Is Mr. Cordell paid by you for his attendance, or does he merely act as a friend of Mr. Dunston's?—As a friend of Mr. Dunston's.

What do you pay for all the medical treatment you have at the asylum?—Five hundred and fifty pounds a year.

Does that include medicines?—Including medicines.

You pay Mr. Dunston £550 a year?—Yes.

Is Mr. Dunston the surgeon of Saint Luke's hospital?— He is.

Is he the resident surgeon of Saint Luke's hospital?— He is not resident; he is not required to reside.

Then you mean that Mr. Dunston has sufficient time not only to attend all your patients but to be the surgeon of Saint Luke's Hospital?—He has.

Who is Mr. Cordell; is he a practising surgeon?—A regular practitioner, living in Broad-street.

No register, you say, is kept of the treatment of the patients; to whom are directions given for their diet, and for such management as the surgeon thinks proper?—To the superintendent of the house, Mr. Jennings, and by him to the servants; and I believe no instance ever occurs of a patient being neglected in consequence of want of diet and want of care.

The Committee found that the good Mr. Warburton handled lunatics on a considerable scale. The White House was only one of his interests, but it was the largest, and he visited it twice a week.

How many establishments have you for the reception of lunatics, besides the Bethnal Green establishment?—Only one, Whitmore House, except private individual patients under my care.

Have you no interest in any other?—None whatever.

At what distance is that other establishment from that in which you receive pauper lunatics?—About a mile and a half.

What surgeon attends that other establishment?—Each patient in that establishment who chooses to have his own medical man, has him.

Can you mention the name of the surgeon who is most usually employed at that establishment?—Mr. Dunston.

Do you mean to say, that you have no insane persons under your care, except those belonging to this establishment at Bethnal Green, and the other establishment at Whitmore House?—Except in private lodgings.

Will you have the goodness to state how many persons you have under your care in private lodgings?—Eight, I think, at this time.

Are they all in separate private lodgings, or is there more than one person in each house?—Only one.

Who attends those eight patients that you have in private houses?—Myself and Dr. Warburton my son.

Does Mr. Dunston attend them?—No.

Who furnishes them with medicines?—The apothecary in the district, if it is at a distance, if not, the prescriptions are sent to Mr. Dunston.

It appears by the return that you have four houses?—

There are licences taken out for the two establishments, which are called six houses, but they are all together, they are all No. 1.

There is one house at Hoxton, and is not there a house at Highgate?—No.

Then you have only the house at Hoxton, and the house at Bethnal Green?—No more.

And eight private patients in private lodgings?—Yes, no more.

Have you any in your own house?—Yes, one old patient, who has been many years there.

You have one in your own house, and eight patients besides in private lodgings?—The patients vary, I may have ten or a dozen at times.

How many do you happen to have at this moment?—Eight.

Eight private patients living in distinct lodgings, exclusive of those at Bethnal Green and Whitmore House?—Yes.

From the account you give of your very short attendance at stated times, would it not be very possible that your regulations might be departed from in the intervals of your absence?—I think not, I have such confidence in the superintendent, Mr. Jennings.

The Committee took the opportunity of asking a little more about the background of Jennings, who was himself due to appear before them.

On what grounds do you place such a complete confidence in Mr. Jennings?—He has been many years with me, and I have great confidence in him.

What was his education?—A common education.

Before he came into your service, was he in any manner particularly adapted for or at all experienced in the management of lunatics?—He had been a keeper for a length of time.

Had he been a keeper before he came into your service as agent?—I do not know.

Had he a medical education?—No.

What was his situation in life before you appointed him

your agent?—He was brought up in that business as a keeper.

Do you mean to say, that he had served as keeper elsewhere before he came into your service as your agent?—I do not know.

Then what do you mean by saying that he was brought up in that line of life?—He had lived in that establishment.

From what age had he lived in your establishment?—I should suppose three or four-and twenty.

In what capacity did he live there before you appointed him your agent?—Keeper under the direction of Mr. Talbot.

How long did he serve with you as keeper before you appointed him to the office of your agent?—Five years, I think.

You state, that you have turned your attention to the curative process of mental disorders?—I have.

Do you apply your own knowledge with regard to this curative process to any of the patients under your care at the White House or at the Hoxton establishment?—I do.

How do you contrive to apply your knowledge as to the curative process, when you have already stated to the Committee, that the only attendance you give to that establishment at the White House, consists of two hours in the week?—I only apply it by examining the patients as other people do; I presume that my knowledge of insane cases is equal to any man's in England.

Without doubting your knowledge, the Committee merely wish to ask how you contrive to superintend the curative process of 500 patients by merely visiting them two hours in the week, having during those two hours all the other duties to perform which fall upon you as proprietor of the house?—I place confidence in Mr. Jennings as to provisioning the house, seeing those provisions myself, which are of an excellent quality; that part I do not take any interest in beyond deputing to him the direction of it, and seeing to it myself after that is done.

If you yourself are supposed to superintend the curative process used for the recovery of insane persons, how do you contrive to do that, only visiting your house two hours in the week?—I conceive the surgeon to be the person, whose constant attention in that way is essential, and he does it at his visitations; but with regard to myself, I see the patients and examine them, and if I see it necessary, give directions accordingly.

The number of Jennings' paid assistant keepers was firmly given by Mr. Warburton as ten.

This figure assumed considerable importance in subsequent stages of the Committee's inquiry. Their questions on this point became pressing.

How many regular keepers, not patients, have you in your establishment at Bethnal Green?—Five men and five women.

What are their names?—There is one Dalby, another Barker; the names of the servants I seldom inquire into, although I know the people when I am there; that is in Mr. Jennings' department.

Then in point of fact, ten servants, five male and five female, are the whole of your establishment?—There are five appropriated to the pauper men, and five to the pauper women.

Who are not patients themselves?—Who are not patients themselves.

How long have five been appointed to the pauper men and five to the pauper women?—For years; Mr. Jennings will give the names of each.

What other servants have you in your establishment?— There are four other men; there are nine, two keepers besides the porter and house servants.

Are they patients?—Not one patient is a keeper; they are never desired or made to attend to any patient, it is done for the benefit of their health, and the promotion of their cure.

What number of male servants have you in your establishment?—I should think fifteen male servants.

Will you have the goodness to give their names to the Committee?—Mr. Jennings has the names of the servants.

You state that the pauper patients are never employed,

except by their own wish and inclination, in attendance upon other persons?—Never.

Have you not in your establishment, to every crib-room, what is called a crib-room man?—No.

You mean to say, that to each crib-room, there is not a convalescent patient who is appointed as a crib-room man?—I do.

Do you mean, that in no instance, is there a convalescent patient appointed to the duty of crib-room man?—I do.

Do you know, of your own knowledge, the manner in which your crib-room patients are placed at night in their cribs?—I do.

How long is it since you ever saw at night, the violent patients placed in their cribs?—That I leave to Mr. Jennings.

Did you ever witness the manner in which those persons are so placed?—Repeatedly; I have repeatedly gone to them.

Within how many years have you done so?—Within less than years or months.

Then the Committee are to understand, that although you stated before, that you only visited your establishment on Tuesdays and Fridays, from ten to eleven o'clock occasionally, you have visited your establishment at other periods?—I have visited it at other times.

Have you ever visited your establishment at the period when those patients were so placed in their cribs?—I have.

Can you state positively, of your own knowledge, that it is not a fact that a convalescent patient is appointed as a crib-room man, and that the business of that crib-room man is to undress the crib patients, and to put them in their cribs?—That question can be better answered by Mr. Jennings.

If you have been present yourself at the placing of the patients in their cribs, the Committee wish you to answer whether that is or is not the fact?—I did not see them put to bed.

The Committee understood that you had been at the house at the period when the crib patients were placed in their beds, and that you yourself had seen the manner in which they were so placed?—I have seen them in their crib beds, but never saw them placed there.

Then you do not know by whose direction, and under whose superintendence they are so chained down, and placed in their cribs?—That part is under Mr. Jennings' direction.

Do you not consider yourself as proprietor, responsible for the treatment of the patients?—I do.

Then if you should understand that great neglect had taken place, should not you consider yourself to be culpable?—I should.

If great cruelty occurred, should not you consider yourself blameable for it?—I should.

If that be the case, unless you take greater care to examine this establishment than you appear to have taken, how can you ascertain whether cruelty or neglect takes place or not?—My confidence is in Mr. Jennings.

That is your only security?—That is my chief security.

Then are the Committee to understand, that whatever Mr. Jennings may hereafter state to the Committee, about the treatment in that house, you will abide by?—I have that confidence in him, that I am sure he would not use any person with cruelty or hardship.

Then whatever Mr. Jennings may hereafter say, as to the treatment of the pauper lunatics in your house at Bethnal Green you consent to abide by his answers?—Yes.

But in a final series of questions about the crib patients, the Committee forced Warburton, in his efforts to save himself, to turn against the very man on whom he relied.

The Committee understand that all patients who are called crib patients are periodically confined from Saturday to Monday?—They are not; only the violent ones.

Then all violent patients are confined on that day?—They are.

Do you not think it possible that that confinement from Saturday to Monday has taken place in your establishment for the sake of the convenience of the keepers?—Never.

You said just now that all violent patients were confined from Saturday to Monday?—A number of the violent patients are; the crib patients only.

Do you conceive that the confinement of a violent madman once a week is a good thing in itself, whether he wants it or not for other reasons?—I conceive that the confinement in bed of a violent madman is beneficial to him, and the best mode of quieting and composing him.

Even when that is applied not as occasion requires, but periodically, once a week?—No, not more than at any other time.

Why then do you make it a practice to confine all violent crib patients in your establishment from Saturday to Monday?—I can assign no particular reason for it; perhaps Mr. Jennings can tell the Committee.

If such were the practice, it would be a very great abuse, according to your ideas, since you can assign no reason for it?—Unnecessary confinement at any time is an abuse.

If all the violent crib patients in your establishment are confined from Saturday to Monday, do you consider that an unnecessary confinement?—I consider it necessary to confine them.

Do you consider it necessary to confine all violent crib patients in your establishment from Saturday night to Monday every week?—They were not confined under my direction certainly.

Do you consider it necessary?—(*The Witness hesitated.*)

Do you decline answering the question?—I do.

The Committee wish to ask you, upon your professional reputation with regard to the treatment of insane persons, whether you do not consider the indiscriminate confinement of furious persons a bad mode of treating them?—Indiscriminate confinement I should think not correct.

Will you have the goodness to state on what Sunday you have ever been present at that pauper asylum for lunatics standing in your name at Bethnal Green?—I very seldom go on Sunday.

Have you ever been there within the last twelve-month on a Sunday?—Yes, repeatedly.

Will you mention any particular Sunday on which you were there?—Three months ago perhaps it is since I was there on a Sunday.

When you were there three months ago, on a Sunday, did you go into any of those crib-rooms?—Certainly I never did; I left them to the management of Mr. Jennings.

You have a great number of private patients of the same description of madness; do you confine them every Sunday in the same manner in which those pauper patients are described to be confined in your house at Bethnal Green?—No.

Is madness so different with regard to the higher and the lower classes of society, as to render that treatment good in the one instance which is bad in the other?—It is not.

Then do you not consider that it is a very extraordinary circumstance that the pauper patients should be treated in this manner on a Sunday at Bethnal Green, when your system is directly contrary with regard to other patients more immediately under your own charge?—That part of the Bethnal Green establishment is under the direction of Mr. Jennings.

Do you consider yourself as responsible for Mr. Jennings' conduct with regard to those persons for whom you contract to provide properly?—I do.

Then if that statement is correct with regard to the treatment of those pauper lunatics at Bethnal Green, you acknowledge that a very improper conduct has been pursued?—I do not admit that it is intentionally improper.

Is it, in your opinion, right or wrong, that such treatment should be shown towards those lunatics?—I do not think it wrong, where the necessity of the case requires it.

Do you consider that necessary universally with regard to paupers which is not necessary with regard to persons in a higher station in life?—I do not.

Did you ever know that those patients were confined during the whole of Sunday till your attention was called to it by the inquiries that were going on?—I did not.

Then till within the last three months you did not know that those patients were so confined?—No.

Has this circumstance which has now come to your knowledge weakened your confidence in Mr. Jennings?—It has.

The Committee understood you to state that you had the most perfect confidence in Mr. Jennings?—I had previous to that circumstance coming to my knowledge.

And that circumstance coming to your knowledge has weakened your confidence in Mr. Jennings?—It has, very much.

It was now the turn of Jennings himself to be called, and he was questioned for nearly the whole of one day.

A farmer's son who left home on account of his father's second marriage, Jennings worked and slept in a warehouse in King-street, Cheapside, until he entered Warburton's establishment as a keeper. He had no medical knowledge beyond what he had picked up in the total of eighteen years which he had now been at the White House.

Asked about the patients' diet, which was one of his main responsibilities, Mr. Jennings was at once evasive:

Can you give to the Committee the name of any individual of the pauper patients, who at any former period or the present time, is receiving sick diet?—I will give you a list to-morrow.

That is not the point; can you now?—No.

You keep books of the expenses?—Not of the things we give out in this way.

You must account for the sums you pay?—Yes, in the cash book; it is entered as sundries. Sometimes I go out and buy a dozen different things, I say sundries three or four pounds.

Is Mr. Warburton satisfied with that?—Yes.

Can you furnish the Committee with an account of money spent in the purchasing of those articles?—No, I cannot.

And you cannot furnish the Committee with the name

of any person of whom you have ever purchased those articles?—None, because I always pay ready money for them.

Answering the Committee's main charge that he kept the pauper lunatics in chains between Saturday and Monday, Jennings retorted:

> That is as false a statement as ever was made. . . . I never heard a more exaggerated or barefaced falsehood in all my life.

The Committee failed to weaken Jennings' story that all the patients were washed and well-cared for, and that only the violent paupers were chained on Sundays. He was a tougher and wilier witness than Warburton, and after over 200 questions on this one topic, he remained unshaken.

Jennings was closely examined on many other matters: his defence varied between thinly veiled prevarication and hypocritical innocence, but the Committee could not break through it.

Their questions were prolonged, but his astute answers gave away little. The only regular absence to which he admitted, for example, was on those occasions when he 'took his children to church'.

The Committee now turned their attention to the two doctors, Mr. Dunston, the son-in-law of Warburton, and Mr. Cordell, his friend, who were immediately responsible for supervising the health of the patients and for seeing that they were properly cared for by Jennings. Dunston began smoothly, but the first few questions were only the prelude of a gruelling examination, by which the Committee exposed his almost total neglect of his responsibilities.

> With regard to the mental disorders of the patients, what steps are you in the habit of pursuing?—Such steps as the individual cases appear to call for.
>
> Will you state what steps you take?—I do not know how exactly to answer the question; if the case is one of

high excitement the steps are to reduce that excitement, if it be one of depression, the steps naturally to be taken are to remove such depression, if it be dependent upon any bodily disease, to direct the attention particularly to that bodily disease which superinduces the infirmity of mind.

Then you expressly declare that you do turn your attention to the cure of the mind as well as the body of the lunatic pauper patients?—Yes.

Do you not consider that variety of diet is of considerable importance in the care and management of such patients?—There are some cases that require peculiarity of diet, in which case it is directed and attended to.

Are you in the habit of directing pauper patients to be placed upon an improved diet in that establishment?—Very frequently.

Will you state the name of any one individual whom you have so directed to be placed upon a sick diet within the last fortnight?—I have a wife who is unfortunately dying, and I believe for the last six weeks I have not been in attendance there; my friend, Mr. Cordell has been in attendance for me; I came up to London for the purpose of attending this Committee yesterday; but the cases are very numerous in which I have so done.

Is Mr. Cordell a partner of yours?—No.

Is it your custom to superintend the care of a patient for a certain portion of time, and then to leave the further care of that patient to the care of Mr. Cordell?—Under the circumstances I have mentioned I have so done, it is not my custom.

Do you keep any register of the nature of the cases under your care and of the medicines by you administered?—No.

Then, how is it possible for Mr. Cordell who assists you in the superintendence of that house, if he shall come to take up the further cure of a case which has been commenced by you, to be able satisfactorily so to do?—From a previous communication with him upon the subject of that case in which I detail to him the history of the case and the treatment which has been adopted.

Then are the Committee to understand that you know
by heart the cases of all those 500 patients that are placed
under your care?—I have never 500 patients under my
medical treatment at one time, the house does not contain
above 450; and perhaps out of that number one in ten may
be under my care.

Then under whose care are the rest placed?—I mean to
say there are not more than one in ten either mentally or
bodily requiring attention; the others are confirmed cases
of derangement in which nothing more can be done
medically than paying attention to the bowels.

You must be aware that at one period there were upwards of 570 persons in that establishment?—In the two
houses there might be.

After strenuous questioning, Dunston was forced to
admit that the crib patients lay chained and naked. His
answers became briefer as the questions grew more pressing.

How long have you been aware of that practice in the
establishment of confining the crib patients from Saturday
evening till Monday morning?—It has held ever since I
have known the establishment.

Does that exist in the other establishment at the Red
House?—It does.

Are you aware of that practice having been altered
lately?—I am not.

You are not aware of Mr. Warburton having expressed
any disapprobation of it?—No.

You are not aware of any representation having been
made by the parish of St. George's, and the practice having been discontinued in consequence?—No.

Are they washed on a Sunday?—Yes.

You say that you have been present at the washing of
crib patients on a Sunday morning; at what hour was
that?—I cannot say.

Finally, Dunston was asked about the number of keepers,
and here he told what was soon to be revealed as a deliberate lie:

How many regular male keepers are there attending
upon the pauper lunatics in Mr. Warburton's establish-

ment?—The average number of keepers is one for about 25 patients.

Little Mr. Cordell, Dunston's assistant, was now called. In spite of his standing as a qualified surgeon, he did not hesitate to lie even more unscrupulously than Dunston. Cordell began by explaining that, as Dunston's assistant, he attended the White House whenever Dunston was out of town.

And you occasionally attend for him during his absence?—Always.

It frequently happens, therefore, that you attend when Mr. Dunston is out of town?—Always.

In case Mr. Dunston has commenced a curative process either of mind or body upon any patient, how are you acquainted with the system which he has pursued?—Most readily, I have access to his books; and I am always furnished with a list containing the names of the patients and the particular nature of the disorder, with the course of medicine they are pursuing; it is done in a very laconic and in a very correct way, because it would not be competent for me or any other person merely seeing a composition of pills or powders to know what it was.

Then the Committee are to understand that that written statement which is given by Mr. Dunston to you contains the medicines that have been administered to those patients, and a general statement of the case?—Exactly so.

When you commence the treatment of a patient that Mr. Dunston has not seen, do you follow the same plan in returning this written paper to him?—Identically so; I put down the patient's name, the nature of the disease, and prescribe the medicine and send it to his house where every thing is prepared, and from his house they are furnished.

What sort of register is it that Mr. Dunston keeps of the patients?—A very correct one.

Is it in a book?—A large folio volume, and I believe for neatness as well as correctness of detail it is a pattern for every professional man to adopt.

Now Dunston, it will be recalled, had told the Committee

he kept no register whatever, and merely told Cordell verbally what treatments were in progress. On being recalled, Dunston repeated his original evidence, and the Committee were able to confront Cordell, on his second appearance, with the disgraceful discrepancy between the two stories; they were now to prove Cordell a shameless liar:

You were asked, 'Are you quite sure about all those things being contained in the register?—Most undoubtedly; if I have occasion to refer to it, I find it correct.' Do you mean to say that that statement is correct?—I mean to say that it is not correct.

You said that the register contained the name of the patient, the complaint, and the medicine; do you mean to say that you ever in one instance have found that it contained the name of the complaint, and the medicine?—No, it does not.

Therefore that answer of yours is incorrect?—Yes.

You were asked, 'Have you ever seen that register?' To which you answered, 'I have constant access to it.' Have you, in fact, constant access to it?—I presume that I could have.

Then, in fact, you have no access to it?—No.

Do you mean to state that the whole of the evidence you gave to the Committee on the 21st of this month relative to the existence of this register, is perfectly incorrect?—Perfectly so; for upon inquiry I find it is so.

Do you or do you not believe that there is any permanent memorandum or register kept of the treatment of those pauper patients by Mr. Dunston?—I believe certainly none; that is my firm belief, that there is not a permanent memorandum kept.

On the former occasion you were asked 'Therefore you have the book in your possession?' to which you answered, 'No, I do not have it in my possession, I only have it when I want to use it; the book is at his house, I take an extract from it; the book is a voluminous one, and I send it immediately back to Mr. Dunston'; how do you reconcile that with your present statement?—I never had it in my hand, that is quite a mistake of my own.

Are the Committee to understand that this answer which has now been read to you is utterly untrue?—It must be so.

As it is perfectly clear that your evidence to-day is utterly contradictory to that which you gave on a former day, the Committee wish to know which they are to believe?—The evidence of to-day; because I have the means of information which I had not then.

Then you stake your veracity upon the evidence of to-day?—Yes.

You mean to say, that the evidence you gave on Thursday last is incorrect, and that the evidence you have given to-day is correct?—Perfectly so.

Is the rest of the evidence true or false that you gave on Thursday; is what you stated with reference to the management of Mr. Warburton's establishment true or false, as far as your knowledge went?—It is perfectly correct as far as my knowledge goes.

Then how do you account for making so many errors regarding this book, while you maintain that the rest of your evidence is perfectly correct?—That must rest with the Committee rather than with me; I have merely stated my apology for being led into an error by supposing that that book was continued; but I find it was not continued, and that the extracts that were made were made from the small book.

Do you mean to say that in that small book there was any account given of the state in which the patients were? —No.

In your former evidence you described the book you referred to as a book giving an accurate account of the treatment of the patients?—I only meant with reference to the medicine that was given.

You are aware that this Committee have power to report your evidence to the House if they think fit?—I am perfectly aware of that.

You are also aware that this Committee, by reporting you to the House, may place you in an unpleasant situation if you do not state the fact?—I believe I have stated everything that I know, but I have been led into an error.

Dunston's story of the number of keepers was next proved false by the testimony of one of the only two keepers regularly employed. No doubt Jennings had given this man some coaching in advance on his replies, but he was unable to resist the pressure of the Committee's relentless questions. It might be argued indeed that the erudite members of the Committee were unduly hard on an obviously ignorant man, but if their inquiry was to elicit the whole truth the Committee could not stop halfway. There is a tendency to-day to avoid inquiries into matters of detail as time-wasting, but this has been proved to be the only effective method where it is desired to expose the worst abuses.

Accordingly, William Barnard was called in and examined.

What are you?—I am one of the servants at the White House, Bethnal Green.

How long have you been there?—I have been there eight years or upwards.

Is it your particular business to attend the male pauper lunatics?—Yes.

Who attends with you?—There is Thomas Dolby, James Essex, Samuel Painter, and Charles Beech.

How long have Beech and Painter been servants in the establishment?—Beech, I believe, has been upwards of three months, and Painter not so long.

Whom had you in your establishment, in the room of Painter and Beech, at Christmas last?—There was one of the name of Sharpe, and we had not another; there were four of us then.

At what time did Sharpe leave your establishment?—I think some little time after Christmas.

Do you mean to say, that after Sharpe left you, there was not a considerable time when there was nobody in the establishment but you, Dolby and Essex?—Not any considerable time.

You mean to say that there was not a space of a month or six weeks before you had any additional keeper?—I believe there was not that space.

Was there a space of two months between the time that Sharpe left you, and any additional keeper being hired?—That I am not positive of.

You must know how that was?—I think it could not be so long.

Will you state when either Painter or Beech were engaged in that establishment?—I think it is about three months, or a little better, since Beech came.

You must be able to state to the Committee, whether from the period that Sharpe left you, you had only Dolby, yourself and Essex, or how long after Sharpe left you, either of those men were engaged?—I believe it might be a month or six weeks.

Was either of those men engaged before the beginning of March?—I believe not.

Was either of those men engaged till after the intention of removing the Middlesex paupers from that establishment was made known?—I am not positive as to that.

Was Essex living with you before Sharpe came?—To the best of my memory, I think he was.

How long has Essex been with you?—I think he came about last autumn.

Before Essex came, whom had you, besides Dolby and you?—There was no other one with us then.

How did you manage when there were only two of you to so many pauper lunatics?—The patients used to assist us.

Could not you trust the convalescent patients with the lunatics as well as you could yourselves?—No, we were always looking after them backwards and forwards.

That is to say, you set them to work in a room to take care of the patients in that room, and then you went to another room?—Yes, and came and unlocked some of them myself.

You set the convalescent patients to get up others?—Yes.

You used the term 'looked after them', do you mean to say you are in the room the whole time?—No, I cannot say that.

Then you have such confidence in the convalescent

patients that you would not have the least scruple in leaving them with the other patients?—Certainly not, because if I thought he was an unfit person, I would not allow him to be there.

Sometimes when you had a convalescent patient that you thought a good steady man, you would let him go and undress the crib patients and put them to bed?—Yes.

Sometimes, when you had so many patients in the crib-rooms, did you not give them a little sort of authority by calling them crib-room men?—We used to call him the man that helped at such a number, for instance, No. 7.

To a patient that you thought a steady man you would give a little sort of direction over a crib-room?—Over some of those that he could manage.

The picture of the White House was now fairly complete; it was already obvious that Warburton, his son-in-law and Jennings had all deliberately lied in a vain attempt to deceive the Committee but the latter checked and cross-checked the statements made against them by calling other keepers, other inmates and other doctors.

Finally, to put the place in perspective, the Committee again called the secretary of the Commissioners appointed to inspect asylums, Dr. John Bright, and asked him for a comparison between the White House and other similar institutions. His evasive attitude in declaring it to be no better and no worse than others forms a good commentary on the treatment of insanity in 1827, as well as on the ease with which a person might be 'put away'.

Inadequate though the Act of Parliament which governed the inspection of asylums was, one of its positive directions to the commissioners was that they should hang up in the Censor Room of the College of Physicians any report on an asylum deserving censure. The doctor admitted that this direction had been disobeyed since 1815, giving as the lame excuse of the commission the fact that they thought it 'inefficient'.

It was only too apparent from Bright's evidence that the

commissioners had not taken the initiative even within the limits of their slender powers, or displayed the smallest sense of public duty in making any communications either to the Secretary of State or the Lord Chancellor, or any other public authority.

In the fortnight in which they sat, the Committee brought to light many minor matters. The whole of the evidence which the Committee presented to the House of Commons is perhaps about twenty times as long as the summary and extracts given here. They discovered a love affair which the disreputable Dr. Dunston had carried on with Mrs. Park, after first certifying her jealous husband Archibald. They traced the housekeeping lapses of Mrs. Elizabeth Jennings, who never kept accounts and whose tea was so bad that the lunatics preferred oatmeal.

Thomas Warburton, his son-in-law Dunston and his creatures and servants of the White House were all utterly discredited. The stories told in 1815 by the dismissed keepers, and then repudiated, must now be assumed to have been true. It was true then that Warburton had refused to dismiss the keeper who virtually murdered Captain Dickinson of the Royal Navy. Dunston, the son-in-law, was looking through the paling of the yard when he saw this keeper raining blows on Dickinson, whose leg-gyves and handcuffs prevented him warding them off. Although Dickinson died shortly afterwards, Warburton, to whom Dunston reported the matter, did not dismiss the keeper because it was difficult to find a replacement. Warburton must have known and approved of the forcible feeding—often unnecessarily applied—which smashed the teeth and even the palates of many inmates. He must have known that thousands of bugs crawled on the walls of the White House at night and that rats were so prevalent that thirty or forty at a time would swarm over the gangrened legs of the lunatics. If he did not approve, at least he did nothing to check the frauds in the linen room whereby even the pauper patients had their new flannel petticoats abstracted and cut up for sale, leaving them to shiver in their cribs without the clothes which had been provided by the parish. He knew that the White House had an old flagged stone slaughterhouse in which twenty or thirty 'recalcitrant' paupers were locked. He knew that in a place of punishment, called Bella's Hole, Charles Green, an insane sailor from *H.M.S. Canopus*, was shut up like an animal, naked, with very little straw, and with no outlet except by the planks above his head, which were pierced by a few gimlet holes.

*

In their report to the House of Commons, the Committee disdained censure on any of the individuals who had lied to them. About the White House they contented themselves with this observation:

> From the Registers of the Visitors appointed by the College of Physicians, and from other testimony, Your Committee might infer, that however great its defects may be, Mr. Warburton's Establishment has hitherto been considered as good as the generality of Licensed Houses where Paupers are received in the neighbourhood of the metropolis; but if the White House is to be taken as a fair specimen of similar establishments, Your Committee cannot too strongly or too anxiously express their conviction, that the greatest possible benefit will accrue to Pauper Patients by the erection of a County Lunatic Asylum.

The Committee went on to say that, as the present law relating to asylums was obviously deficient, a new Act should be passed by Parliament extending and improving the system of regulating and visiting private lunatic asylums, and making further provision for building County Asylums. The brief report ended with an outline of the proposed Act, which would supersede eight earlier and obviously ineffective Acts passed in the reigns of George II, George III and George IV.

The Act which Parliament passed in the next summer,

1828, brought all asylums under the general control of the Home Secretary, to whom annual reports on all patients had to be made. For London and Middlesex a new body of Commissioners were allowed to grant licences, and in other parts of England applications for licences had to be made to the Justices at Quarter Sessions. A plan of any house which sought a licence had to be submitted and it was made a misdemeanour to conceal any insane person from these authorities on their visits of inspection. It was compulsory for houses accommodating more than 100 lunatics to have a resident medical practitioner; while those with fewer patients were to be visited by a medical man twice a week.

The Lord Chancellor was empowered to send visitors to lunatics being cared for by relatives. Before a lunatic could be certified for admission to an asylum, two medical men were to examine him, neither of them being on the asylum staff.

This Act was not the last word in legislation for the insane; some of its provisions were obscure and had to be clarified within a few years, but the protection which it gave has endured as the framework of present-day administration.

Select Committees of the House of Commons have no power to punish those whom their investigations expose. That must be left to the Courts, and no criminal proceedings were taken against the criminally negligent and perjured Warburton. His asylum, however, was henceforth controlled by the new Act of Parliament, and the conditions under which lunatics were boarded were perforce improved as the price he had to pay for the retention of his licence. When he died, discredited but full of years, he was able to hand on a going concern to his son, Dr. John Warburton, who lived to see the beginning of mid-Victorian prosperity before he too died, in the year 1850.

It was not the end, either of the Warburtons or of the White House. As each generation produced its tragic crop of idiots and insane, the White House continued to harvest its share. There was no more flogging and robbery within its walls, but the jangle of keys and the lacing of strait waist-coats to the sound of moans continued to echo down the years. Meanwhile the name of Bethnal Green, once so fashionable that mansions were built there, declined till it became synonymous with slum-land. The advertisements for the asylum tactfully stated that it was situated at Cam-bridge Heath, E.20. Nothing remained now of Kirby's Elizabethan mansion; and the use of the blunt term 'mad-house' was no longer an adequate description of the premises which replaced it. In the edition of the *Encyclo-pædia Britanica* of 1911, the treatment of lunatics throughout Europe was acclaimed as a tribute to the level of civilization attained by the modern world. Every country vied with its neighbour in humane administration; ironically, Germany was specially commended for its enlightened treatment of lunatics—the country that within a handful of years was to assent to the gassing or other means of extermination of the mentally weak. In those quiet years before 1914 a handsome brochure, circulated in response to chance inquiries, showed that the claims of the *Encyclopædia* were well founded so far as Bethnal Green was concerned. Bethnal House had regained its old name and something too of its old respectability. Announcing terms of from '25*s*. to £3 3*s*. a week . . . for persons suffering from mental disorders', the brochure showed from handsome photographs that there was a ladies' garden, a gentlemen's garden—both with wicker garden seats—a concert hall, a billiards room and many other pleasant amenities.

From the heartbreaking inquiry of a century earlier and from the Acts which Parliament had passed as the result of the disclosures, a genuine reform had been brought about. The photographs in the brochure were not bogus. The official reports of the Visitors of Lunatics paid tribute to the cleanliness and efficiency of the house and to the cures effected there.

At last, one winter morning in 1921, the few inmates who then remained were discreetly driven away in ambulances or closed cars to continue their shuttered lives in the more rural setting of Salisbury. Trustees had sold the premises, once so notorious, latterly so respectable, to the local authorities of Bethnal Green, who celebrated their acquisition by pulling down the still imposing Red House. But the name of Warburton was not forgotten. Indeed, though the grandchild could not be expected to take much interest in what the trustees did in his name, he was the sole beneficiary. But for Parliament's vigilant control, his fate might have been less enviable; he was Thomas Frederick Warburton, a certified lunatic.

VI

THE CASE OF
THE TORTURED CHILDREN

And in the morn and liquid dew of youth
Contagious blastments are most imminent
(HAMLET, Act I, scene 3.)

RULED BY an insatiable avarice for gain, the un-
checked factory system of industrial England in 1831
knew no pity. Human beings were regarded merely as
parts of the machinery they kept in motion; and as the population increased, wages were lowered until they were calculated on how little the movements of a pair of hands could
be supported. For the purpose of swelling already over-
grown fortunes, children and adults were crowded together
in circumstances which bred disease and vice. They were
not slaves, but in fact the conditions in which they worked
were even less dignified and less happy than those from
which the Negroes in our West Indian colonies had lately
been freed.

As many people died before their twentieth year in districts where the factory system prevailed as before their
fortieth year elsewhere. It was this appalling revelation
which encouraged the efforts of reformers, who contended
that the success of the system as a source of wealth should
be subordinated to the moral and physical welfare of the
employees. Prominent in the crusade for factory legislation

was the Yorkshire landowner, Richard Oastler. It was due to his determination and that of other humanitarians that the plight of children employed in factories was first brought to the notice of Parliament.

Oastler began his case against the employers of children with violent energy. A series of flaring denunciations in letters to the Leeds press were headed 'Slavery in Yorkshire'. His statements were sensational and public opinion was excited.

Oastler's aim in arousing pity for these children was the legal protection of the adult worker, for as the number of children employed in factories was so great in proportion to the number of adults, it would have been impossible to restrict their working hours without also restricting the hours for adults.

Neither of the two political parties were prepared to remedy the conditions of child labour. The Whigs believed that the economic machine should be allowed to run freely, without interference from the State; and although Oastler himself was a Tory, that party as a whole resisted any change on principle. There were, however, a few members of Parliament who put humanity before political or economic theory. In the session 1831–32 the Tory member for Leeds, Michael Thomas Sadler, introduced a bill which set a limit of ten hours on the working day of children under eighteen employed in mills and factories. The modest proposals of the ten-hours bill were considered Utopian and unworkable by many practically minded men. The arguments advanced in debate against Sadler by Mr. John Hope seemed cogent to many members of the House. Hope declared that interference with free labour was unwarrantable, and while admitting that 'the labour of children must, in some degree, be considered of a compulsory nature', he argued that the remedy lay with the parents.

'If these natural ties are unavailing, legislative action will prove equally useless and unavailing.'

He argued that the hardships, the youth and the numbers

of children involved were all greatly exaggerated by Sadler. Why did Sadler single out mills, where children were no worse off than in other industries? He showed that the number of hours worked in other trades were the same or longer than in the cotton and woollen mills. Children employed in earthenware and porcelain factories worked from twelve to fifteen hours a day, those in calico printing worked up to sixteen hours a day and in arms factories fourteen hours a day.

As for their morals, health and education, Hope said he had certificates from several clergymen from industrial districts that the children employed in the mills were as well conducted as the agricultural population.

Finally, foreign cotton manufacturers, particularly the Americans, trod closely upon the heels of our manufacturers, and a rise in prices here might have ruinous consequences. He believed that 'the Bill would be productive of great inconvenience, not only to persons who had embarked large capital in the cotton manufacture, but even to workmen and children themselves'.

Several other Members spoke in similar terms; but those who supported Sadler argued very forcibly against such complacency.

'It would be a libel upon cannibals or the worst savages of the human race,' declared Mr. Hunt, 'to suppose that they would voluntarily suffer their children to be so treated.'

In its wisdom the House took the course it has so often followed on occasions when opinion on some new issue is sharply divided. It referred the whole question to a Select Committee.

It was to appear before this sometimes sceptical Committee of 37 members that Richard Oastler made the long coach journey from Fixby Hall, near Huddersfield. In his own words, he told the story of how he first came across the hideous facts of children's labour in factories:

> The immediate circumstance which led my attention to the facts [said Oastler] was a communication made to me

by a very opulent spinner, that it was the regular custom, to work children in factories thirteen hours a day, and only allow them half an hour for dinner; that that was the regular custom, and that in many factories they were worked considerably more. I had previously observed a difference in the working classes of the West Riding of the county of York, I mean in the clothing districts. I had observed an amazing difference from what they are now, in comparison of what they were when I was a youth; but I must say that my attention had not been particularly called to the subject of the factory system, until I had that fact communicated to me, which certainly startled me considerably; and although it was communicated to me by an individual who must have been acquainted with the fact that it was true, I think I was three times pointedly addressing him, 'Is it really true? Is it really true?' Being assured that it was so, I resolved from that moment that I would dedicate every power of body and mind to this object, until these poor children were relieved from that excessive labour; and from that moment, which was the 29th of September, 1830, I have never ceased to use every legal means, which I had it in my power to use, for the purpose of emancipating these innocent slaves. The very day on which the fact was communicated to me, I addressed a letter to the public, in the *Leeds Mercury*, upon the subject. I have since that had many opponents to contend against: but not one single fact which I have communicated has ever been contradicted, or ever can be. I have certainly been charged by the opponents of the measure, in general terms, with exaggerations, but on all occasions I have refrained from exposing the worst parts of the system, for they are so gross that I dare not publish them. The demoralizing effects of the system are as bad, I know it, as the demoralizing effects of slavery in the West Indies. I know that there are instances and scenes of the grossest prostitution among the poor creatures who are the victims of the system, and in some cases are the objects of the cruelty and rapacity and sensuality of their masters. These things I never dared to publish, but the cruelties which are inflicted personally upon the little children, not to mention the immensely long hours which they are subject to work, are such as I am sure would disgrace a West Indian plantation. On one occasion I was very singularly placed; I was in the company of a West Indian slave master and three Bradford spinners; they brought the two systems into fair comparison, and the spinners were obliged to be silent when the slave owner said, 'Well, I have always thought myself disgraced by being the owner of black slaves, but we never, in the West Indies, thought it was possible for any human being to be so cruel as to require a child of nine years old to work twelve hours and a half a day; and that, you acknowledge is your regular practice.' I have seen little boys and girls of ten years old, one I have in my eye particularly now, whose forehead has been cut open by the thong; whose cheeks and lips have been laid open, and whose back was almost covered with black stripes; and the only crime that that little boy, who was 10 years and 3 months old, had committed, was that he retched three cardings, which are three pieces of woollen yarn, about three inches long. The same boy told me that he had been frequently knocked down with the billy-roller, and that on one occasion, he had been hung up by rope round the body, and almost frightened to death; and I am sure it is unnecessary for me to say anything more upon the bodily sufferings that these poor creatures are subject to; I have seen their bodies almost broken down, so that they could not walk without assistance, when they have been 17 or 18 years of age. I know many cases of poor young creatures who have worked in factories, and who have been worn down by the system at the age of 16 or 17, and who, after living all their lives in this slavery, are kept in poor-houses, not by the masters for whom they have worked, as would be the case if they were negro slaves, but by other people who have reaped no advantage from their labours.

Oastler went on to make an interesting comparison with eighteenth-century cottage industry, a subject on which economic history is almost undocumented. Referring to what he remembered from his own youth in the West Riding, Oastler said:

It was the custom for the children at that time, to mix learning their trades with other instruction and with amusement, and they learned their trades or their occupations, not by being put into places, to stop there from morning to night, but by having a little work to do, and then some little time for instruction, and they were generally under the immediate care of their parents; the villages about Leeds and Huddersfield were occupied by respectable little clothiers, who could manufacture a piece of cloth or two in the week, or three or four or five pieces, and always had their family at home; and they could at that time make a good profit by what they sold; there were filial affection and parental feeling, and not over-labour; but that race of manufacturers has been almost completely destroyed; there are scarcely any of the old-fashioned domestic manufacturers left, and the villages are composed of one or two, or in some cases three or four, mill-owners, and the rest, poor creatures who are reduced and ground down to want, and in general are compelled to live upon the labour of their little ones; it is almost the general system for the little children in these manufacturing villages to know nothing of their parents at all excepting that in a morning very early, at 5 o'clock, very often before four, they are awakened by a human being that they are told is their father, and are pulled out of bed (I have heard many a score of them give an account of it) when they are almost asleep, and lesser children are absolutely carried on the backs of the older children asleep to the mill, and they see no more of their parents, generally speaking, till they go home at night and are sent to bed.

Every word of Oastler's formidable indictment was confirmed not once but a score of times by the great body of witnesses who appeared before the Committee. In the course of the inquiry, which lasted from April to September, 1832, a hundred people were questioned by the Committee;

in all, eleven thousand, six hundred and eighteen questions were answered. In addition, the physical testimony of stunted bodies and twisted limbs supported the spoken word.

William Cooper, a man of twenty-eight who began work in a Leeds flax mill at ten years old, was only five feet tall. His father had been five feet seven. Here was the reason, as it was explained by him to the Committee.

> The wet fleeces which I had to turn are very heavy and full of water. You have to stand in a crouching position to support them and turn the fleece over. If you are not over strong it makes you rather deformed in your legs.

That Cooper was not over-stating the effects of hard factory work on children's bodies was soon proved. James Kirk, aged seventeen when he gave evidence, had been doing the same task as Cooper since he was nine years old, in which time his pay had risen from three shillings to six shillings a week.

On being invited by the Committee to state the effect his work had had on his health, he replied:

> I began to be very weak in my knees; one of my knees gave way.
> Was it observed by anybody in the mill, that your knees were bending?—Yes.
> What did you think this bending of your knees was owing to?—Owing to working such long hours.
> Were you perfectly straight limbed before?—I was.
> And a very strong youth?—Yes.
> You still continued to work, did you not?—I did.
> Until your limbs became quite bent?—Yes.
> Will you show your limbs?—(Here the Witness showed his knees and legs.)
> What did you do then?—I was so weak that I was forced to give over.
> You could hardly walk, could you?—No.
> Did you make use of a stick in walking?—No.
> To whom did you apply?—To the Leeds Infirmary.

mmended you to it; your employer?—No.

of Bath Square.

medical gentleman attended you in the Infirmary?

Samuel Smith.

did he say your distortion was owing to?—To

such long hours.

your employers inquire after you, or pay any

on to you after you became thus weak and de-

d.—No.

You heard nothing more about them?—No.

It was not only the fact that the work was strenuous which destroyed the physique of young workers. Children can stand a momentary strain as well or better than adults; but they need more sleep—and this was constantly withheld from them. Kirk's evidence continued:

What were the hours of labour at the gigs?—We began at five o'clock on Monday morning, and went on to Tuesday night at nine.

What age were you at that period?—About 16.

You began on Monday morning?—At five o'clock.

When did you rest?—At eight o'clock.

For how long?—For half an hour.

From half-past eight to when did you work?—Till twelve.

How long did you rest then?—For an hour.

Was that for dinner?—That was for dinner.

Go on?—We then went on from one till five, and stopped half an hour; from half-past five to nine, and stopped half an hour; from half-past nine to twelve, and stopped an hour; from one to half-past four, and stopped half an hour; from five to eight, and stopped half an hour; from half-past eight to twelve, and stopped an hour; from one to five, and stopped half an hour; and from half-past five to nine, and then we went off.

Then you worked for forty successive hours, including the intervals you have stated?—Yes.

Of course you had no time to go to bed?—We laid down at 12 o'clock at night.

For how long?—For an hour.

Was that the only rest you could take?—Yes.

What was your daily work on Wednesday?—From five o'clock in the morning to nine o'clock at night.

With two hours rest?—Yes.

And what was it on Thursday?—The same.

Then on Friday, will you state what your usual labour was?—We began at five o'clock on Friday, and went on till eight, stopped half an hour; from half-past eight till twelve, stopped an hour; from one to half-past four, stopped half an hour; from five till eight, stopped half an an hour; from half-past eight till twelve, stopped an hour; from one till five, and then came home.

What were your wages at this time?—Eight shillings a week.

What description of work was this; was it hard or easy work?—Hard work.

The long hours became even longer when, through poverty, the families had no clock or watch to get up by. Elizabeth Bentley described how her day began at the mill at which she was employed first when she was six years old:

Did you live far from the mill?—Yes, two miles.

Had you a clock?—No, we had not.

Supposing you had not been in time enough in the morning at these mills, what would have been the consequence?—We should have been quartered.

What do you mean by that?—If we were a quarter of an hour too late, they would take off half an hour; we only got a penny an hour, and they would take a half-penny more.

The fine was much more considerable than the loss of time?—Yes.

Were you also beaten for being too late?—No, I was never beaten myself, I have seen the boys beaten for being too late.

Were you generally there in time?—Yes, my mother has been up at four o'clock in the morning, and at two o'clock, in the morning; the colliers used to go to their

work about 3 or 4 o'clock, and when she h
ring she has got up out of her warm h
and asked them the time; and I hav
Hunslet Car at 2 o'clock in the m
streaming down with rain, and we h
mill was opened.

Supposing your hours of lab
could you have awoke regularly?—

Was it a matter of anxiety and di..
rouse yourself to be early enough for thos
labour?—Yes.

You are considerably deformed in your person in consequence of this labour?—Yes, I am.

At what time did it come on?—I was about 13 years old
when it began coming, and it has got worse since; it is
five years since my mother died, and my mother was
never able to get me a pair of good stays to hold me up,
and when my mother died I had to do for myself, and got
me a pair.

Were you perfectly straight and healthy before you
worked at a mill?—Yes, I was as straight a little girl as
ever went up and down town.

Did the deformity come upon you with much pain and
weariness?—Yes; I cannot express the pain I had all the
time it was coming.

Do you know of any body that has been similarly
injured in their health?—Yes, in their health, but not
many deformed as I am.

You are deformed in the shoulders?—Yes.

It is very common to have weak ankles and crooked
knees?—Yes, very common indeed.

That is brought on by stopping the spindle?—Yes.

Do you know anything of wet-spinning?—Yes, it is
very uncomfortable; I have stood before the frames till I
have been wet through to my skin; and in winter time,
when we have gone home, our clothes have been frozen,
and we have nearly caught our death of cold.

Were you permitted to give up your labour at any time
to suit your convenience and your health, and resume it
again when you were more capable of it?—Yes, we have

stopped at home one or two days, just as we were situated in our health.

If you had stopped away any length of time, should you have found a difficulty to keep your situation?—Yes, we should.

Were the children constantly beaten to their labour, as you have described?—Yes.

Where are you now?—In the poor house.

Where?—At Hunslet.

Do any of your former employers come to see you?—No.

Did you ever receive anything from them when you became afflicted?—When I was at home Mr. Walker made me a present of 1*s*. or 2*s*., but since I have left my work and gone to the poor-house, they have not come nigh me.

You are supported by the parish?—Yes.

You are utterly incapable now of any exertion of that sort?—Yes. (*Her age was twenty-three.*)

You were very willing to have worked as long as you were able, from your earliest age?—Yes.

And to have supported your widowed mother as long as you could?—Yes.

State what you think as to the circumstances in which you have been placed during all this time of labour, and what you have considered about it as to the hardship and cruelty of it? (*The witness was too much affected to answer the question.*)

Long hours and hard work left their mark on adults also. Their nerves became frayed, and supervisors tended to lose their tempers with sleepy, or as it doubtless seemed to them, lazy children. In this way cruelty, fortuitous or deliberate, became an additional burden of factory employment.

A middle-class clothier, Mr. Abraham Whitehead, lived in the centre of thirty or forty Yorkshire woollen mills and for twenty years had had constant opportunity of observing the manner in which the mills had been conducted. The chairman of the Committee asked him:

What has been the treatment which you have observed that these children have received at the mills, to keep them attentive for so many hours at such early ages?—They are generally cruelly treated; so cruelly treated, that they dare not hardly for their lives be too late at their work in a morning. When I have been at the mill in the winter season, when the children are at work in the evening, the very first thing they inquire is, 'What o'clock is it?' if I should answer 'Seven', they say, 'Only seven! it is a great while to 10, but we must not give up till 10 o'clock or past.' They look so anxious to know what o'clock it is that I am convinced the children are fatigued, and think that even at seven they have worked too long. My heart has been ready to bleed for them when I have seen them so fatigued, for they appear in such a state of apathy and insensibility as really not to know whether they are doing their work or not; they usually throw a bunch of 10 or 12 cordings across the hand, and take one off at a time; but I have seen the bunch entirely finished, and they have attempted to take off another when they have not had a cording at all; they have been so fatigued as not to know whether they were at work or not.

Do they frequently fall into errors and mistakes in piecing when thus fatigued?—Yes, the errors they make when thus fatigued are, that instead of placing the cording in this way (describing it), they are apt to place them oblique-ly, and that causes a flying, which makes bad yarn; and when the billy-spinner sees that, he takes his strap or the billy-roller, and says, 'Damn thee, close it—little devil, close it' and they smite the child with the strap or the billy-roller.

You have noticed this in the after part of the day more particularly?—It is a very difficult thing to go into a mill in the latter part of the day, particularly in winter, and not to hear some of the children crying for being beaten for this very fault.

How are they beaten?—That depends on the humanity of the slubber or billy-spinner; some have been beaten so violently that they have lost their lives in consequence of their being so beaten; and even a young girl has had the end of a billy-roller jammed through her cheek.

What is the billy-roller?—A heavy rod of from two to three yards long, and of two inches in diameter, and with an iron pivot at each end; it runs on the top of the cording over the feeding cloth. I have seen them take the billy-roller and rap them on the head, making their heads crack, so that you might have heard the blow at the distance of six or eight yards, in spite of the din and rolling of the machinery; many have been knocked down by the instrument. I knew a boy very well, of the name of Senior, with whom I went to school; he was struck with a billy-roller on the elbow, it occasioned a swelling, he was not able to work more than three or four weeks after the blow, and he died in consequence. There was a woman in Holmfirth who was beaten very much, I am not quite certain whether on the head, and she also lost her life in consequence of being beaten with a billy-roller. *This* which is produced (*showing one*) is not the largest size; there are some a foot longer than that: it is the most common instrument with which these poor little pieceners are beaten, more commonly than with either a stick or a strap.

The cruelty was part of the factory system; even humane men were forced into it. Another witness made this clear:

Have you yourself been beaten, and have you seen other children struck severely with that roller?—I have been struck very severely with it myself, so much so as to knock me down, and I have seen other children have their heads broken with it.

You think that it is a general practice to beat the children with the roller?—It is.

You do not think then that you were worse treated than other children in the mill?—No, I was not, perhaps not so bad as some were.

In those mills is chastisement towards the latter part of the day going on perpetually?—Perpetually.

So that you can hardly be in a mill without hearing constant crying?—Never an hour, I believe.

Do you think that if the overlooker were naturally a humane person it would be still found necessary for him to beat the children, in order to keep up their attention and vigilance at the termination of those extraordinary days of labour?—Yes; the machine turns off a regular

quantity of cardings, and of course they must keep as
regularly to their work the whole of the day; they must
keep with the machine, and therefore however humane
the slubber may be, as he must keep up with the machine
or be found fault with, he spurs the children to keep up
also by various means, but that which he commonly
resorts to is to strap them when they become drowsy.

At the time when you were beaten for not keeping
up with your work, were you anxious to have done it if
you possibly could?—Yes; the dread of being beaten if we
could not keep up with our work was a sufficient impulse
to keep us to it if we could.

When you got home at night after this labour, did you
feel much fatigued?—Very much so.

Had you any time to be with your parents, and to
receive instruction from them?—No.

What did you do?—All that we did when we got home
was to get the little bit of supper that was provided for us
and go to bed immediately. If the supper had not been
ready directly, we should have gone to sleep while it was
preparing.

Did you not, as a child, feel it a very grievous hardship
to be roused so soon in the morning?—I did.

Were the rest of the children similarly circumstanced?—
Yes, all of them; but they were not all of them so far from
their work as I was.

And if you were too late you were under the apprehension of being cruelly beaten?—I generally was beaten
when I happened to be too late; and when I got up in the
morning the apprehension of that was so great, that I
used to run, and cry all the way as I went to the mill.

That was the way by which your punctual attendance
was secured?—Yes.

And you do not think it could have been secured by
any other means?—No.

At this point it might be asked whether parents were
heedless of their children's suffering and why they did not
intervene to prevent it. An answer was given by the
working-class father of a girl aged fifteen:

How old was the child?—She was then about 15 years of age.

How did she bear that labour?—They put her into the preparing room, and it had a very bad effect upon her health; they call it the carding-room.

Did you find that she could bear that length of labour in the carding-room?—No, she was generally sick every night; but whether well or not, we gave her a vomit once a week.

In certain departments of flax-spinning, is not there a good deal of dust thrown out?—Yes, there is.

Does it not sometimes affect the health permanently?—It is the case with mine; she has never been able to breathe like other children since.

How long was she so employed?—About six weeks; and then the over-looker beat her severely, and I took her away.

What is the matter with her?—She is deficient in her breathing, as though she was troubled with a kind of asthma.

What did the over-looker beat her with?—I believe he beat her, and kicked her with his foot.

You say that this (other) child of yours, who was a scribbler-filler, was reproved by the over-looker because there was some dirt in the doffer, and the over-looker ordered her to clear out the doffer; is it usually the business of the scribbler-filler to clear out the doffer?—Yes; but they ought to have a sweep to fling the machine out for this purpose; and at Brown's mill there are machines thrown by straps, and at that time it was not boxed off, but it was open to every thing that might come in contact with it.

Then she took hold of the crank, and not being strong enough, she got her hand wounded?—Yes.

When your eldest daughter met with the accident in her hand, did you make any complaint to the master of the factory?—I went to the over-looker of the scribblers and he went and showed me how it happened.

Was he ever reprimanded for it, or did you get any compensation?—No; and I was only paid for the half day that the child worked; they did not even pay the day's wages.

You say you would prefer moderate labour and lower wages; are you pretty comfortable upon your present wages?—I have no wages, but two days a week at present; but when I am working at some jobs we can make a little, and at others we do very poorly.

When a child gets 3s. a week, does that go much towards its subsistence?—No, it will not keep it as it should do.

When they got 6s. or 7s. when they were pieceners, if they reduced the hours of labour, would they not get less?—They would get a halfpenny a day less, but I would rather have less wages and less work.

Do you receive any parish assistance?—No.

Why do you allow your children to go to work at those places where they are ill-treated or over-worked?—Necessity compels a man that has children to let them work.

Then you would not allow your children to go to those factories under the present system, if it was not from necessity?—No.

Supposing there was a law passed to limit the hours of labour to eight hours a day, or something of that sort, of course you are aware that a manufacturer could not afford to pay them the same wages?—No, I do not suppose that they would, but at the same time I would rather have it, and I believe that it would bring me into employ; and if I lost 5d. a day from the children's work, and I got half-a-crown myself, it would be better.

How would it get you into employ?—By finding more employment at the machines, and work being more regularly spread abroad, and divided amongst the people at large. One man is now regularly turned off into the street, whilst another man is running day and night.

You mean to say, that if the manufacturers were to limit the hours of labour, they would employ more people?—Yes.

Another parent with three daughters expressed a similar opinion:

Do you conceive that, circumstanced as you are, you

have no alternative but to subject your children to this labour, though it is extremely distressing to your feelings?
—Yes; I can say that from the very ground of my heart, that it is; and I have been repeatedly solicited by my employers to apply to the parish for relief; they have repeatedly said that it was impossible for me to live as I was, but I have never done so yet, and I can positively state that my wife and I have been weeks and have had nothing but what the girls have brought in from the mill.

William Swithenbank, a cloth dresser aged thirty-nine, had seven children. He showed that if the children were fit to work, there was no possibility of parish relief:

Have you known the men to be many months out of employ when they have lost their shops?—Yes, I have been twenty-six weeks out myself.

Not being able to get a shop?—Yes.

Supposing that you, or the individual to whom you have been alluding, had applied to the parish, stating that he was obliged to ask relief, as he could not stand his work, would the parish relieve him if he had left his employment?—No, he would have a note to take from the parish to his master, to know if he had any work; and if he had got a note from his master, saying he could not or would not stand the long hours, he would not have any relief; he would have been told he was too idle to work.

In point of fact, are not similar inquiries made at the parochial board when a man applies for relief, in consequence of poverty and having a large family; is it not made a matter of inquiry whether his children are old enough to go to a mill, and if so, and they are not sent when there is employment for them, would he be relieved?
—No, he would not.

No regard being had to the number of hours such children would have to be employed?—No, there would be no relief if they did not work up to their hours; and they must leave their employment if they do not work the hours; and then if they go to the parish they would not get any relief.

Have you had any children in your family that have

met with accidents at their work?—Yes, I have one boy that met with a very serious accident, my eldest boy; he is a cripple, and will be all his life.

What part of his body was hurt?—It was at a machine called a crab that the stuff goods go through; it pulled him in, and caught his arm, and it tore it all to bits; it tore the veins from the arteries, and tore the muscles of the arm out; it was all torn.

Is it his right or left arm?—His right arm.

He is a cripple for life?—Yes.

Have any other accidents of that sort happened there? —Yes another boy at the same crab got killed, and another got his arm torn off.

Would it not be possible to fence off these dangerous machines?—I should think it would.

Again, Samuel Cooke, an orphan of fourteen when he came before the Committee, showed how powerless parents were under the prevailing system:

Have you ever been beaten severely with a billy-roller?—Yes; when I worked at William Woodhead's, I had my head broke with it.

Do you mean till it bled?—Yes.

What age were you when you were thus beaten with a billy-roller?—Between 10 and 11.

Were you struck with it till your head was broken?—Yes.

And you perhaps had to defend yourself from the blow?—Yes.

Did he keep laying on you still?—Sometimes.

Who did this?—It was the slubber.

How long is it since your mother died?—It is about two years since my mother died.

Did your mother ever make any complaints as to your treatment?—Yes.

What was said to your mother when she complained?— The slubbers all said, if they did not like it they might take us away.

In what situation was your father?—My father was lame, and he could not work then; he had hurt his shoulder.

Where had he got lamed?—At work, when he was twining.

In the factory?—Yes.

Was he disabled from going on with his work?—Yes.

Would you not have been starved at home if you had been taken away?—Yes.

How long is it since your father died?—A fortnight after Christmas.

After last Christmas?—Yes.

What age was he when he died?—Between 46 and 47.

How long had he been ill?—He had been ill two years before he died.

What did he say his illness was brought on by?—He said it was brought on by working.

Was he ill as well as crippled?—He was.

Was he in any club?—Yes.

How much had he a week, after a certain time, from the club till he died?—Two shillings a week.

Finally the Committee called a parent with eight children, who was himself an overseer named by one young witness as having used cruelty. This man was asked:

Have you had much experience regarding the working of children in factories?—Yes, about twenty-seven years.

Have you a family?—Yes, eight children.

Have any of them gone to factories?—All.

At what age?—The first went at 6 years of age.

To whose mill?—To Mr. Halliley's to piece for myself.

What hours did you work at that mill?—We have wrought from 4 to 9, from 4 to 10, and from 5 to 9, and from 5 to 10.

What sort of mill was it?—It was a blanket-mill; we sometimes altered the time, according as the days increased and decreased.

Were your children working under you then?—Yes, two of them.

State the effect upon your children?—Of a morning when they had to get up, they have been so fast asleep that I have had to go up stairs and lift them out of bed, and have heard their crying with feelings of a parent; I have been much affected by it.

Were not they much fatigued at the termination of such a day's labour as that?—Yes, many a time I have seen their hands moving while they have been nodding, almost asleep; they have been doing their business almost mechanically.

While they have been almost asleep, they have attempted to work?—Yes; and they have missed the carding and spoiled the thread, when we have had to beat them for it.

Could they have done their work towards the termination of such a long day's labour, if they had not been chastised to it?—No.

You do not think they could have kept awake or up to their work till the seventeenth hour, without being chastised?—No.

Will you state what effect it had upon your children at the end of their day's work?—At the end of their day's work when they have come home, instead of taking their victuals, they have dropped asleep with the victuals in their hands; and sometimes when we have sent them to bed with a little bread or something to eat in their hand, I found it in their bed the next morning.

Has it affected their health?—I cannot say much of that; they were very hearty children.

Do you live at a distance from the mill?—Half a mile.

Did your children feel a difficulty in getting home?— Yes, I have had to carry the lesser child on my back, and it has been asleep when I got home.

Did these hours of labour fatigue you?—Yes; they fatigued me to that excess, that in divine worship I have not been able to stand according to order; I have sat down to worship.

So that even during the Sunday you have felt fatigue from your labour in the week?—Yes, we felt it, and always took as much rest as we could.

Were you compelled to beat your own children, in order to make them keep up with the machine?—Yes, that was forced upon us, or we could not have done the work; I have struck them often, though I felt as a parent.

If the children had not been your own, you would have chastised them still more severely?—Yes.

What did you beat them with?—A strap sometimes; and when I have seen my work spoiled, with the roller.

Was the work always worst done at the end of the day? —That was the greatest danger.

Do you conceive it possible that the children could do their work well at the end of such a day's labour as that? —No.

Matthew Crabtree, the last witness examined by this Committee, I think, mentioned you as one of the slubbers under whom he worked?—Yes.

He states that he was chastised and beaten at the mill? Yes I have had to chastise him.

You can confirm then what he has stated as to the length of time he had to work as a child, and the cruel treatment he received?—Yes, I have had to chastise him in the evening, and often in the morning, for being too late; when I had one out of the three wanting I could not keep up with the machine, and I was getting behind-hand compared with what another man was doing; and therefore I should have been called to account on Saturday night if the work was not done.

Was he worse than others?—No.

Was it the constant practice to chastise the children?— Yes.

It was necessary in order to keep up your work?—Yes.

And you would have lost your place if you had not done so?—Yes; when I was working at Mr. Wood's mill, at Dewsbury, which at present is burnt down, but where I slubbed for him until it was, while we were taking our meals he used to come and put the machine agoing; and I used to say, 'You do not give us time to eat;' he used to reply, 'Chew it at your work;' and I often replied to him 'I have not yet become debased like a brute, I do not chew my cud.' Often has that man done that, and then gone below to see if a strap were off, which would have shown the machinery was not working, and then he would come up again.

Was this at the drinking time?—Yes, at breakfast and at drinking.

Was this where the children were working?—Yes, my own children and others.

Were your own children obliged to employ most of their time at breakfast and at the drinking in cleansing the machine, and in fettling the spindles?—I have seen at the mill, and I have experienced and mentioned it with grief, that the English children were enslaved worse than the Africans. Once when Mr. Wood was saying to the carrier who brought his work in and out, 'How long has that horse of mine been at work?' and the carrier told him the time, and he said, 'Loose him directly, he has been in too long,' I made this reply to him, 'You have more mercy and pity for your horse than you have for your men.'

Did not this beating go on principally at the latter part of the day?—Yes.

Was it not also dangerous for the children to move about those mills when they became so drowsy and fatigued?—Yes, especially by lamp-light.

Do the accidents principally occur at the latter end of those long days of labour?—Yes, I believe mostly so.

Do you know of any that have happened?—I know of one; it was at Mr. Wood's mill; part of the machine caught a lass who had been drowsy and asleep, and the strap which ran close by her catched her at about her middle, and bore her to the ceiling, and down she came, and her neck appeared broken, and the slubber ran up to her and pulled her neck, and I carried her to the doctor myself.

After the Committee's report was published, it was criticized by some as exaggerated and unfair, and this is the verdict of some historians upon it. It might seem, from the bare record of question and answer, that some of the witnesses took the chance of getting sympathy, but child after child supported his evidence with an actual demonstration of premature deformity which could be accounted for in no other way than ruthless overstrain brought on by work. Time after time the Committee called on a witness to show his limbs; time after time the short-hand note is interrupted by Gurney's sombre entry: 'The witness exhibited the same, which appeared to be deformed.' Occasionally the entry reads 'excessively deformed'. Not one of the children showed that they did not come forward eagerly to make public complaints against their employers. Indeed, although Parliamentary privilege should have protected them, they came to London at their peril, and loss of employment and starvation faced them on their return as the penalty for having spoken; this was the price Eldin Hargrave, aged fifteen, had to pay for telling the Committee the story of his childhood:

What age were you when you were sent to the mill?—I was about eight years old.

You come from Leeds?—Yes.

To whose mill did you go?—I went to Messrs. Shaun and Drivers.

Did you work there as a premer?—Yes.

What were your hours of labour there?—I worked from 6 to 7.

You worked 13 hours, with two hours for meals?—Yes.

How long did you stop at that work?—A year.

What wages did you have for that?—Three shillings a week.

Where did you go to then?—I went to Lord and Robinson's.

What did you do there?—I was a carper there.

What is a carper?—There are some prickles on the top of the tassels, and they had a pair of scissors to clear them off.

Did you find that work easier?—Yes.

Had you less wages for that?—I had half-a-crown.

How many hours did you work at Lord and Robinson's?—From 5 to 9.

Why did you leave Shaun and Driver's?—Because they went to a fresh mill, and one of the master's cousins went in my place.

How long did you stop at Lord and Robinson's?—About half a year.

Why did you leave that?—Because I could not clip tassels fast enough.

Did they discharge you?—Yes.

Where did you seek for employment then?—At Mr. Brown's mill.

What age were you then?—About 10 years old.

After a year as a sweeper the boy was promoted to mind Lewis machines. On these he worked from five in the morning till ten at night, including compulsory overtime.

Did you work at the broad or the narrow Lewis?—I worked at the broad.

What had you for working at the Lewis?—I had 5s. a week and over-hours.

How much had you for over-hours?—I had a penny an hour.

Will you describe the labour you had to do in attending to the Lewis?—I had a stool to stand on, and then I had to reach over as far as I could reach to put the list on.

Did you find that harder work than brushing?—Yes, that was harder work than any that I had.

In attending to this machine, are you not always upon the stretch, and upon the move?—Yes, always.

Do you not use your hand a good deal in stretching it out?—Yes.

What effect had this long labour upon you?—I had a pain across my knee, and I got crooked.

Was it the back of your knee, or the side of your knee?—All round.

Will you show your limbs?—(*Here the witness exposed his legs and knees.*)

Were your knees ever straight at any time?—They were straight before I went to Mr. Brown's mill.

Had you had bad health generally, besides the pain in your knees?—Yes; I have been very weak and poorly sometimes.

What sort of clothes had you before you put these on? They were middling good trousers.

You had no better suit for Sunday?—Not before I got this.

You say that you worked for 17 hours a day all the year round; did you do that without interruption?—Yes.
Could you attend any day or night school?—No.
Can you write?—No.
Can you read?—I can read a little in a spelling-book.
Where did you learn that; did you go to a Sunday-school?—No, I had not clothes to go in.
Are you still working at Mr. Brown's?—I have got turned off for going to London.
Till you came, did you work at Mr. Brown's, at the Lewis?—Yes.
How came you to be turned off, what did they tell you?—They told me I was to go no more.
Did you ask for leave to go away?—Yes, I told the over-looker a day or two before.
When they turned you away, did they tell you that you could not come back because they must put another boy in your place, or did they seem angry with you for going?—They looked very cross with me for going.
Did they say anything?—They said I was not to come any more again, if I went.

As the procession of little deformed bodies passed in and out of the Committee room, the evidence against the mill-owners grew constantly blacker. It was no longer a question of hours of work which the Committee were studying in their inquiry; they seemed rather to be examining the effects of torture upon the human frame. It was revealed, for example, that children employed to piece worsted in the woollen mills worked till their hands were raw, an injury which, though temporary, was more immediately painful than the permanent deformities which the work was also causing.

What is the effect of this piecening upon the hands?—It makes them bleed; the skin is completely rubbed off, and in that case they bleed in perhaps a dozen parts.
The prominent parts of the hand?—Yes, all the prominent parts of the hand are rubbed down till they bleed; every day they are rubbed in that way.
All the time you continue at work?—All the time we

are working. The hands never can be hardened in that work, for the grease keeps them soft in the first instance, and long and continual rubbing is always wearing them down, so that if they were hard they would be sure to bleed.

Is it attended with much pain?—Very much.

Do they allow you to make use of the back of the hand? —No; the work cannot be so well done with the back of the hand, or I should have made use of that.

Yet the permanent injury, when it came, was worse. Benjamin was a lad of sixteen who worked at Mr. Cozens's in Bowling-lane in Bradford. The rest of his story is briefly told:

What age did you go into the mill?—About 9 years old.

What sort of a position do you stand in, in order to piece worsted goods?—If we are higher than the frames, we have to bend our bodies and our legs, so: (*Here the witness showed the position in which he worked.*)

Have you always to bend your body?—Yes, always.

Were you a healthy and strong boy before you went to the mill?—Yes.

Could you walk well?—Yes; I could walk from Leeds to Bradford when I was eight years old.

Without any pain or difficulty?—Yes.

You felt no fatigue from it?—Not much.

How long did you work at that mill for those long hours before you found your limbs begin to fail?—About a year.

Did it come on with great pain?—It did.

Have you ever been beaten?—Yes, till I was black and blue on my face; and have had my ears torn.

Were you generally beaten at the end of the day more than at any other time?—Yes; at the latter end, when we grew tired and fatigued.

Will you have the goodness to show the Committee your limbs? (*The witness did so, and they appeared to be excessively crooked.*)

Can you stand at all without crutches?—Not without crutches or a stick, or something to lean against.

Can you walk at all?—No.

Can you get up stairs?—Perhaps I might creep up.

Must it be upon your hands and knees?—Yes, or backwards way.

Do you get up stairs backwards way?—Yes, every night.

As the inquiry drew towards its close, it became clear that the comparatively undramatic matter of hours of work was more serious in its effect than physical violence. The beatings which were common to all factories were accepted as the only means of keeping exhausted children going. The girls, therefore, could not be treated better than the boys. Eliza Marshall, a seventeen-year-old girl from Leeds, gave evidence which was supported by many similar accounts. Her widowed mother had not been able to find work, and at the age of eight Eliza herself had had to begin working in a flax mill:

How much did you get?—Four shillings; and then I got 3*d*. myself, and I had to clean the engine.

The four shillings went to your parents?—Yes; but I had no father then.

Your mother was very poorly off at the time?—Yes.

You and your sister did what you could for her?—Yes.

Did not you think this treatment very cruel?—I have cried many an hour at the factory.

You were exceedingly fatigued at night, were you not? —Yes, I could scarcely get home.

Had you to be carried home?—Yes, to be trailed home.

How were you waked in the morning?—The bell in Mill-street rang at half past 5, and we got up by that.

That was not a pleasant sound to you?—No, it was not.

Was the fatigue gone off in the morning?—No; I was worse in the morning.

You thought the bell a very doleful sound?—Yes, it was a doleful sound to me.

Did your mother wish for your hours to be rather altered?—Yes; she would rather I worked regular times, for I was unable to work as I did; I have taken 6*s*. 5*d*. for one week, including the over-hours, before I left.

What were the regular hours of work?—From 6 in the morning till 7 in the evening.

What age were you when you left; when you got this 6s. 5d.?—I was nearly 17; I was turned 17 when I left.

Your mother could not get you those extra hours off?—No, I was obliged to work the hours or else leave; my master could not do without someone doing it.

Did this begin to affect your limbs?—Yes, when we worked over-hours I was worse by a great deal; I had stuff to rub my knees; and I used to rub my joints a quarter of an hour, and sometimes an hour or two.

Were you straight before that?—Yes, I was straight before that; my master knows that well enough; and when I have asked for my wages, he said that I could not run about as I had been used to do.

Did he drop your wages in consequence?—No, but he would not raise my wages, as I hoped he would; I asked, 'Could not I mind my work?' and he said, 'yes, but not so quick.'

Are you crooked now?—Yes, I have an iron on my right leg; my knee is contracted.

Was it not great misery for you to do your work?—Yes, it was.

You could hardly get up to your bed of a night sometimes, could you?—To speak the truth, my sister has carried me up many a time; she is larger than I am; I have gone on my hands and knees many a time.

Have you been to Leeds Infirmary, to have, if possible, your limbs restored?—Yes, I was nearly twelve months an out-patient; and I rubbed my joints; and it did no good; and the last summer I went to the Relief, and that did me no good, and I was obliged to have a machine; and this last winter I have been into the Infirmary six weeks.

Under whom are you?—Mr. Charley.

They have put irons on your legs?—Yes, they cost £3.

Have any of the surgeons in the Infirmary told you by what your deformity was occasioned?—Yes, one of them said it was by standing; the marrow is dried out of the bone, so that there is no natural strength in it.

The terrible accidents which the children suffered were also mainly attributable to the hours of work which they were compelled to maintain.

A seventeen-year-old boy said:

There was a boy who, to fettle the machine, was kneeling down, and a strap caught him about his ankles, and carried him round the wheel, and dashed his brains out on the floor.

Do you think these accidents usually happen at the latter end of the day, when the children get tired?—Yes, that boy got killed at a quarter past 7 at night.

Did you not state that you met with an accident in the mill?—Yes, I had one of my arms broke.

What were you doing when that occurred?—I was working at what is called a brushing mill; there is a pin they put into the roller to make it run round and the pin caught my sleeve, and twisted my arm round and broke it—and another boy has had his arm broke in the same way.

Another case:

He was standing alongside of a card, and there was a belt that was hanging over one of the big shafts, and he happened to be putting his arm forward in this position, and his arm got entangled, and he went up to the shafts, and both his feet were knocked off, and his left arm was dislocated at the shoulder, and broken in three different places; he lived twenty-four hours after he got the accident, and then died.

That was attributed to his over-fatigue, in consequence of excessive labour?—Yes.

The picture presented by Dr. Green, of St. Thomas's Hospital, suggests the effect of this accumulation of over work and ill-treatment on the human body:

Take, for instance, a healthy child from an agricultural district in the bloom of health, animated, cheerful, lively, strong, active and free-limbed, and place it in a factory; let it work for twelve hours a day in the stifling heat of some of the work-rooms, confined in the impure air breathed by hundreds of others, without any provision for ventilation; let it learn to drink ardent spirits to support its enfeebled frame and depressed feelings under over-labour and harassing tasks, with a proportionate disrelish for wholesome food; let it then be turned out of this heated factory on a damp, foggy November evening, to rest its fevered and debilitated frame in some dank and close cellar of an over-peopled manufacturing town, and shall we be surprised, is it not rather a certain consequence, that the unfortunate child becomes the victim of disease?

Not even the enlightened medical witnesses suggested what today seems obvious on the evidence presented, that is to say, that no child should be employed at all in a factory. They only put forward, as the extreme limit of the reformer's case, the desirability of a reduction in hours to ten a day, as proposed by the bill, and that only light work should be undertaken before the age of nine was reached.

But the truth was that damage to health was not the only damage inflicted on children who worked in factories, and shorter hours alone could not be calculated to remove the bad moral conditions about which many witnesses spoke.

Matthew Crabtree, aged twenty-two, who was himself working without payment in a woollen mill, in order to redeem his father's debt, spoke on morals:

Can you speak as to the effect of this labour in the mills and factories on the morals of the children, as far as you have observed?—As far as I have observed with regard to morals in the mills, there is everything about them that is disgusting to every one conscious of correct morality.

Do you find that the children, the females especially, are very early demoralized in them?—They are.

Is their language indecent?—Very indecent; and both sexes take great familiarities with each other in the mills, without at all being ashamed of their conduct.

Do you connect their immorality of language and conduct with their excessive labour?—It may be somewhat connected with it, for it is to be observed that most of that goes on towards night, when they begin to be drowsy; it is a kind of stimulus which they use to keep them awake; they say some pert thing or other to keep themselves from drowsiness, and it generally happens to be some obscene language.

Have not a considerable number of the females employed in mills illegitimate children very early in life?—I believe there are; I have known some of them have illegitimate children when they were between 16 and 17 years of age.

How many grown up females had you in the mill?—I cannot speak to the exact number that were grown up; perhaps there might be thirty-four or so that worked in the mill at that time.

How many of those had illegitimate children?—A great many of them;—eighteen or nineteen of them, I think.

An overseer from a Dundee mill said:

There are more crimes committed in Dundee than there were in former times, as far as I can remember; and as to the streets, I believe they are mostly all mill people that are prostitutes.

A Sunday-school teacher from Keighley also referred to morals in the factories:

There are factories (I can speak to one in particular) where there is a man in the situation of an overlooker, who is a very bad man, and who keeps an old female who has had three illegitimate children, as a procuress for his own lustful ends.

Do you think this long and exhausting labour has a great tendency to increase the crime of drunkenness?— Yes, I do think so, because there are young men that are very much addicted to drinking; and when they get a little time they learn to smoke and drink; and when their bodies become exhausted, they go to the dram shop and get spirits, and they say that they do them good.

It seems strange that the mill owners themselves did not come forward to refute the great body of evidence which was daily being built up against them. Several rich and

humane manufacturers, like John Wood of Yorkshire and
John Fielden, member of Parliament for Oldham, were
themselves leading the agitation for reform. But the men
who thought the present system good enough remained
silent: they were not, however, unaware of the inquiry and
their actions suggested they were men with uneasy con-
sciences. The Committee drew from one witness a somewhat
pathetic story which proved that mill owners were reluctant
to display to strangers' eyes the everyday sights of their factories. Indeed, they hoped to deceive the Committee. Eliza
Marshall, the girl who had already given the lucid evidence
quoted above, was asked:

State whether, when your mill has been shown, and
when people have come to look at it, there has not been a
great deal of preparation before it has been seen by a
stranger?—Yes, there has.

Has there been a great deal done to make it appear
clean and nice, and the children tidy?—Yes, a great deal.

Have any other mills been prepared for people coming
to them, to your knowledge?—We live in Leeds, at the
Bank, nearly opposite Holdforth's silk mill; there was a
Parliament gentleman going on the Saturday, and the
children kept on till 12 o'clock on the Friday night, and
then they had an hour given them on the morning of
Saturday to go and dress themselves.

When was this?—I cannot tell rightly, two or three
weeks since, as nearly as I can recollect.

Did the children come in their Sunday clothes then?—
Yes.

Were all the children there?—Yes, for anything I know.

Were any of those who were ill-looking or unwell kept
away?—There were some of them sent home.

That were not to return?—Yes.

What were they sent home for?—I do not know, but
there was a gentleman going there.

Were they sent home because they did not appear to be
in good health?—Yes, that was the purpose, I believe.

You saw those persons, did you?—Yes.

Did not you think it very wrong for people, who wish to show the condition in which children are, to make those sort of preparations previously?—Yes, it was to deceive the gentleman.

What did the neighbours say of that?—They said it was a shame; that they could not always be so, in their Sunday clothes, and so on.

Did they wash and scrub themselves for the occasion? —I do not know whether they scrubbed themselves; they washed themselves.

What you speak of is what you heard among your neighbours?—I live near there; I saw the gig there with a footman.

Did you see the gentleman?—I cannot say that I did; the footman went riding backwards and forwards a good while.

You perceived that the children were dressed quite differently?—Yes, they had got their curls out and their lace caps on.

You saw that yourself?—Yes, I did.

So that would give no idea whatever of the general state or the cleanliness of the children?—No; they could not always be that way.

The Committee found that in most cases the education of the frail and exhausted children of the factories was totally neglected; but a few mills engaged a schoolmaster to hold a night school for an hour or so at the end of each day. Working time was never shortened to allow for schooling, however, and as the working day began at about half-past five and ended at eight, it was not surprising that children who attended evening classes fell asleep. Indeed, the Committee wondered why the children attended at all in such circumstances, till a witness pointed out that the parents were compelled by the mill owner to pay for such classes.

Questions and answers brought out the motive behind this unlooked for humanity by the mill owners:

Have not the masters recently appeared very wishful

to have those children in some sort educated?—Yes, since the agitation of the Bills for regulating the hours in mills and factories.

Do they suppose, then, that it will reconcile the children or the parents or the public to this system, to add another hour or two's confinement and general suffering to the already extravagant hours of labour which they extract from those children and young persons?—Undoubtedly so: but I know parents who shrink at the idea of sending their children, who work at the mills, to get education at night after their work is done, for when they get their suppers they will be sitting with a potato in one hand and something else in the other, and go to sleep, and after this they will go to school; and those parents who are more humane than others will abhor the idea of sending them off to school, knowing that the poor creatures have been standing the whole day upon their feet, for thirteen or fourteen hours, and that it is impossible that they should receive any education. The mill masters have been in the habit, in Dundee, of drawing up lists, that the people can all read and write. I have known those at 16 years of age that could not say A B C; and I have known some at that age who never were in a church.

Peter Smart, the overseer of Baxter's flax mill at Dundee, explained what education meant to the hands at this mill.

Have those children any education?—Some of them have and some of them have not.

In what time can they get that education?—There is a night school that commences at 8 o'clock at night, and goes on till 9.

What time do the children start in the morning?—Five minutes before 5, the mill begins.

What time do the children leave their homes?—At 4.

And work till when?—Till half-past 7.

Are they forced afterwards to go to that school?—Yes; I even got an order from their master, that if they did not attend the school they would be obliged to leave, and some girls told me they were not able to go from fatigue, and others that they had no clothes to go in.

Do you mean to say that they have got up from their beds at 4 o'clock in the morning, and have worked from 5 to 8 at night, and then that the master has compelled them to go to his night school?—Yes.

A teacher at a mill's school reported:

I have frequently observed the languid state of those children when in school; some of them, through the fatigue of the day, fall asleep in writing their copies . . . it is therefore very difficult to communicate instruction to them.

This dry and pedantic verdict was borne out by another teacher's picture of worried parents, who would sometimes set out late at night to search for a missing child, only to find it at last asleep in the corner of the deserted and locked-up school. The longest day has its end; but to some of the young workers at the mills even this hackneyed reflection could bring no comfort. Painful though it was for many of the over-wrought children to make their way at last back to their parents' homes, there was a worse alternative.

This was reserved for orphans or children employed at small, remote country mills; they had to live in a bothy—'a house with beds all round'.

For several reasons, Mr. Braid, who kept a mill at Duntruin, found the bothy system advantageous; he had mainly orphans in his employment. His overseer, who had the duty of thrashing them by night as well as by day, was asked:

Had some of those orphans been in that mill for a considerable length of time?—Yes; I believe there were some from Edinburgh, that had been in it four or five years.

Were those children beaten, in order to compel them to work for that length of time?—Yes; whenever they refused to do anything, they were taken and beaten.

Were they capable of performing their labour well towards the termination of such a long day's toil?—No, they were not.

Then their fate was to be awoke by being beaten, and to be kept to their labour when awoke by the same method?—Yes.

How were they kept in the premises under that method of treatment and labour?—They were all locked up.

While they were at work?—Yes; they were guarded up to their bothies to take their meals, and they were locked up in the bothies at night, and the master took the key away with him to his own bed-room; they were guarded to their work and they were guarded back again, and they were guarded while they were taking their meat, and then they were locked up for rest; the windows of the bothies where they slept had all iron stanchions on the outside, so that they could not escape.

Were they allowed to go to a place of worship on a Sunday?—No, they were not.

Were they guarded on the premises on the Sunday?—Yes; they were guarded by the master or by his son.

How many children were there in that mill?—I think there were twenty-five or twenty-six of us together.

Were the sexes always divided in those bothies?—No; there was one bothy for the boys, but that bothy did not hold them all, and there were some of them that were put into the other bothy along with the girls.

At what ages were the boys that were put into the girls' bothy?—The boys might be, I should suppose, from 10 to 14.

What were the ages of the girls?—Perhaps from 12 to 18.

Did the children and young persons attempt to escape from their labour and confinement, and, in fact, from the incarceration that you have described?—Yes; and I have gone after them on horseback and brought them back myself.

What was done with any of the hands that were brought back?—They were taken into the mill and got a severe beating with a strap; sometimes the master kicked them on the floor, and struck them with both his hands and his feet.

The mill-owner Braid's high-handed treatment of his employees was even given some legal backing, as it was customary to extract a contract which tied a child to the mill for at least a year. His overseer's evidence explained the result:

> Were those of them that had made engagements for a length of time ever prosecuted?—Yes; whenever they ran away, if he could not find them before they got home to their relations, if they had any, he sent after them, and put them in gaol.
>
> Did you ever know any put in gaol?—I knew a woman put in gaol, and brought back after a twelvemonth, and worked for her meat; and she had to pay the expenses that were incurred.
>
> For how long a period were the engagements made?— There were some engaged for two years, and some as far on as three years; and some of those girls sent from Edinburgh I heard them say were engaged for five years.
>
> So that when that girl was sent to prison, the master indemnified himself for the loss of her time while she was in the course of punishment, by compelling her to work a year after for nothing?—Yes, there were two years she had to work for nothing.

In this mill it was impossible to say how many hours were worked except that they were 'unmercifully long'. There was no clock, and when one adult operative was found with a watch, it was taken into the mill master's custody, because the worker had told the other men the time of day. And for the children in the bothy, the unmerciful treatment went beyond that required to keep them working.

> When the hands worked those long hours, how were they roused in the morning?—The master came himself; and those that could not rise, I have seen him take a pail of water and throw it upon them, to make them rise in the morning.
>
> Are any means taken to secure those children and young persons from running away; is any part of their property constantly kept back, if they have any?—Their clothes are locked up; they cannot get their clothes; and they cannot get them given them, but just as they require

them; and if they do run away, they can only run away with what is on their backs.

You state that those children are beaten very violently? —Yes, I saw one girl; I do not know what had been the occasion of it, but the master was kicking her along the floor, and she was bleeding at both mouth and nose; I asked what was the matter; and she said he wanted familiarities with her; this was in the forenoon, in the winter time.

This system gives a very great and very improper control over those young women to such individuals; have you, upon your own knowledge, reason to suspect that improper advantages are taken of that control, and of the defenceless situation, especially of the female hands?— Yes, I have every reason to believe that such is the case; for this same gentleman had a considerable number of females that have been working under him that have had children by him.

*

The end of the story is a little happier. Once again the reforming ardour of a few single-minded men overcame the lethargy of the majority. Sadler's immediate reward for his untiring labours on the report of the Select Committee was to lose both his Bill and, in the next General Election, his seat as well. But the evidence of the children, the overseers and the medical men was too strong to be denied by any fair-minded observer.

If it had achieved nothing else, the report brought conviction to a great philanthropist whose name will always be connected with work for children, the seventh Earl of Shaftesbury. At this time he was Lord Ashley, Tory member for the pocket borough of Woodstock. He had taken no interest in the case presented by Oastler and did not even know that Sadler had obtained a Committee of Inquiry in 1832. But the terrible evidence, when published, changed his attitude completely. In 1833 he took over the cause in

Parliament which Sadler could no longer plead. The Bill which Lord Ashley introduced limited the working day to ten hours for all below the age of eighteen and forbade the employment of children less than nine years old. It provided also for the appointment of factory inspectors and for the education of employed children.

Though sympathetic to reform, Lord Althorp (who was once described as 'the tortoise on whom the world rests') knew that in this form the bill would not get through; it was too harsh for the manufacturers. When Ashley, in understandable indignation, refused to betray the interests of the children, Althorp, as Chancellor of the Exchequer, adopted the Bill as a Government measure, but while children of over thirteen had still to work a twelve-hour day, or sixty-nine hours per week, those under thirteen were given an eight-hour day. In this form, the first important Factory Act was passed into law.

VII

THE CASE OF
THE SCUM OF THE EARTH

*It is a Shameful and Unblessed thing, to take the Scumme of the People,
and Wicked Condemned Men, to be the People with whom you Plant:*
FRANCIS BACON, *Of Plantations.*

TWO MONTHS before Queen Victoria succeeded to
the throne a young dandy of twenty-seven, with fair
hair falling below his collar, and an eyeglass, rose to
address the Commons. His customary dress was a long frock
coat, a high, starched collar, and a black stove-pipe hat.
He proposed an inquiry which should stretch for 16,000 miles
to remote Van Diemen's Land, and even to a speck in the
Southern Seas called Norfolk Island; upon which the House
agreed that a Committee should 'inquire into the system of
transportation, its efficacy as a punishment, its influence on
the moral state of society in the penal colonies, and how far
it is susceptible of improvement'. The delicate young man
who thus set in motion one of the most important Select
Committees which ever sat was Sir William Molesworth,
eighth baronet, of an ancient Cornish family. As possessor
of wide estates and £11,000 a year, he had enough, in those
untaxed days, to live on. But in his veins was the blood of
the West Country—blood that had flowed in victory from
the Spanish Main to the Nile and in defeat from Exeter to
Sedgmoor. Molesworth was typical of his countrymen,

quick in thought, impatient of authority, unconquerable in
spirit. His career began in the mood which was to continue
for the whole of his life; at Cambridge he disagreed with his
tutor and quarrelled with him so forcefully that both men
crossed the narrow seas in order to fight a duel.

The fact that this episode ended his scholastic career was
incidental: Molesworth continued to read for nine to ten
hours a day in his own study. Soon he came across matters
which were irreconcilable with his conscience and pursued
his quarrel to the very steps of the throne.

Molesworth's supreme clash with authority came early.
Some great men, like Gladstone, wait till their reputation is
reasonably secure before they risk it in an unpopular cause.
Molesworth knew no such restraint. Entering Parliament as
a Radical, his reforming zeal soon outstripped the opinions
of his constituents, even of his political friends. In his
maiden speech he departed from custom by introducing
inflammatory material: he advocated election of members
by secret ballot. In 1872, when he had been dead nearly
twenty years, it became law in England; even now some
nations have not reached this point in political maturity.
Nothing ever satisfied Molesworth. He was always pressing
on to new reforms, pursuing them simultaneously. He
advocated the abolition of slavery, self-government for the
colonies, national education, and every species of reform in
church and state, separately or all together. His energies
flowed out in all directions. He founded the *London Review*
and the Reform Club. To all these causes he brought a pene-
trating intellect, supported by a surpassing memory, a reck-
less audacity of attack and an unrelenting determination
which were all the more effective because they were sustained by accurate and detailed facts. His enemies called
his speeches 'a kind of biltong of blue-books and statistics',
but they were often delivered with a sustained passion
which left permanent effects on the House.

As a politician he was that rare creature, a true independent. The solitary luxury he demanded from politics was

the right to speak and vote as his conscience dictated. 'I will vote with them,' he said of any party, 'when to the best of my judgment they are right.'

The origins of the inquiry into transportation furnish a good example of the energy and determination of Molesworth's methods. Since 1833 he had been deeply interested in the subject of colonial settlement by his friendship with Edward Gibbon Wakefield. Next year six poor ignorant labourers from neighbouring Dorset were sentenced to seven years' transportation. They were sentenced under an obsolete statute designed to deal with naval mutiny, ostensibly for administering illegal oaths to their fellow labourers (accompanied by puerile ceremonies of drawn swords and bandaged eyes); but their real crime was an attempt to form a nation-wide trade union. Molesworth was stung first into two years of laborious research and then into violent action. While others moved to the rescue of the six 'Tolpuddle martyrs'—they were granted a free pardon in 1837—he decided that the treatment prepared for the Dorset labourers should now be applied to the King's brother.

Briefly, the case was this. Just before George IV died, his brother the Duke of Cumberland professed to believe that since the next heir, Clarence, was insane, and the next, Victoria, was 'not alone a female but a minor', the crown would be seized by a usurper unless he himself were placed upon the throne. To ensure this convenient arrangement he endeavoured to extend the intensely loyal Northern Irish Society know as Orangeism, of which he was Grand Master, to England. Many Lodges were established by the Duke's agents in the Army and Navy, and oaths administered with exactly the same sort of childish ritual as had been used by the Dorset labourers.

The Radicals raised the matter in the House of Commons, but the royal duke stood firm. Some months later the attack was renewed, but Joseph Hume's motion for an Address to the King to discharge all Orangemen from all employments was a sadly confused performance. In a packed House

Molesworth then seconded the motion with shattering success. The scene is well described by the artist Duppa:

> He rose, not with the diffidence which generally characterises and so well becomes one of his age, but with a degree of self-confidence worthy the Great Dan himself. . . . He then expounded the laws relative to Orange and other societies using secret signs and oaths, told them those who frequented such societies subjected themselves to transportation—that the Duke of Cumberland and his clique ought not to be spared because they were rich and well educated, whilst the poor ignorant Dorchester labourers were suffering for the infringement of those laws which they were unable to understand.
>
> William gave out the names of the titled criminals, as he termed them, with exquisite bitterness, and clenched his red pocket handkerchief in his fist as though he were tearing up Orange Societies by the root. Tremendous cheering followed his speech. . . . After *the* speech, for it was assuredly *the* speech of the night, William Arscott, and your humble servant adjourned to Bellamy's Kitchen, where we demolished sundry mutton chops, Welsh rabbits, bottles of porter and sherry—no bad finale to the night's fatigue, for, by Jove, it is a monstrous bore to sit in the same place for ten consecutive hours. Thank God, I am not an M.P.

The great sensation of the speech had been the reference to the Duke of Cumberland by name. As a result the Duke surrendered, the Orange Lodges were disbanded and Molesworth's triumph was complete.

When, therefore, the House agreed to the setting up of the Select Committee on transportation, Molesworth, who had also spoken brilliantly upon his motion for the Committee, was elected chairman. Though it was a young committee (a majority of its fifteen members being under forty), this was a decided compliment, for among those nominated to the Committee were the Home Secretary (Lord John Russell), the Leader of the Opposition (Sir Robert Peel), two other Ministers, two other ex-Ministers, and several distinguished members of all parties. The then Under-Secretary for the Colonies (Sir George Grey) and Lord Howick were the chief advocates of transportation, but it is clear that from the start most of the other members took the opposite view.

The Select Committee were indefatigable, meeting day after day through the best part of two parliamentary sessions. Molesworth never missed a sitting, each of which frequently involved four or five hundred questions, mostly put by himself.

Before this Committee there stepped a procession of characters steeped in experience of the wildest passions of mankind. The historical account of transportation given by the Committee forms a background for their evidence:

> The punishment of Transportation is founded on that of exile, both of which are unknown to common law. Exile, according to the best authorities, was introduced, as a punishment, by the Legislature in the 39th year of Elizabeth; and the first time that Transportation was mentioned was in an Act of 18 Charles II, c. 3, which empowered the judges to exile for life the moss-troopers of Cumberland and Northumberland, to any of his Majesty's possessions in America. The punishment, authorized by this Act, is somewhat different from the one now termed Transportation, inasmuch as the latter consists not only of exile to a particular place, but of compulsory labour there. It appears, however, to have been the practice at an early period to subject transported offenders to penal labour, and to employ them as slaves on the estates of the planters. . . . With the war of independence, transportation to America ceased. . . . It was not deemed expedient to offer to the colonies, that remained loyal in America, the insult of making them any longer a place of punishment for offenders. It was determined, therefore, to plant a new colony for this sole purpose; and an Act was passed in the 24th year of George the Third, which empowered his Majesty in Council, to appoint to what place, beyond the seas, either within or without his

Majesty's dominions, offenders shall be transported; and by two Orders in Council, dated 6 Dec. 1786, the eastern coast of Australia and the adjacent islands were fixed upon. In the month of May 1787, the first band of convicts departed, which, in the succeeding year, founded the colony of New South Wales. . . .

Against 27,831 convicts in New South Wales there were at this date 49,831 free souls. In Van Diemen's Land the proportion was similar; in each case, of course, the free included many who had been convicts. Sentences ran for seven years, for fourteen years or for life. Let us see at once what kind of criminals were concerned. A small proportion of the whole number were agricultural labourers and workmen driven into crime by hunger or by political fervour. The return of those transported on board the *Elphinstone* from the hulks at Woolwich and Chatham in May, 1836, however, provides a more characteristic sample. Here are a baker's dozen of average rogues:

Name	Age	Birth-place	Crime	Sentence	Trade	Character from the Gaoler
Charles Modley	22	Nether-stowe	Stealing above £5 from a shop	life	Confec-tioner	A traveller to fairs; behaviour in gaol good.
George Cox	35	Worcester	Horse stealing	life	Higgler	Temper and behaviour in prison good.
William Pegg	20	Lough-borough	Robbery	life	Chair-maker	Ditto.
John Leach, alias William Bewick	30	Dublin	Stealing above £100 in a dwelling house	life	Pipe-maker	Not known; supposed to be one of the swell mob.
Thomas Smith	17	Blackburn	Stealing a drawer, etc.	life	Sweep	Twice convicted before, and twice imprisoned as a vagrant.
James Regan	25	Leeds	Stealing a purse and money	14 years	Hair-dresser	Convicted before.

Name	Age	Birth-place	Crime	Sen-tence	Trade	Character from the Gaoler
Isaac Williamson	22	Invergordon, Ross	Robbery and assault	14 years	Brazier	Behaviour in prison tolerable.
Thomas Magill	22	Tullow	House-breaking	14 years	Sailor	Imprisoned as a vagabond; idle, dissipated and very bad in every respect.
William Winterbottom	21	Honslet	Stealing various articles	14 years	Labourer	Convicted before; idle and drunken, of the worst-description in every respect.
William Broadley	29	Huddersfield	Stealing from the person	14 years	Weaver	Transported before, and bad in every respect.
James Patterson	14	Toxteth Park	Stealing various	14 years	Shoe-maker	Convicted three times before.
William Smith	21	Liverpool	Stealing a key	14 years	Cooper	Connections decent; transported before.
Thomas Owen	13	Ditto	Stealing 6 spoons and 1 pair of tongs	14 years	Errand-boy	Twice convicted before, and twice imprisoned as a vagrant.

A last confession made to a gaol chaplain at Hobart in 1831 would seem to fix for ever in one's mind the background of one such thief: this catalogue of juvenile delinquency was made by George Thomson, alias Nutt, on the evening preceding his execution for a burglary in Van Diemen's Land:

When I was between eight and nine years old, I used to sleep with my mother, and wanting some money I put my hand in her pocket and stole 6d.; and as I was not discovered, a short time afterwards I stole something else, and from that time I was always pilfering. My father was very indulgent, and died when I was about 11 years of age. Soon after I ran away from school; I had frequently, done so before. I went into the fields and saw some chickens; I stole two of them; a boy whom I had known upwards of two years advised me to steal the fowls. I sold them to a man who lived in our neighbourhood, to whom my companions introduced me, for 3s.; he kept an old iron shop, and used to buy stolen things from boys. I gave my companion half the money; I was always stealing and mixing in bad company. When I was between 12 and 13 years old, I became acquainted with bad women. I was introduced to them by my companions. Shortly after I stole the fowls, I went with my companion to Clapham Common; we there stole six ducks, and sold them to the same man for about 9s. I used to tell my mother that I got the money by going to work. I was afterwards introduced to another companion by my first. One night we went, all three together, for the purpose of shop-lifting; I was then not 12 years old. We went into a shop in the Kent Road, no person was in it; we stole a pair of scales and ran away; taking them down Kent-street in the Borough, a patrol met me named 'Ruby', and took me into custody. I was sent to Horsemonger Gaol, and as no owner could be found I was discharged. (I had told my sister, and she had paid the owner for the scales.) In less than a month after I was discharged, myself and one of my companions went to Epping Forest. We there stole two sheets and a table-cloth, which were hanging in the yard of a man's house; we had watched the servant out before we stole the things; he met us with a bundle; we were apprehended and tried at Chelmsford in 1823; we were confined twelve months in the house of correction. When we were discharged we separated. I had partly lost the use of my leg in gaol, which hindered me for about a month or five weeks. When I recovered I went with two fresh companions to commit a burglary in Russel-street, Bermondsey. We got in by a window at the back part of the house, between 11 and one at night; it was a tailor's shop; we stole a great many articles of wearing apparel. We got clear away, and sold them to another man who kept an old iron shop. Three or four nights after that, I committed another burglary, with the same companions in

East-lane, Walworth; it was a grocer's shop; we entered there by boring holes in the window shutters; we took plate, money, tea, sugar, tobacco and a large looking-glass; we got clear away; we took them to the same iron shop. We staid in the house until nearly five in the morning, till the watch went off, which I suppose is the reason we were not apprehended. We ate and drank there until we were half intoxicated; we got between £5 and £6 for what we took there. About three or four nights after this, I committed a burglary with one of the same persons in a street in the Grange Road; it was a corn-factor's; we entered by breaking through a shutter in the back parlour; we took the things to the same man; he lived in Bermond-sey-street; I forget his name; he has removed from thence; we got between £12 and £13 for these things. By buying clothes suspicion was excited, and I was apprehended, examined and discharged for want of proof. Previous to my apprehension I committed a burglary in company with the same man in the Kent Road, in a private house. We took from there a quantity of plate, about 150 ounces, some wearing apparel and tea. We left about 4 o'clock in the morning. We sold these things to the same man.

When I was discharged for the former robbery, I met with two other companions, (the name of one was 'William Rice', who suffered at Newgate in July 1828, the other is alive, I do not wish to name him); we committed a burglary in the Grange Road; Rice would not go; we got in by wrenching off a bolt from the back-door; it was a private house; the gentleman's name was Porter; we took there a quantity of plate, wine and Irish linen not made up; we got clear off; we sold that to the same person. Three or four nights after this Rice joined us; we broke open a house in Grange-walk (Mr. Hooper's, a tanner) we there took a quantity of plate; we broke the plated articles to convince us they were not silver; we sold these things to the same man; we got about £20. (I was now cohabiting with a female.) Within a week after this we committed a burglary in the house of Mr. Woodward, in the Kent Road, a private house; we there took some plate, about 150 ounces, a timepiece and wearing apparel; we got clear off, and sold the things to the same man. About three or four nights after this, myself and Rice committed a burglary in Prospect-place, near Dock-head; it was a captain's house; we there got only a little plate; we got clear off, and sold it to the same man. In the morning, while at breakfast with the girl I lived with in London-street, Dock-head, I was apprehended for Mr. Woodward's robbery. I was confined in Horsemonger-lane three weeks, when I was discharged for want of proof. After this I met with another man, and committed a burglary with him in East-lane, Walworth; we got a quantity of plate, and escaped clear off; we sold this to another man, a Jew, in Petticoat-lane, Whitechapel; I do not wish to mention his name. After three or four nights after this, myself with my last-mentioned companion, attempted to commit a burglary in the Kent Road, near the Green Man turnpike; we were apprehended in the yard between one and two in the morning; we had three months in the house of correction at Brixton. . . .

Thus the melancholy catalogue continues, short spells of liberty devoted entirely to crime, and punctuated at ever shortening intervals by prison sentences:

About five or six weeks after I came out of the House of Correction, myself and companions were taken in the Kent Road; my companion escaped. I was confined three months in Brixton for having implements of house-breaking in my possession; I had a small crowbar, a dark lantern, a small centre-bit, a box, some false keys and phosphorus box; I could carry them all out of sight. . . . When I came out I returned to my old place of residence. (When I was taken it was generally away from home, and I never told where I lived.) . . . The next night I committed a burglary with two other men, in the New Road, Bermondsey; I knew how to take pannels out of doors and windows now. . . . Four nights after this, which was on the 27th December, 1827, one of my former companions, named 'Harper', with myself, committed a burglary in the Kent Road, near the sign of the Lord Wellington; we took some money, about £10, some old gold and silver

coins, and some plate; we got clear off, sold these things
to two Jews, half to each, for about £30. . . . About a
week afterwards Harper and myself committed a burglary
on Finsbury-pavement, near London-wall; Harper was
taken there; I escaped, and got £15 for what I brought
away; Harper was executed for this robbery in 1828. I
committed the robbery at Mr. Young's, Limehouse; was
taken in the fact, convicted and received sentence of
death, and was afterwards transported for life. I have
committed many robberies which I do not recollect. I
was always thieving. I do not think that I have stated
more than three-fourths of the robberies I have committed. I am not quite certain as to the dates. I have spent
the money in drunkenness and debauchery of all kinds. I
was much among prostitutes. The robbery for which I am
about to suffer is the only one that I have committed in
this colony; Mr. Gregson's servant proposed the robbery
to me, and I proposed the robbery to Newman; we were
all concerned in it.

This human magpie was aged twenty when hanged for
this offence, but it was by no means his last; the chaplain
who took down the statement makes the final ironic comment: 'He acknowledged committing many thefts while he
was confined in the gaol.'

*

After sentence at home the convict waited in a gaol or
hulk until he sailed in a convict ship, under the authority of
a surgeon-superintendent. Upon the prisoners' occupations
at sea we have the evidence of the Very Reverend William
Ullathorne, Roman Catholic Vicar-General of New Holland
and Van Diemen's Land, and perhaps the most humane,
earnest and compelling witness of all whom the Committee
heard:

Will you be so kind as to state to the committee your
opinions with regard to the condition and conduct of the
convicts, beginning first of all with those on board ship?
—I should distinguish between the male prisoners and

the female prisoners, who, of course, go out in separate ships. The male prisoners have little or nothing to do, except to keep themselves and their apartments below clean. Having nothing whatever to do, they of course occupy themselves in conversation, and in amusing themselves as much as they can, and I believe it is the case, that the subjects generally conversed upon are of a very corrupting character; for instance, they converse much on the subject of their past crimes, and the manner in which they have effected their past crimes; they converse much likewise on the manner in which they have succeeded in perpetrating all kinds of immoralities. They converse likewise on board with regard to their future prospects. And there is likewise a good deal of petty theft from the provisions in their passage through the hands of the cook, and from the hands of the cook to the prisoners; also they pilfer provisions and little necessaries from each other; and, of course, wherever a great number of bad men are brought together, anything of a virtuous character does not appear; it is not at all the tone of the men, and they would put it down immediately if a man were to attempt to say anything tending to moral reformation. I do not think that bad men of that kind will allow such things to be spoken of; in short, there is a sort of spirit of bravado, a spirit of pride, and an *esprit du corps*, which leads them to converse much on their crimes, and to mix their conversation with a good deal of obscenity.

What is your opinion of the effects of the association of hardened criminals upon the minds of those unhardened? —The effect on board ship is very bad indeed; I have known it complained of frequently. We find the injurious effects of the hardened criminals, and particularly the criminals from the hulks and the large towns in England, much complained of; I believe the effect is very bad indeed. I would remark upon one point more with regard to the prisoners on board ship; they are put together four on the same couch generally, and I think that a great deal of evil, not only from their conversation, but from other causes, arises from that. The boys have a separate compartment below, but they mingle on deck with the men, and are much corrupted by the converse and remarks of the prisoners on deck. The huddling of the boys together below is likewise accompanied with a great deal of moral pollution.

Upon arrival, convicts were either retained to work for the Government or distributed among private colonists as 'assigned servants'. If they had committed some further crime on board ship, they might be committed to the punishment chain gangs or sent to the penal settlements. But in this allocation or assignment hardly any attention was paid to whether a man was young or old, sensitive or callous, transported for seven years, for fourteen or for life. Often his very crime was unknown to the Assignment Board. Thus the thing was a vast lottery, and a man's whole welfare and happiness depended upon whether he found a good or a bad master. At this time, too, the demand for convict labour greatly exceeded the supply, especially for tradesmen or artisans—'mechanics' as they were called. But during the few days when the Board were determining their fate, Dr. Ullathorne showed that they had the chance in the convict barracks of remedying any deficiencies in their criminal education which remained after the voyage:

Are the boys separated from the men in the barracks?—They have, I believe, a separate apartment, but they mix in the yards with the men during the time of recreation. . . .
What is the effect of permitting the boys to associate with the men during the day?—The effect is very bad; the moral contamination upon the boys is very great indeed. . . .
What is the general conduct of the convicts in the barracks?—There is, I believe, a great deal of very bad language, and a great deal of pilfering from each other; and I am afraid that when they are locked up there is a great deal of crime of a monstrous character.
Are the less hardened convicts, do you think, liable to ill-treatment and outrage and ridicule from their more hardened associates?—Undoubtedly; many men have

come to me a day or two after they have been in the barracks, for the purpose of going through their religious
exercises, and some of those men have been absolutely
heart-broken. The scenes of that kind have been exceedingly harassing which I have witnessed; those men who
have been rather accidental criminals than habitual (and
there is a considerable class of prisoners of that kind from
Ireland, many of whom pass through my hands) have
expressed to me, in a manner which has completely har-
rowed my soul, the sufferings that they had to undergo
from the conduct of the other prisoners when they
arrived there at first.

*

Assigned convicts who were lucky might be sent to Mr.
James Macarthur's 'well-regulated establishment'. He was
the son of that John Macarthur, whose family remains one of
the best-known in Australia to this day, who during a
violent and adventurous career, achieved more for that
country than perhaps any other single man, by founding its
principal industry and source of wealth.

In Van Diemen's Land, too, there were good employers.
Obviously well treated, an assigned convict named Henry
Tingley wrote home to his parents at Uckfield, Sussex:

Ansley, 15 June 1845.

Dear Mother and Father,

This comes with my kind love to you, hoping to find
you in good health as, thank God, it leaves me at present
very comfortable indeed. I have a place at a farmhouse,
and I have got a good master, which I am a great deal
more comfortable than I expected. I works the same as I
were at home; I have a plenty to eat and drink, thank God
for it. I am allowed two ounces of tea, one pound of
sugar, 12 pounds of meat, 10 pounds and a half of flour,
two ounces of tobacco the week; three pair of shoes, two
suits of clothes, four shirts, a year; that is the allowance
from Government. But we have as much to eat as we like,
as some masters are a great deal better than others. All a
man has got to mind is to keep a still tongue in his head,

and do his master's duty, and then he is looked upon as
if he were at home; but if he don't, he may as well be hung
at once, for they would take you to the magistrates and
get 100 lashes, and then get sent to a place called Port
Arthur to work in irons for two or three years, and then
he is disliked by everyone. . . . This country is far
before England in everything, both for work and money.
Of a night, after I have done my work, I have a chance to
make a few shillings; I can go out hunting or shooting of
kangaroo, that is about the size of a sheep, or ducks or
swans, tigers, tiger cats or native cats; there is nothing
that will hurt a man but a snake, they are about five or six
feet long, but they will get away if they can. I have dogs
and gun of my own, thank God for it, to make me a few
shillings, anything that I want; thank God, I am away
from all beer-shops, there is ne'er a one within 20 miles of
where I live. . . . I am doing a great deal better than
ever I was at home, only for the wanting you with me,
that is all my uncomfortableness is in being away from
you. . . .

Dear Mother and Father, I have eight years to serve
with my master, and than I shall have a ticket of leave,
that is to work for myself, and then to keep that for four
years if no trouble, and to have my emancipation, that is
to be a free man in this country; I am now a prisoner then
in this place and then after that I shall have my free
pardon to come to England once more. But I should be a
deal more comfortable if you could get the parish to send
you out, as it would be the making of you if they would
pay your passage over, and give you about £60 to land
with, you would do well. A farming man gets 5s. a day
at day-work; if you was to come you could take me of
Government for £1 for eight years to work for you, and
then we should be more comfortable than ever we have
been. . . .

A harder master, though by no means the worst, was
James Mudie, a landed proprietor resident in New South
Wales from 1822 till 1836. He had been a magistrate, was
relieved of his office probably on account of too great

severity, and had left the colony in fear of his life. He was an excellent and ready witness who appeared to hold nothing back:

What number of convicts should you say you had assigned to you?—During the harvest I had occasionally as many as 120.

Will you now state in what occupations you employed the men under your estate?—A certain number were employed as shepherds, a certain number as ploughmen, a certain number as bullock drivers, a certain number as mechanics, and a certain number in looking after the horned cattle, and also in looking after pigs.

What were their hours of work?—Upon my establishment, it being a very large one, I believe the most extensive in the colony as an agriculturist, I had a very large bell; I found it very difficult to get them to turn out at the proper time; some would say they did not know the hour, and others made other excuses; and I kept a watchman all night, and I gave directions that he should ring this bell about perhaps an hour before sunrise as a warning; then he would ring it again about half an hour after that, and it was then rung for the third time just as the sun was rising. It was expected that the men would be all out at sunrise; they could hear the bell all over the establishment; it was rung again at eight o'clock.

What was that for?—For breakfast.

How long a period were they allowed for breakfast?—One hour; and then again at nine o'clock it was rung for them to turn out to work.

How long did they work?—Until one.

One was their dinner hour?—Yes.

When did they cease work?—Then they had from one to two; but I should wish to state, that in the summer, when the weather was very warm, I used to give them an hour and a half instead of an hour.

What time did they end work?—At sunset; in the winter time the bell rang at eight; it was expected then that the men should be in their huts; they go to bed in the summer at nine.

You have stated their hours of work; what were their hours of leisure?—What I have stated to the committee, the time of their diet and after sunset.

What were their occupations during their hours of leisure?—That is rather difficult for me to detail; I will endeavour to do it as far as I can. There is a traffic carried on amongst them in plaiting straw hats, which they dispose of, and some of them gamble; indeed they all gamble if they can get cards; it seems to be a universal propensity among the convicts; and one out of 20, perhaps, will read; but the greater portion, after dark, slip out, and go prowling about robbing in the neighbourhood.

The greater proportion of your convicts, after the hour of dark, went prowling about, robbing?—Yes, I can speak of my own estate, and from having acted as a magistrate.

Have you reason to believe that the same thing is common upon all the other estates?—I should think so.

Have they any means of obtaining spirits?—Decidedly, they have.

Did you ever allow your men spirits?—I have; and I will state upon what occasions. . . . The thing is notoriously known in the colony. During the time of harvest the weather is excessively hot; in fact I have often wondered how the men can stand out in the sun; and they drink a vast quantity of water; to those men I allowed after breakfast, a glass of colonial gin; then, after dinner, I allowed them another; and I was told by the medical men that it was very proper and desirable, on account of the great quantity of water that they drank. Then, at harvest home, I have always made a point of having a dinner cooked expressly, something similar to what is done in England, at least I know that to be the practice in Scotland, and they had one day given them for what they called a jollification; then the dinner was cooked, and as much as the men could eat was given to them; and in fact I, and other persons with me, attended as waiters upon them; then upon those occasions I gave them a certain quantity of spirits, which, of course, I reduced, and sometimes wine; and indeed I purchased London porter for them, and recommended it strongly, and offered to give them a quart of London porter a day during the harvest, but they preferred spirits.

In all respects, therefore, the condition of your convicts was as good as that of the labourer in England?—I believe that I should have no difficulty in showing that it was far superior.

Sir George Grey: Do you mean in all respects, or with regard to the quantity of food allowed them, and the quantity of labour exacted?—I should say with regard to the food, but with regard to the labour, I have no hesitation in saying, that one English labourer, or Scotch labourer, upon the same rations, (for I have had them agree to work for me, and contented with the rations that I gave my convicts) would do as much in one day as most convicts would do in a week.

Have you been in the habit of employing mechanics?— Yes.

Do you find it possible to extract the skill which they possess from them?—Only by a species of bribery.

Is it not the case that wages are necessarily given to assigned servants in the colony for the interest of the master, and in order to obtain from them that work that they cannot do in another way?—I have been obliged to do it myself. I erected a windmill upon my estate, and I had an ingenious fellow, a carpenter. . . .

An assigned servant?—Yes; and he was particularly fond of dress; I gave him superior clothing; he was also very musical; he told me that he wanted a flute, and I purchased a flute for him, and little temptations of that kind, and I got the work done by him; I should not without.

On the other hand, many witnesses showed that a bad master could, and often did, by cruelty and injustice render an assigned servant's life unbearable. The Reverend Dr. John Dunmore Lang, for instance, a Minister of the Church of Scotland, stated:

. . . The master often employs a degree of severity which the law does not contemplate. . . . So strong is this felt to be the case by the convicts themselves, that there are many instances of convicts committing crimes, or rather misdemeanors, for the express purpose of being turned into Government, as it is called; that is, being sent to the road parties, or the road gangs, in order that they may have a chance of assignment to a milder master after their period of punishment has expired. As an instance of the tyranny that is practised, and of the feeling it gives rise to in many instances in the colony, I would just relate a circumstance which fell within my own knowledge. A master complained before a magistrate of his servant for having stolen a quart of skimmed milk; the magistrate dismissed the complaint as frivolous, but the convict's sense of injustice being roused, he took an opportunity, very shortly afterwards, when his master and the other men were engaged in killing bullocks for the establishment, and when he was desired to carry the half of a carcase of a bullock across the court-yard, to pretend that something had tripped his foot, and he let the carcase fall in the dirtiest part of the court-yard. This system of tyranny on the one hand and of revenge on the other prevails in a great many establishments in the colony, and is quite inconsistent with any plan of reformation; indeed the thing is hopeless under such circumstances.

Broadly speaking, almost all the witnesses corroborated each other's evidence, but upon one matter they were perfectly unanimous: the worst of all the convicts, they averred, were the women, about whom James Mudie gave this verdict:

What is the character and description of female assigned convicts?—Of their character I should say, in fact, that they are worse than the men in all descriptions of vice; you can have no conception of their depravity of character. If you apply, for instance, for a dairywoman or a housemaid, perhaps you will have a lady sent to you that has been walking the lobby of the theatres; this is your dairymaid.

Have you had any such sent you?—Yes.

Will you state any particulars of that?—I had one sent; in fact she was, as far as regards dress, and manners and affectation, what you would expect to meet in one of the lobbies of a theatre; and I asked her what she had been accustomed to do. 'Nothing'. I said: 'You must work here, you must do something'; she said she could not. She brought a lot of band-boxes. I told her, 'You cannot make use of these things here.' She asked me where was her room; I showed her a room where another convict woman was; she said she was accustomed to nothing of that kind; was there not another room for her? 'No,' I said, 'that is your room, and that is your bed.'

How did she behave herself?—She behaved herself by, I think, the first or second night absenting herself; and the overseer reported to me that there were nine of the men missing. I asked what was the meaning of that, and he said he supposed it was with the new woman that had gone.

Do you find, on the whole, that the convict women are generally continent or incontinent?—I should say, of almost the whole of the convict women that arrive in New South Wales, that there is hardly an exception amongst them; there are some sent out for bigamy that have been in better society; but others that have attended the theatres, and the lowest girls possible that have been street-walkers, all sorts; but they all smoke, drink, and in fact, to speak in plain language, I consider them all prostitutes.

He gives us a glimpse, too, of the very occasional exception, possibly the victim of a tragic miscarriage of justice:

I had only one woman that I considered really well-behaved; she was recommended to me by the doctor of the ship. I went on board for the purpose of getting a servant, and he recommended several I could see, by looking at them, what they were. He said, 'Here is a woman, a remarkably well-behaved woman, but she has a child.' I said, 'What is the age of the child?' He said, 'A

very nice little boy.' I asked, 'Can he walk?' The child
was brought; it was two or three years old. I said, 'If the
woman is well-behaved, and of course partial to her child,
the object of the child's food and clothing is nothing to
me, and I will take the woman.' I took the woman, and I
found her a remarkably well-behaved woman; so much
so, that if my daughters complained at any time, I used
to talk of sending her to the factory, when she used to
cry, and hoped she should not be sent away; but the
others made a point of doing what they could in order to
be sent to the factory, and said, 'Why not send me to the
factory? I wish to go to the factory.'

Mr. Baring: Do you know what this woman was transported for?—Yes, I know all her history: she was a
simple, ignorant woman, a lace-worker in Nottingham,
and some other female, an acquaintance of hers had
stolen some property, and asked her if she would let her
leave her trunk in her house; and I believe the woman to
have had no more to do with the robbery than I had.

Peter Murdock agreed that it was impossible to reform
these women:

Will you enter a little more into particulars?— . . . I
may mention the first woman we received. . . Mrs. Murdock saw her and almost wished herself at home again;
however, nothing else could be done, and she got a little
room made up for her, and put her in it; and she went in
one day, and found her lying on the bed, with what she
called a yard of clay in her mouth, and drinking a pot of
porter, and blowing a cloud; that was her own expression
to Mrs. Murdock, when she went in.

How did she conduct herself after that?—I think I sent
her back to the factory that night. The next was a remarkably clever woman; but I understood afterwards that she
had attempted to poison herself three or four times; she
at last ran away from us, got married on a false certificate,
and a year or two ago was found dead in her bed, through
drink; and I suppose, if I could follow the history of them
up, they would, no doubt, be all much the same.

The great difficulty in dealing with the women was the impossibility of overawing them. The men were dominated by the lash, but practically the only punishment applicable to females was to place them in the penitentiary, or 'Factory', as it was called, at Parramatta near Sydney, of which James Mudie gives his usual colourful and corroborated description:

When a convict ship arrives with females, they are assigned to as many settlers or emigrants as apply. It is generally announced that a convict ship has arrived; in fact, there is a gazette notice, and they apply, and then the women who are not applied for are forwarded to Parramatta, to the place that is called the factory; why it should be called a factory I do not know; the factory is a very large building, something like that of the poor-houses here, an excellent building, with a large garden connected with it, and court-yards; and there the women remain until they are applied for as assigned servants or wives. I have known some of the sailors that have come out in the ship with a convict woman, and taken a fancy to her, get married to her immediately; there is no time required. . . .

Sir George Grey: Is it not in fact notorious, that a number of the female convicts do become with child by male convicts?—Yes; and a great many become with child by their masters.

Is it not equally notorious, that female convicts who become with child are generally sent to this factory, and are there confined?—Yes.

Therefore the fact of illegitimacy of children is a fact of notoriety, and not resting upon particular instances?— Yes, they never think of asking those women who is the father; and if they were to state, they would not be believed; they might state, 'I cannot tell whether it is clergyman so-and-so, or aide-de-camp so and so,' although they never saw the woman.

Chairman: Do female convicts dread being sent to the factory at Parramatta?—The very reverse. . . . I remember particularly one very young woman indeed; I had sentenced her to 10 days' solitary confinement on bread and water, and I said to her, 'You appear a very young woman, and therefore I shall be very lenient with you;' and we generally tell the clerk to look if they have been there before, and I found that she had not. I was sitting in this sort of way, with my hand over my eyes, and I suppose she did not fancy that I saw her; she turned round; and actually spat upon her master. I said 'You appear to be, though young, a very abandoned woman, and I shall give you 30 days instead of 10, on bread and water.' She then said, 'Oh, thank you, I am much obliged to your worship; 30 days; I am very fond of an odd number, would you be kind enough to indulge me, and make it 31 days; do, your worship, I should like to have 31.' I could not give her more than 30, and she knew that well; this was done merely to insult me.

Mudie also shows how Parramatta was the convicts' marriage-mart:

What is the usual mode of a convict getting a wife?— The usual mode is, if they do not marry a convict woman upon the estate where they belong, to be allowed to get a wife from the factory at Parramatta.

Will you state full particulars upon that subject?—If a master has a convict that he is anxious to keep, and whom he believes to be well behaved, it is considered a great indulgence if he gives him permission to get a wife from the factory; but the master must enter into an engagement with the government (and have permission from the government) to feed and support the woman, and, in fact, the offspring, to prevent its being a burden upon the government. This being done, the man goes and gets an order to the matron at the factory, and, of course, that is for a wife. There are a certain number of the women that are not allowed to marry; but with respect to those that are not under punishment, Mrs. Gordon (I have been there and seen the ceremony) says, 'Well, turn out the women of such a class:' they are turned out, and they all stand up as you would place so many soldiers, or so many cattle, in fact, in a fair; they are all ranked up. It is requisite for me to state that the same sort of ceremony and the same mode occur with a free man; for there are free men that go to the factory to select a wife. The convict goes up and looks at the women, and if he sees a lady that takes his fancy, he makes a motion to her, and she steps on one side; some of them will not, but stand still, and have no wish to be married, but that is very rare. Then they have, of course, some conversation together, and if the lady is not agreeable, or if the convict does not fancy her from her conversation, she steps back, and the same ceremony goes on with two or three more. I have known an instance of convicts going and having the pick of 100 or 200 without finding one to please them; the lowest fellows you can fancy have said it would not do; they could not get one to suit. But if he finds one to please him, they get married, and, on returning to his master's estate, he knocks up a hut for himself and his wife, and they live together, when he is not at work; the master allows generally what is called half a ration for the wife, in addition to the man's ration.

How do you find that the wives of those convicts behave?—With few exceptions, very bad; in fact, when the man is out at work, there is a regular trade carrying on. But a great many of them get tea and sugar; in fact, many of the husbands make a boast that they have two bags behind the door, one for tea and another for sugar; and if they find that the two bags are well supplied, they are not particularly jealous; they consider that they ought not to be 'greedy' and that they cannot expect to engross a woman to themselves.

While studying the feminine side of their problem the Committee encountered a very equivocal yet formidable personality—Mr. Ernest Augustus Slade, ex-police magistrate at Sydney.

Among the greatest of transportation evils was the disparity of the sexes in the colony; to remedy this disparity an Emigration Committee had been appointed with Government backing to select young women emigrants of irreproachable character in Britain and ship them to Australia;

the development of this theoretically excellent scheme was described bluntly by a witness:

Do you know what became of the free emigrant women that were sent out by the Female Emigration Society?—From report I have heard that many of them have become prostitutes.

More than one half?—I cannot answer as to the number; in the inquiry which took place before the committee of the legislative council, it appeared that out of one cargo of females, or one expedition, there were 41 that were prostitutes, and turned out to be so before they embarked from England.

Of all the ships which transported these ladies the *David Scott* was the most notorious, and part of the evidence of Mr. Slade showed the kind of dealings which followed. Mr. Slade admitted to the committee that he had been living with a free girl by whom he had a child, and had applied to Mr. Marshall, the superintendent of the *David Scott*, upon her arrival at Sydney, for a domestic servant to help in his irregular ménage. Slade continues the story:

I went on board the ship, then at anchor in the cove; upon my arrival on board that vessel, Mr. Marshall sent for a girl called Lavinia Winter, and upon her arrival in the cabin he said, 'This is the only girl I think I could recommend, as most of the girls I have brought out in the ship are prostitutes or rogues; I cannot give you an irreproachable character of this girl, because she has been guilty of stealing lace on board this vessel, and from the circumstances of her having been brought on board by a person who I have reason to believe was not her father; I consider that she was an illegitimate child, and that the object of the parents in sending her out was the fear that she should be transported.' . . . Whilst she was preparing to go on shore I walked on the deck, when one of the sailors came up and asked permission to land one of the girls; this girl was what would be called pretty; and he said, 'My object in taking away this girl is because she is my cousin, and I wish to take her on shore;' Mr. Marshall

replied, 'Will you pay her passage?' he said 'Yes;' I
replied, 'Mr. Marshall, you little know this colony; I have
little doubt in my own mind that that girl is not the
sailor's cousin, and that his object in taking that girl on
shore is for the sake of prostitution;' Mr. Marshall
replied 'I know that she is a bad girl, but what is that to
me? Our object is merely to obtain the repayment of the
passage money, and as he has promised to pay that money,
I shall consent to the girl landing.' I then took Lavinia
Winter on shore with me. . . .

There follows a sordid story of how Marshall met Slade
in the street and first demanded the girl's passage money
(already paid by the Emigration Committee) and then
accused him of forcibly detaining Miss Winter for prostitution, an accusation which he denied. The incident eventually
cost Slade (whom we shall meet again) his office as third
Police Magistrate. His character, as illuminated by the
evidence from various angles, was probably not unique in
those rough days and shows how authority was occasionally
attracted down to the boundary line of crime.

Early in their inquiry the Committee had grown accustomed to angry condemnations of the activities of the
Emigration Committee and their indignation was evidently
piling up during the eleven months which elapsed before
they examined its members. Apart from minor hesitances
and prevarications Molesworth's Committee met with sur-
prisingly candid and forthright witnesses—until they encountered Mr. John Marshall, Secretary to the Emigration
Committee and not to be confused with the Mr. Marshall
who superintended the emigrants on board the *David Scott*.
From the fine type of the old report one may still clearly
sense the eagerness with which the members of the Committee fell upon this long-awaited witness. They were taut
with cold fury and a remarkable duel took place. When
Marshall was called in it was as if a wily fox had entered, at
his own request, a kennel of experienced and remorseless
hounds:

Chairman: What situation do you hold?—I am engaged at present in the promotion of emigration to New South Wales, and was during the period that the Emigration Committee was in existence, their agent.

Will you state to the Committee, what Emigration Committee you refer to, and when it was first formed, and what your duties were?—The Emigration Committee I refer to was appointed by Government, to select and send out females to the Australian colonies. The committee's existence commenced very early in the year 1833, and terminated by the resignation of the trust confided to them at the close of 1836. May I be permitted, before the Committee put such interrogatories to me as they may think proper, to offer a few preliminary observations. In appearing before this honourable Committee, I deem it due to myself to state, that I do so at my own earnest desire, and that the wish recently expressed to that effect to the Chairman by an honourable Member in the House of Commons, was in accordance with such desire on my part, though not at my immediate instance. This Committee has not now to learn that I appear before them under peculiar circumstances; that I have been for a considerable period attacked in various quarters on the alleged ground, that my responsible duties as the agent of the late Emigration Committee have not been performed with fidelity and uprightness: but that I have abused the influence which, my calumniators assert, I possessed in that station, in inducing the committee to sanction the embarkation of females in the ships sent out by them to the Australian colonies, whose previous habits and character should have excluded them from that privilege; that in consequence many females of known previous disreputable character are stated to have obtained passages to New South Wales, contrary to the wise and benevolent objects which the Government had in view, in appointing the Emigration Committee, to the injury of the colonies, and in violation of my duty as the agent of the committee. To all this and to every allegation which has been levelled at me with reference to the discharge of my duties in the difficult and arduous position

in which I have stood, I give the most unqualified denial;
and I court, on the part of the honourable and enlightened
tribunal, to whose jurisdiction I now respectfully submit
myself, the utmost possible scrutiny into all and every
part of my conduct as the agent of the late Emigration
Committee.

How many ships have the committee, under which you
acted, sent out?—Fourteen ships.

How many females altogether?—There were 4,088
souls, men, women and children, went out in the ships
sent by the Emigration Committee, of which 2,703 were
single females, between the ages of 15 and 30.

The Chairman's clear, cold intellect struck at the witness
from every angle. Back came the answers, always perfectly
phrased, consistent, cool, suave and unctuous:

Upon what principle did you go in selecting the females
you sent out?—The system on which the committee
invariably and strictly acted in the admission of females,
who were candidates for emigration, was as follows: In
every individual instance, where the person applying lived
in London, or within an inconsiderable distance of it, she
was requested to appear personally before the committee
at their office, where they met twice in each week for that
purpose, and to bring with her the best testimonials she
was able to procure, explanatory of the knowledge which
the parties certifying had of her. The committee then personally investigated the circumstances in which the appli-
cant was placed; her means, past and present, of maintaining herself; her connexions; who and what the persons
were who recommended her; and all was done by the
committee which cautious and sensible men could do to
ascertain all the facts essential to enable them to decide
correctly as to her fitness, as a moral and well-ordered
person, to be allowed the bounty of Government. She
was then directed to come again on a fixed subsequent
day; meanwhile a respectable and intelligent individual,
past the meridian of life, who was employed by the committee for that express purpose, took the testimonials,
called on each person who had given them, ascertained

the degree of credit due to their representations, probed every case to the bottom, and then reported, in writing, the result of his investigations in each case; and upon all the circumstances before them, the committee admitted or rejected the party applying. In country cases, no female was ever admitted without such a clear voucher from a minister, or other person of known unexceptionable standing, where she resided, for her moral conduct and habits, as could leave no reasonable doubt on these points; and in every case of a dubious representation, or where the parties were not well known to be quite above lending themselves to deception, the application was uniformly rejected. I am quite at a loss to conceive what more could be done, what more efficient guards, what better practical arrangements could be adopted by sensible and conscientious men for the practical guidance of their conduct, and the best possible working of the important duty devolved upon them.

Were you very careful in examining the characters of the females you sent out?—As careful as it was possible to be.

Did you carefully reject all whom you considered to be mere prostitutes?—It has been stated that prostitutes have not found it difficult to get a passage; I never knew a person that came before the committee that bore the appearance of a street prostitute.

Do you recollect the ship *David Scott*?—I do.

Are you aware, that upon an inquiry directed by the local government of New South Wales, into the character of the young women sent out by the *David Scott*, previous to their distribution, it appeared that out of the total number of 247 emigrants, 41 were common prostitutes?— I am aware that that statement has been made.

Do you doubt that a very considerable portion of them turned out ill?—I do; and I doubt it upon the representations which have been made to me by various persons who came home from New South Wales, from the surgeons of convict ships, and others, who have said that the representations with regard to the number that turned out ill were greatly overcharged.

Then you consider that the statements before this committee, that a considerable portion of them turned out ill, were unfounded?—I do not mean to say that they were unfounded; that they are partly true, I have no right to question. I am not justified in questioning it; but that they were true to the extent alleged, I do not believe.

Were any steps taken by the committee to furnish them with clothing, or to give them any other assistance?—The committee had no funds from which they could supply deficient clothing, but there were instances of individual benevolence, which, if I were at liberty to state, could not but raise the individual members of the committee who displayed those instances very highly in the opinion of every thinking man.

The fund that was formed to assist them was one entirely deriving its source from private charity?—I do not like to blow the trumpet of any such actions I may have done, but I myself expended, upon the average, £100 by every ship that was sent out, to supply deficient clothing; it was no part of my contract to do so, but which I paid for out of my own pocket in order that the women might go in that state, that cleanliness and health would be preserved on board, and that they would be reasonably clothed on their arrival in the colony.

Occasionally damaging admissions were extracted, usually when the questions veered towards financial aspects of Mr. Marshall's activities, but the position was quickly re-established. The Government, it appeared, paid a fixed sum of £17 per head for each emigrant:

To whom was the £17 per head paid?—Sixteen pounds per head was paid to me. Perhaps I had better read to the Committee the contract which I made with the Emigration Committee: 'The terms on which I propose to convey these females out, is £16 per head; £10 per head thereof to be paid on the ship sailing from Gravesend, and £6 per head to be paid by an order from the Secretary of State on the colonial governor of Van Diemen's Land, for such number as may embark, without any deductions for death on the voyage, if any.

Then you were the chief contractor?—The committee contracted with me to supply fit and proper ships, and to equip and victual them in a fit and proper manner at a certain rate per head upon the number the ship actually carried. The contract itself, I will put in, with the permis sion of the Committee.

Had you any salary?—None.

Then your profits were made upon this £30,000 or £40,000, which passed through your hands?—The advantage which I derived from my devotion to the duties 1 undertook, was derived from the difference between the amount it cost and the amount which I received.

You say 'devotion to the duties you undertook.' Those duties were of two different descriptions, the one in selecting the emigrants?—Not in selecting; I did not select in any case.

Did you assist in selecting?—I gave information of the conditions on which only the committee would grant the passage, and it was for the parties themselves applying to comply with those conditions if they could; in other words, 'to satisfy the committee that they were fit and proper persons;' and it was for the committee, in every case, either to admit or reject them, as they saw proper.

It was through you that the recommendations passed, and the correspondence took place?—Through me the correspondence took place, to afford all necessary explanation, but no recommendation ever proceeded from me in any case.

You did not consider yourself in any manner responsible for the description of females that went out?—In no one single instance.

That depended entirely upon the committee?—Solely.

The defence was consummate to the last:

You have stated, in reply to a question from Mr. Hawes, that it was not improbable that the general immorality in New South Wales caused what you consider to be exaggerated complaints of the conduct of the females?—I think it has been a cause.

Do you mean to apply that opinion to the gentlemen

whose testimony has been quoted to you, and to state that you believe that to have been the cause of their sending home those reports which you state were exaggerated?—I am not personally acquainted with any of the individuals whose names have been mentioned, except one, and I am quite incapable, from anything I know of them, to give an opinion as to whether they would be influenced by any particular considerations in giving such a report as they appear to have done. They fill highly responsible situations. I have every reason to believe that they are men of high character and honour, and I cannot allow myself for an instant to have the impression upon my mind, that they would make a statement that they did not quite believe to be true. Beyond that, I know nothing of those individuals, and can only judge as any other individual would do.

Then the opinion you expressed, in answer to the question by Mr. Hawes, does not refer to those gentlemen?—I should be extremely sorry to charge any one of the individuals whose names have been mentioned, as having lent himself to a representation not in his judgment consistent with fact.

With that final masterpiece of effrontery the triumphant fox bowed himself out, but the hunt continued, and the evidence of H. W. Parker, Esq., a member of the Emigration Committee, began to show something rather different from the warm-hearted altruist which Mr. Marshall had represented himself to be:

Did you ever on any occasion, when he (Mr. Marshall) pronounced a female to be fit, reject her?—Yes, certainly.

If Mr. Marshall's judgment had been strictly followed by the committee, more females would have been sent out than were sent?—There would certainly; because those the Emigration Committee rejected, would have been sent out if Mr. Marshall's opinion had been acted upon.

Was it to his advantage to have a good number of females to carry out?—Certainly; or I do not suppose he would have continued it.

And the more female emigrants he had, the better

profit he would obtain?—I can hardly know that ; because he had a certain space allowed him for stores, and those stores I am aware, from consulting the price-current and the Sydney papers, it must have given him an amazing profit, when he had a freight provided for him, which would be the case where the whole ship was not appropriated to emigration purposes.

Were there any complaints made of the arrangements on board ship, or of the supply of food?—Once, on board the *David Scott*. I was not a member of the committee when the *David Scott* went out, but I conducted an examination after she returned. A son of Mr. Gilmore, who was one of the officers on board, complained of the provisions, as well as of the impositions of Mr. Marshall, in respect of the young women who had been put on board. The complaint, with relation to the provisions, was, that the beef had contained more shin bones than the casks ought to have contained; it did not at all affect the quality of the meat. The complaint in respect to the persons put on board was, that Mr. Marshall had sent on board a person between 60 and 70, several between 40 and 50, a great number between 30 and 40, and a great number much below 15; and he had charged the Government as for the passage of persons between 15 and 30. I collected from him the names of the persons he so represented to have been put on board, and I then sent for the books of the committee, and showed him that not one of those persons had been charged for to the Government, and that the committee had allowed Mr. Marshall to send those persons on board, after inquiring as to their character, as usual passengers proceeding on board ship.

Then, in addition to the female emigrants whom Government sent out, the committee allowed Mr. Marshall, in the same vessel, to carry passengers?—The committee were rather desirous, indeed very desirous, to bring the emigration to family emigration; and wherever several young women who were eligible to the bounty presented themselves, they allowed the families, if they could satisfy Mr. Marshall for the passage-money, to proceed on board.

Then suddenly the Committee were confronted once again with Mr. Slade and Lavinia Winter:

I may state the case of Lavinia Winter, on board that ship, as an example of the characters of the young women put on board that ship. She was exposed to very great temptations on her arrival at Sydney.

On what ground do you state this?—On the statement of Lavinia Winter herself, who is now in England. I learnt from Captain Owen, that when he arrived at Sydney, he became acquainted with Mr. Slade, the police magistrate, in consequence of some proceedings relating to his first officer, and that, whilst he was in the police office, Mr. Slade wrote a note to Captain Owen, inquiring whether any young women of good character could be sent to his house, one as cook, and the other as companion to his wife. Captain Owen replied in the affirmative, and Mr. Slade on the evening of that day went on board the vessel, and after taking wine in the cabin with himself and Mr. Marshall, who was the superintendent of the emigrants, had before him several of the women, and he selected Lavinia Winter and another young woman to enter his service. It was not stated at the table by Mr. Slade that he was a married man, but Mr. Marshall and Captain Owen several times spoke of his wife, and said that as Lavinia Winter was a quiet girl, she would not disturb her nor inconvenience her during her confinement. Mr. Slade allowed the whole of this conversation to pass, and then said, as his wife was so unwell, he should take the young woman with him that night. She was lowered into the boat; and as they were leaving the ship, another boat came up with a gentleman, whose name I do not now remember, an acquaintance of Captain Owen's. This gentleman then said to Captain Owen, What is Mr. Slade going to do with that young woman? And Captain Owen replied, that he wants her as a companion to his wife. The observation then was, He is not married; his mistress, when her confinement is over, is going to leave him, and he wants her for the purpose of prostitution. Captain Owen immediately communicated this statement to Mr. Marshall, and they went on shore; but finding some difficultly in proceeding in the matter, they returned, and determined to go to Mr. Slade's house next morning. They went there next morning, and he refused to allow them to see the young woman, or to give her up. They then went to the police-office, and a warrant was refused. They then applied to an attorney, and an application was made to the Supreme Court for a habeas corpus to bring up Lavinia Winter. She was brought up before Mr. Justice Burton; and there the young woman stated that she was not detained by force, and on that Mr. Justice Burton refused to make any order; but the young woman returned to the ship. I have seen her since she returned to England, and she has told me, that she was so flurried and so alarmed at the threats that had been made to her, that she did not know what she said before Mr. Justice Burton, and that she has no doubt that Mr. Slade intended that she should occupy the place of his then mistress; because, when she had left his house, and sent for her clothes, he put three letters into her carpet-bag, requesting her to come and live with him at his house.

But though the hounds continued tireless, their quarries scattered, and in the major hunt the egregious Mr. John Marshall was never finally run down.

*

The fate of those convicts asigned to Government service instead of to a private settler was another lottery. There were many comparatively easy and comfortable jobs such as clerks, messengers and storemen. Some of the best-behaved from each shipload were chosen as sub-overseers and police over their fellows. Others were employed as artisans upon the public works, while the remainder laboured in road parties, unencumbered, or in chain gangs with irons fastened to their ankles, upon the tasks of road-making, timber-felling, etc. Most of those in the road parties had been returned by their masters from assignment as unfit for service or had been convicted of some fresh offence after transportation. Almost all in the chain gangs were under.punishment.

The compassionate Dr. Ullathorne testified as follows:

What is the nature of the road-gangs, and what are their effects upon the persons who are sent to them?—The gangs are employed out of chains on the roads; the effect is of course the same as in all cases where a number of bad men are brought together. Their mutual converse creates mutual corruption, until the best are levelled down to the worst in disposition and corruption.

Has it a tendency to produce an equality in degradation?—Yes, decidedly.

Is the same the case in the chain gangs?—The same in the chain gangs; but the evil result is much greater in the chain gangs, for particular reasons, than in the road-gangs.

Why so; will you state to the committee the particular reasons?—One reason is, the degradation arising from their being in chains, and from the distinguishing dress of degradation; but another very serious evil is, their being packed very closely together at night after their work is over. I remember once visiting a chain gang near Parramatta, on a Sunday, for the purpose of administering religious consolation, and when I came to the gang I found a series of boxes, and when the men were turned out, I was astonished to find the numbers that were turned out of each of those boxes; I could not have supposed that those boxes could have held such a number. I found that they were locked up there during the whole of the Sunday; likewise during the whole of the time from sunset to sunrise. On looking into those boxes I found that there was a ledge on each side, and that the men were piled upon the ledges, and others below on the floor; and I believe from the bringing together of such numbers of men, heated as they are and excited, the consequences are of a very immoral kind. As I left the colony in haste, I put a question to a clergyman, who has had much experience there, as to the space allowed to each convict in those boxes; the answer given was, that the average was about 18 inches each man, but that they varied considerably.

Eighteen inches square?—Yes; there are two shelves, so

that some are piled above and some below. He stated to
me at the same time, that in the hulks he believed it was
not more than 16 inches, and that they were so closely
piled, some 10 or 14 being put in a small cell, that they had
not room to lie on their backs, and were obliged to lie
sideways.

Having described the alternative destinations which
awaited a convict upon arrival in the colonies, let us now
trace his progress. Some got themselves assigned to their
wives or husbands, who had followed them out from England as free settlers. A famous colonial administrator, at that
time Lieutenant-Governor of Van Diemen's Land, Colonel
George Arthur, describes the well-known system of
tickets of leave:

> A ticket-of-leave man receives so much exemption of
> sentence as takes him out of the hands of the principal
> superintendent of prisoners; he works for his own bene-
> fit, but he can only move from one district to another by
> permission; he is subject to attend a muster regularly on
> the first Monday, or one day of every month, and he
> musters to attend Divine Service every Sunday; that, I
> think, terminates his liability.
> Upon what depends his obtaining the ticket-of-leave?—
> A convict has strictly no claim to a ticket-of-leave, but he
> becomes eligible to it, if he were sent out to the colony
> for life, at the termination of eight years.
> If he were sent out for 14 years, how is it then?—He
> is eligible to receive a ticket of leave at the expiration of
> six years; and if sent out for seven years, he is eligible to
> receive a ticket at the expiration of four years.
> Is the condition of the ticket-of-leave men, then, on the
> whole, an agreeable or disagreeable one?—The most
> advantageous one, as a convict, that a man could be
> placed in.

If a convict survived his ticket-of-leave period or served
out his original sentence without mishap, he then became
an 'emancipist', on which the Committee received this

astonishing piece of evidence from the Chief Justice of New South Wales:

> Have not some of the emancipists gained a great amount of wealth?—Very great indeed.
> Some of them have £20,000 or £30,000 a year, I believe?—The richest person in the colony is reputed to have about £40,000 a year.

Regarding emancipists James Mudie as usual gave the most descriptive evidence. He deplored 'the tone of society' which the emancipists set:

> Are they very punctilious in point of honour; are there many duels there?—Very few; there may have been during my fourteen years' residence there perhaps three ór four; I have heard of a good deal of horsewhipping, and a little science and fighting displayed, but very few callings out.
> Yet party runs very high there?—Prodigiously with regard to the emancipists and the free people.
> Is there a marked line of distinction between the emancipists and the free people?—Certainly; I would not invite any of that class to my table. When I went out I had several letters of introduction with me, and I showed these to a friend of mine, and he told me, you must not deliver some of these letters, if you do you will be ruined quite; I asked why; he said, you have got a family of daughters in the colony; these people have been convicts; yet, although they are people of fortune, no one will associate with them.
> Have these people with £10,000 a year the means of getting a service of plate?—I know some of them, the most notorious fellows, and could name them, who have been twice transported in the colonies, have been to penal settlements, have returned and made fortunes afterwards, and sport their plate.
> They must have been well-conducted to have amassed these fortunes?—Quite the reverse.
> How can a man beginning with nothing acquire £20,000 a year, without being an industrious well-conducted man?—I could explain that.

Explain it then?—In the first place, there is a sort of masonry amongst these men. Supposing a free emigrant arrived in Sydney and he was to keep an inn, and a man who had just become free, but only returned from Norfolk Island, was to set up next door to him, or on the opposite side of the street, he would have the whole of the custom, with the exception of the genteeler custom, which they do not wish to have, but what they call the tap custom, fellows who go in and spend £20 or £50 at a sitting. A ticket-of-leave man will drink or spend that at a sitting. . . . A certain ex-convict's house was more frequented by these sort of people than any other in the colony; a great portion of these men would get drunk and remain at his house a day or two (he did not tell me this part of it, I heard it from others, and know it to be correct); he would say, 'Are you aware how much your bill is?' 'No.' 'Perhaps £40 or £50.' 'Why, how is that?' 'You were so drunk you do not recollect what you have been doing; you told me to give a gallon of rum to Peg Such-a-one, a convict woman, and another to such a person.' 'I cannot pay it.' 'Never mind, I must trust you till you come again; in the mean time you must sign this.' He used to keep warrants of attorney ready filled up in his drawer, and these ignorant people used to sign warrants of attorney; and he went on this way till he thought there was a risk in the value of the property they possessed, and then they were sold off; the consequence was that he carried this on for a number of years, until he got possession of a very great portion of the whole cultivated part of the colony at that time.

But supposing the convict turned for a moment off the path of obedience and docility, what was his fate? Colonel Arthur replies:

Now, with regard to the punishment of the assigned convicts, will you inform the committee what the punishment of the assign-convicts is, if they are negligent in the performance of their duties?—I should apprehend that a kind and prudent master is, in the first place, in the habit of admonishing his servants, and that his interest depends very much indeed upon his reforming the servants he has; and I have no reason to doubt, but, on the contrary, I am fully persuaded that a great majority of the settlers in Van Diemen's Land do take pains with their assigned servants, and that they do admonish and advise them; if, however, a prisoner again misconducts himself, and is habitually negligent, he is then taken before a magistrate.

What is the punishment to the convict in that case?— The magistrate punishes him according to the circumstances of the case which are brought under his notice; if his neglect has been of apparently a wilful nature he subjects him, according to the nature and degree of it, either to be whipped or sent to a road party, in or out of chains, according to the nature and the circumstances of the offence.

May he likewise be punished in the same manner for insolence of expression?—Yes, he may.

And for insolence of looks also?—Yes, for insolence in any way whatever it may be. . . .

To explain precisely what flogging meant Mr. Ernest Augustus Slade appeared in his more respectable official character:

You are the son of General Sir John Slade?—I am.

Were you formerly an officer in the British army?—I was an officer in the British army for nine years, and served in the 40th and 54th regiments of foot.

Were you appointed to take charge of the prisoners' barracks in Sydney?— . . . I was appointed by Sir Richard Bourke.

And then what was your appointment?—I then was appointed police magistrate for the town and port of Sydney.

Did you ever receive from Sir Richard Bourke any censure or rebuke respecting your management of the convicts?—I never received any censure from Sir Richard Bourke but in one case. A notorious convict, the greatest scoundrel in the colony, now an emancipist, a Mr. Robert Cooper, notorious for his bad conduct, had two convict servants of his sentenced to receive 50 lashes each. I believe the offence was pilfering. I, as the superintendent of that barrack, was bound to see this punishment carried into effect, and I, being an independent officer, and being anxious to do my duty, was determined to see the law properly administered; the consequence was, that 50 lashes under my superintendence was equal to 1,000 under any other man's ever before in the colony. These men were so flogged that they returned home, and the punishment was sufficient. This man, in reference to that, had influence enough with Governor Bourke to call upon me for an explanation; and although the explanation that I gave to Governor Bourke was so satisfactory that he wrote me back a handsome letter, applauding my conduct, still this man was allowed the indulgence of convict servants.

In spite of some temporary odium Slade's methods of increased severity combined with personal supervision appealed to the governor of New South Wales, Major-General Sir Richard Bourke, who issued the following circular to magistrates and police:

You will have the goodness to superintend, personally, the corporal punishments which shall be inflicted in your district during the ensuing month of September, and report in the column of remarks in the return above alluded to the amount of bodily suffering in every case which the infliction shall appear to have produced, whether evinced by the effusion of blood, or by laceration, or other symptoms of bodily injury. . . .

The subsequent returns show that Mr. Slade had gained his point. Among eighteen cases from Maitland:

Dennis M'Donald, insolence and neglect, 50 lashes: This man's back appeared much lacerated, and the blood appeared at the 20th lash, and continued to bleed much.

Henry Brown, drunkenness, 25 lashes: Back did not appear lacerated, but the offender screamed out greatly.

The floggings supervised and reported by Mr. Slade himself are, as might have been expected, more numerous, detailed and brutal than those of any other official. Between

4th and 30th September, 1833, alone he watched eighty-one 'executions' of which the following are but average samples:

John Lenon, absent one night from barrack without leave; 25 lashes. The skin torn at the eighth, and a slight bleeding at the tenth lash; at the 15th lash the skin was decidedly flayed off, the blood flowing slightly; the flesh much swollen. The severity of this man's punishment was manifest. . . .

Daniel Alone, grossly neglecting his duty; 50 lashes: The prisoner cried loudly at the second, and repeated his cries at every lash; at the 12th lash the blood was flowing largely; the prisoner seemed to suffer intense agony. I am of opinion that this man was sufficiently punished at the 25th lash. . . .

Thomas Holdsworth, pilfering from his master; 50 lashes: At the first lash the prisoner uttered piercing screams, and continued screaming at each succeeding lash, and appeared to suffer greatly; the fifth lash brought blood, and the flesh was considerably lacerated at the conclusion of the punishment. I am of opinion that he was sufficiently punished at the 25th lash, for his bodily strength was nearly exhausted, as was manifested by his staggering gait when cast loose.

Joseph Kenworthy, accessory to pilfering from his master; 50 lashes: The first lash elicited loud cries from this prisoner; at the 18th lash the blood appeared; at the 25th lash the blood was trickling, and at the 32nd flowing down his back; the bleeding continued until the end of the punishment. This man was very severely punished. I am of opinion that he would have been sufficiently punished at the 25th lash. He says he was never flogged before; he was very fat with a thin skin. The sufferings of this prisoner were evinced by his unnerved state of body when cast loose; he could scarcely stand.

Isaac Coates, insubordination; 25 lashes: At every lash this prisoner called loudly for mercy; the blood was drawn but did not flow. He says he was never flogged before; when cast loose he was very pale, and asked permission to sit down, as he felt sick and faint; a sure evidence that his power of endurance of pain had been proved nearly to an extreme.

William Greeg, absent without leave; 25 lashes: This man was punished with 50 lashes about the end of last month, his back was then sore; the unhealed skin broke at the first lash, and at the fourth the blood appeared. This man did not cry out; he is a stout man, and has a thick skin, but the appearance of his back, when the punishment was over, sufficiently proved that he had endured much pain.

Daniel Dickson, disobeying orders; 50 lashes; This man was never flogged before; he cried out loudly at every lash; the skin was lacerated at the 17th lash. He fainted at the 30th lash; he was very severely punished.

Many boys were among Mr. Slade's victims:

John Tree, neglect of duty by feigning sickness, 36 lashes on the breech: at the 11th stroke the blood appeared, and continued running; he cried out loudly at every lash; this was the first time of corporal punishment. This boy suffered most severely; and, in my opinion, 12 lashes would have been sufficient for him.

But even if he felt that the retribution he had drawn down was a shade too heavy, it never appears to have occurred to Mr. Slade to stop the punishment. The effects of flogging, however, were rarely reformatory, as the Revd. Dr. Ullathorne showed:

When a man goes through a scourging once he generally goes through several scourgings. I recollect hearing of a man who had been but three years in the colony, and who had received 1,600 lashes.

Do you think that this brutal punishment tends to produce feelings of vengeance on the part of the convicts towards their overseers, or those who have caused them to be punished?—The feeling of vengeance is general indeed, and much more than would be supposed, because it does not always express itself. . . . I believe if the records of the courts of Australia were consulted, it would be found that a very great proportion of the capital offences arose from the murder of overseers, as a revenge for the evils that they had inflicted upon the parties who murdered them.

Once headed downward, the path usually led by scourgings and the chain gang to one or other of the penal settlements dotted around the shores of Australia and in particular of Van Diemen's Land, established for the express purpose of punishing serious crime committed in the colonies. Among them is Port Arthur, on the Tasman peninsula. At the entrance to the harbour is a peaceful islet, the graveyard of nearly 2,000 convicts. An avenue of English oaks stretches up from the harbour to the now roofless church. Stone buildings stand half-ruined all around, centred by the crumbling powder-house, with sentry towers above and cells below. Seated in the witness-chair in front of the Committee on 19th February, 1838, Assistant-surgeon John Russell described it in its days of terror:

Was there not a chain of dogs, as well as a military post, on the neck of land which runs between Pirate's Bay on the one hand and Storm Bay on the other?—Yes, it was at my recommendation that a military party was first placed there; the neck of land is about 450 yards across; there is a guard of soldiers there under an officer, with lamp-posts and dogs attached, with a deep trench across the neck.

What kind of dogs?—Very fierce, and always kept fed with raw meat.

What, in your opinion, is the effect of the punishment of a penal settlement on the character of the convicts?—I think it hardens them exceedingly, and makes them dead to all sense of honest shame, and careless of trifling punishments.

Did you know of any crimes committed by the convicts for the purpose of getting away from the settlement? —I did.

Crimes of an atrocious nature?—After I left it, there was one man murdered another with a hatchet, I believe for the purpose of getting away. . . .

Was he condemned to death?—He was condemned to death, and executed.

The official regulations for the chain gangs help to explain the wretched men's decision:

> The Chain Gang shall consist principally of convicts who have been sentenced to the gang by the police magistrate, or have been specially sent to the settlement to be worked in chains.

> They are to wear chains and the yellow dress, with the word 'Felon' stamped upon it in several places; they are to sleep in separate cells; they are to go out to work one by one in Indian file, and no conversation is to be allowed among them; they are to be put to the heaviest and most degrading labour than can be found on the settlement. . . .

In the words of the responsible officer:

> The work appointed for them is of the most incessant and galling description the settlement can produce, and any disobedience of orders, turbulence or other misconduct, is instantaneously punished by the lash. . . .

For some convicts, there was one more voyage. Amid scenery which must have reminded them of their homes in England, 16,000 miles away, condemned men from the cells at Port Arthur were rowed over the sparkling harbour to a ship which would carry them round to Hobart Town and death there on the gibbet.

Exhibits in the museum at Hobart form a sombre sort of memorial. There are the paintings of the savage mastiffs, chained nose to nose, each with a barrel kennel and a lantern above it. There are the shapeless grey clothing and caps; the tickets-of-leave and sentences of death; the irons and the chains; the muskets and the cat-o'-nine-tails. But most revealing of all are the photographs of the last convicts. Even though they relate to a much later date, when conditions were ameliorated, the wretched and degraded features, seemingly twenty years older than the actual age, speak more cogently than anything else to the effects of transportation. Worse than Port Arthur was Norfolk Island, far out in the

Pacific. Because this is a natural paradise it is impossible now
to imagine the terror its name once evoked. But it must be
remembered that some future generation will find it equally
hard to associate the gentle climate of Devon with handcuffed men marching in the fog and bloodhounds panting
from a chase. Major Thomas Wright, who was Commandant of the island for a year or two about 1827, described its contrasts:

> When I was there, there were from 200 to 300 prisoners
> under my command; we had 60 or 70 soldiers; we had a
> superintendent of convicts; we had a surgeon, and we had
> a storekeeper, and a superintendent of agriculture, which
> was all, I believe; and there were subordinate people.
>
> What was the description of convicts sent to Norfolk
> Island?—What we term 'out-and-outers'; . . . the greater
> part are what are termed 'transports for life'.
>
> What were the rations allowed to them?—A pound of
> bread and a pound of meat; they had each a garden, and
> therefore were allowed such vegetables as they could pro-
> duce by their own industry; they had a little soap and
> some minute trifles of that kind; soap for cleansing
> themselves.
>
> What mode did you adopt of preserving discipline,
> among them?—The punishment was corporal and im-
> prisonment, and putting them on short rations; diminish-
> ing their rations.
>
> Were any of them worked in irons?—I should think at
> least half of them were worked in irons. . . .
>
> Is Norfolk Island a very fertile island?—It is the most
> beautiful spot I ever saw in the world. . . . It is like a
> paradise.
>
> What is the size of the island?—It is about 15 miles in
> circumference; it is volcanic.
>
> Remote from any other land?— . . . That was the
> cause of its selection, together with its inaccessibility.
>
> Then there was, I suppose, no attempt at absconding
> from Norfolk Island?—Just before I went there the
> prisoners rose and took the island from the preceding
> Commandant, broke down the stockades, murdered the

guard, captured the boats, and the whole body made over
to an island called Phillip's Island, which is about seven
or eight miles off. . . .

Were any other attempts made to take the island?—Yes,
there was an attempt to take the island when I was Commandant; they attempted to murder me and take the island.

Did the convicts commit many offences?—Every
species of offence among themselves, and upon the stores,
and under all circumstances; there was nothing to be got
at to rob that they would not steal.

What was the punishment?—Summary when they were
brought up; the power which I had then was to inflict
50 lashes, or to put them into gaol on short rations; and
the opinion that I entertained when I was there was, that
it was of no use to fellows who had been convicted over
and over again of crimes, for which, if they were committed in England, they would be transported sometimes
for seven or fourteen years; that it would have been an
endless business to send them up to Sydney to be tried,
on every occasion, and I used therefore, to give them
50 lashes, and send them away about their business.

Speaking of a period seven years after Major Wright's
command Dr. Ullathorne concludes the wretched story:

Did you go to administer religious consolation to the
condemned for the conspiracy of 1834?—Yes, I went
under the apprehension that there might be Catholics
amongst them.

Will you briefly state to the committee what that conspiracy was, and the result of it?—It was a conspiracy
amongst the prisoners to take the island from the military,
and to obtain their freedom; that conspiracy was planned
with considerable ingenuity; it was planned that a greater
number than usual of prisoners should report themselves
sick, and those were separated from the rest, and were
placed in a room of the hospital for examination by the
surgeon, others were, on the farm at Longridge, to arm
themselves with the implements of husbandry, and to
proceed down, whilst the third party, who were then proceeding to their labour, should turn upon the guard. The

party which was then proceeding to their labour suddenly assailed the guard, those who were in the hospital broke out, having broken off their chains and the other party was proceeding down, but did not arrive in time; a skirmish ensued, one or two persons were slain upon the spot, and I believe 11 or 12 were dangerously wounded; six or seven died of their wounds afterwards; the consequence was, that a great number of them were implicated in the conspiracy, a commission was sent from Sydney to try them; in this case 31 were condemned to death. Some six months afterwards I proceeded from Sydney for the purpose of attending those who were to be executed, and on board the same ship was a Protestant clergyman likewise.

What did you find was the state of mind of the prisoners under sentence of death?—On my arrival I immediately proceeded, although it was late at night, to the gaol, the commandant having intimated to me that only five days could be allowed for preparation, and he furnished me with a list of the names of the 13 who were to die, the rest having been reprieved; I proceeded therefore to the gaol, and upon entering the gaol I witnessed a scene such as I certainly never witnessed in my life before. The men were confined in three cells.

Mr. Leader: The 31?—The 31; they were then mixed together; they were not aware that any of them were reprieved; I found so little had they expected the assistance of a clergyman, that when they saw me they at once gave up a plot for escape which they had very ingeniously planned, and which might, I think, have succeeded, so far as their getting into the bush; I said a few words to induce them to resignation, and I then stated the names of those who were to die; and it is a remarkable fact, that as I mentioned the names of those who were to die they, one after another, as their names were pronounced, dropped on their knees and thanked God that they were to be delivered from that horrible place, whilst the others remained standing mute and weeping; it was the most horrible scene I have ever witnessed.

Chairman: Then those who were condemned appeared

to be rejoiced?—Those who were condemned; it had been a very common thing with us to find prisoners on their way to the scaffold thanking God that they were not going to Norfolk Island. The Revd. Mr. M'Encroe attended 74 executions in the course of four years, and during that time he remarks, that the greater number, on their way to the scaffold, and upon the scaffold, thanked God that they were not going to Norfolk Island.

Did anything particular strike you with regard to the language of the convicts in Norfolk Island, as evincing a total subversion of all moral ideas and feelings?—I was very much struck indeed with the peculiar language used by the prisoners. When a person has been conversing with me respecting another individual, he has designated him as a good man; I suspected that he did not mean what he said; and on asking an explanation he has apologized, and said that it was the habitual language of the place, and that a bad man was called a good man, and that a man who was ready to perform his duty was generally called a bad man. There is quite a vocabulary of terms of that kind, which seem to have been invented to adapt themselves to the complete subversion of the human heart, which I found subsisting. There has, however, been a considerable reform since that.

In short, by convicts, evil was designated as good, and good as evil?—Yes.

The result of the appalling system was that prisoners no longer feared the death sentence. A later witness described the execution of three men as follows:

Their execution produced a feeling, I should say, of the most disgusting description; the convicts were, on that occasion, assembled around the gallows for the purpose of witnessing the execution; and so buoyant were the feelings of the men who were about to be executed, and so little did they seem to care about it, that they absolutely kicked their shoes off among the crowd as they were about to be executed, in order, as the term expressed by them was, that they might die game; it seemed, as the sheriff described it, more like a parting of friends who were going a distant journey on land, than of individuals who were about to separate from each other for ever; the expressions that were used on that occasion were, 'Good bye, Bob,' and 'Good bye, Jack,' and expressions of that kind, among those in the crowd, to those who were about to be executed.

Some even committed capital crimes to escape from their unendurable agonies. Lt.-Col. Henry Breton, laconic commanding officer of the 4th regiment, was asked:

Do you know anything of the condition of the convict at Norfolk Island?—It is a very miserable condition indeed; they have committed murders to be sent up to Sydney to be hanged.

Even the Chief Justice of New South Wales did not deny the proposition:

Mr. Buller: It is apparently your opinion that transportation may be made one of the most horrible punishments that the human mind ever depicted?—It is my opinion that it may be made more terrible than death. . . . If it were to be put to myself, I should not hesitate a moment in preferring death under any form that you could present it to me, to such a state of endurance as Norfolk Island.

Finally the Committee heard of the vilest settlement of all. John Barnes, surgeon at Macquarie Harbour, told how that penal settlement conducted floggings of exceptional viciousness:

Will you give the committee a description of Macquarie Harbour?—Macquarie Harbour is a large bay, situated on the western coast of Van Diemen's Land, probably about 10 miles in length, and about seven or eight in breadth. There are several small islands scattered about the bay, two of which were occupied as penal settlements. The other islands were generally used, one as a place of burial, another as garden ground, or something of the kind, for the employment of the convicts.

What were the offences for which convicts were sent to Macquarie Harbour?—At the early period of the settlement they were generally . . . drunkenness, disobedience of orders of their masters, neglect of duty, absence from the farm without permission, and petty thefts.

What was the occupation of the prisoners upon those islands?—The occupation was felling timber upon the main; hewing pine, light wood, and myrtle; those were the three valuable kinds of wood which were exported to Hobart Town, and the prisoners were principally employed for that purpose. . . . The most laborious part of the work, that which the convict dreaded the most, was working in water and assisting in building small piers about the island, or any labour of that kind; carrying stones, or even diving for stones, which was frequently an occupation amongst those who could dive.

Was flogging frequent?—Very frequent; daily.

Does it appear (from a return which was handed in to the committee) that on the average of five years there were 245 prisoners, of whom 167 were annually punished by flogging, and that the total number of lashes inflicted was 33,723, and the annual average 6,744?—Yes, that is the statement.

Was the cat with which the floggings were inflicted at Macquarie Harbour of the same description as the ordinary cat-o'-nine-tails?—No, it was a much heavier instrument, and larger; the cat which is generally used in the colony for the punishment of convicts is what is called a single cat, such as is generally employed for the punishment of soldiers and sailors, but that which was used at Macquarie Harbour is what is called a thief's cat, or a double cat-o'-nine-tails; it did not comprise more than the usual number of tails, but each of those was a double twist of whipcord, and each tail contained nine knots; it was a very formidable instrument indeed. . . .

Did you find that the convicts frequently attempted to escape from Macquaire Harbour?—I believe that was their constant desire; a great number of them did escape from Macquarie Harbour, and when ever they had an opportunity they certainly took advantage of it.

16*

Have you a return of the number of convicts who absconded from Macquarie Harbour from the 3rd January 1822 to the 16th May 1827?—Yes, which I copied from the black books of the settlement. From that return it appears that out of 116 who absconded, 75 are supposed to have perished in the woods, one was hanged for murdering and eating his companion, two were shot by the military, eight are known to have been murdered by their companions, six of whom were eaten, 24 escaped, 13 were hanged for bush-ranging, and two for murder; making a total of 101 out of the 116 who came to an untimely fate.

Lord Howick: What is the authority for supposing that 75 perished in the woods?—They never were heard of, and the skeletons of some were found upon the shore, the shore being the only place where they could get food; they went there and frequently perished; sometimes within a mile or a mile and a half of the settlement bodies were found of convicts who, in all probability, were coming to deliver themselves up, and who died from want.

Chairman: Have you a narrative of the case of Pierce?—Yes. . . . This document that I have here is his own statement when he was ill in the hospital, and expecting to die, and it is taken in his own language. There is no alteration whatever; it is just as he described it; it was taken by the clerk of the commandant.

An extract from this remarkable document is enough to impart its flavour. The original party who escaped on 20th September, 1822, was composed, in addition to Alexander Pierce, of John Mathers, Thomas Bodenham, Alexander Dalton, Mathew Travers, Robert Greenhill, Edward Brown and William Cornelius. After a few days wandering:

We were very cold and hungry. Bill Cornelius says, 'I am so weak that I could eat a piece of a man.' Next morning after this, there were four of us for a feast. Bob Greenhill was the first who introduced it, and said he had seen the like done before, and that it eat much like a little pork. Mathers spoke out and said, it would be a murder to do it, and then perhaps could not eat it. 'I will warrant you,' said Greenhill, 'I will well do it first myself and eat the first of it; but you must all lend a hand, so that you may all be equal in the crime.' We then consulted who should fall. Greenhill said, 'Dalton; as he volunteered to be flogger, we will kill him.' Dalton, Brown and Cornelius had a few bushes and made a little break-wind. About three o'clock in the morning, Dalton was asleep; then Greenhill ran and took an axe and struck him on the head, and he never spoke a word after; he called—Mathew Travers with a knife also came and cut his throat, and bled him; we then dragged him to a distance, and cut off his clothes, and tore out his inside, and cut off his head; then Mathew Travers and Greenhill put his heart and liver on the fire and eat it before it was right warm; they asked the rest would they have any, but they would not eat any that night; the next morning it was cut up and divided, and each one got an equal share. . . .

Cornelius and 'little Brown', the weakest member of the party, detected which way the wind was blowing, and staggered back to the settlement, only to die in hospital. Perhaps it was as well for them that they died, for in their pockets they carried pieces of flesh, on one of which was clearly visible a human vaccination pock-mark.

With Dalton killed and eaten the rest of the graceful little group proceeded—and every night or two the axe fell:

John Mathers and deponent went to one side, and Mathers said, Pierce, let us go on by ourselves; you see what kind of a cove Greenhill is, he would kill his father before he would fast one day. We then went on for two or three days after this, through a very fine country, and you could see 70 miles without any bush. We then came to a little creek of fresh water, and a large sugar loaf. We then took and boiled some of Bodenham; Mathers boiled the first, and it made his so sick he then began to vomit. Greenhill started up, and took the axe, and hit him on the forehead; he shouted, 'Murder! Pierce, will you see me killed?' He cut him, but being stronger than Greenhill, he took the axe and threw it to me to keep. We then went on a little further, to another little creek of fresh water, where we took up our lodgings that night. I went to a little distance, and, looking round, I saw Travers and Greenhill collaring him, and they told him they would give him half an hour to pray for himself, which was agreed to; he then gave the Prayer-book to me, and laid down his head, and Greenhill took up the axe and killed him. We then stopped two days in this place. . . .

As their numbers dwindled, life must have presented increasingly exhilarating problems for the survivors—particularly towards the evening. The arrival at a convenient 'little creek' began to have interesting possibilities. At last the powerful figure of Greenhill remained alone with Pierce:

I watched Greenhill for two nights, for I thought he eyed me much more than usual. He always kept the axe under his head when lying down, and carried it on his back in the day-time. One night we came to a little creek, between two hills, where we kindled a fire. I thought he had a bad disposition as to me this night. Near the break of day I found he was asleep; I ran up, and took the axe from under his head, and struck him with it, and killed him; I then took part of his thigh and his arm, and went on for several days after this till all was completely done. . . .

After many adventures Pierce reached civilization. As there was no proof against him beyond his confession, which was not relied on, he was returned to Macquarie Harbour. In the following November he escaped again, this time with a farm-labourer convict named Cox.

*

Five days later, on 21st November, 1823, as the ship *Waterloo* was sailing down the harbour, those aboard her noticed a man on the shore, signalling with a smoking fire.

It was Pierce, anxious to surrender and to confess to murder. There was no question this time of starvation, for his pockets were stuffed with bread, pork and fish; but they also contained a piece of human flesh about half a pound in weight. It was simply a case of preference of taste, for Pierce declared that human meat, and especially the heart, liver and upper arms, was exceedingly delicious. Next day he led a party to his victim's corpse. It was neatly 'dressed' and washed and suspended from a tree, but it was not as a corpse should be found. It was cut in two, 'with the head off, the privates torn off, all the flesh off the calves of the legs, back of the thighs and loins, also off the thick part of the arms; one of the hands was also missing.'

Pierce gave as his reason for giving himself up that he had no hope of ultimately escaping, and that he was so horror-struck at his own inhuman conduct, that he did not know what he was about when he made the signal. The *Waterloo* obligingly carried him on to Hobart, to be tried by the Supreme Court, sentenced to death and executed. But it left behind a ghost, that of a man standing by a smoke-signal on the shore—surely the quintessential product of the misery that was transportation and the ultimate degree of bestiality to which the system reduced its victims.

*

Having examined the nature of transportation and its results upon the prisoners themselves, we may briefly consider its general effect upon the colony. Upon closing the Supreme Court at Sydney in 1835, after a good hundred death sentences had, as usual, been passed, Judge Burton gave a solemn conspectus of the whole question for the benefit of the jury:

> It would appear, to one who could look down upon the community, as if the main business of us all were the commission of crime and the punishment of it; as if the whole colony were continually in motion towards the several courts of justice, and the most painful reflection of

all must be, that so many capital sentences and the execution of them have not had the effect of preventing crime by way of example.

One man particularly had observed, in a manner which drew tears from his eyes and wrung his heart when he was placed before him for sentence, 'Let a man be what he will when he comes here, he is soon as bad as the rest; a man's heart is taken from him, and there is given to him the heart of a beast.'

The Select Committee had completed their investigations except for the effect upon the colony of the only diversion, apart from the sly grog shop, which was open to the convicts. The observant Mudie was once again ready to testify:

Is it a common practice for assigned convicts to cohabit with the native black women?—In the districts, and particularly in the more remote districts, it is quite notorious; you will always find a certain number of them hanging about farms.

Was that the case with your property?—Yes, I used to be tormented with it. When I first went into the district they seemed quite a different class of people altogether in appearance and everything, but the convicts got acquainted with them, and connected of course; and at first there were a great many children of the half-caste; the blacks then were ignorant of the connexion between their wives and the white men, and when a child was produced a half-caste, they used to persuade the blacks that it was owing to the mother having eaten too much white bread, and that it had affected the colour; but latterly the black men became quite acquainted with it, so much so, that they used to make a bargain for a little tobacco or a little provision, and they were quite agreeable.

What is the name the convicts give to the black women? —Gins.

Is the venereal disease common among the native black women?—Extremely so. . . .

By what name does the disease go among the native blacks?—They call it wambush.

Do the natives usually rear or destroy the half-caste

children?—They very often destroy them; in fact, knock their brains out, as you would a cat or dog; and I know an instance upon my farm; I was very much exasperated against the fellow, a black man; his wife was delivered of a child; it was a very small child, and the fellow was in a great rage, and said, 'Narang fellow,' which means 'small fellow;' he took it up at once and dashed it against the wall, as you would any animal.

Was that a half-caste child?—No, he was displeased at the size; whether he thought from that circumstance that it was not his I cannot say.

Sir George Grey: Are they more inclined to kill half-caste children than their own?—No question of it.

Do the natives obtain spirits from the convicts?—Yes.

How do they obtain them?—They would come to my farm and go into the huts, and if the men have any spirits, (it is commonly called 'bull', but in addition they call it 'tumble down') they get it from them; and they are particularly fond of rum and tobacco.

Mr. Lennard: How do they get spirits? What do they give in return?—Nothing but connexion.

That is the only return they have to make?—They have nothing else to give; they are naked, and in remote parts they are just as naked as the cattle; they come into our kitchens perfectly naked.

Sir George Grey: During the 14 years that you were established there, could you trace any perceptible effect upon the character of the blacks from the intercourse that took place between them and the European settlers?— When I first arrived I found them, as far as health and appearance, strong, and they looked healthy and clean, and free from any appearance of disease; but gradually, year after year, young men, who appeared quite young and in the prime of health, became old, and decrepit and diseased; it gradually grew upon them; and I will go further; in all the districts that become inhabited by the Europeans, the blacks always die at a much earlier age than those that live in the bush on what they can get, from the different mode of living, and from the spirits that they get.

*

Thus ended the great inquiry. Six thousand three hundred and forty-seven questions had been asked and answered. A gigantic mass of statements, statistics and tables had been considered. The report created an enormous sensation. It was said that 'probably no volume was ever published in England of which the contents were so loathsome as the Appendix to that report'. When Gibbon Wakefield received a copy he exclaimed optimistically that 'the unclean thing had got its death warrant'. In view of the nature of the evidence it seemed almost superfluous for Molesworth and the Committee to recommend that transportation be ended forthwith.

But not all the members were whole-hearted in their support of this view. Lord Howick remained an impenitent believer in transportation in spite of all that he had heard, and as Colonial Secretary in 1849 stirred the colonists of the Cape of Good Hope to a threat of rebellion by endeavouring to foist it upon them. Certainly within two years transportation to New South Wales was for ever abolished. But a great body of opinion still favoured its retention or was at least neutral. *The Times*, which printed the report in instalments, sneered petulantly at 'these sages' on the Committee, and contrived somehow to find their resolutions 'vague and almost unmeaning suggestions'. Possibly with the story of poor 'Thomson, alias Nutt' in mind they may have expressed the not unnatural feelings of many of their readers:

All moral reform must begin by the careful and religious . . . education of the children of the poor . . . any hope that a man of 20 or 30, bred in vice, and who knows of no duty to others but to steal from them without their knowledge, and of none to himself except to avoid if possible the hulks or the gallows, will by some moral conjuration all at once become right-principled is as baseless as it would be for a surgeon to expect to make an adult, distorted and hump-backed from his infancy, as straight and shapely as an Apollo.

From another quarter the Committee received less encouragement than they might have hoped. Lord Glenelg, the Secretary for the Colonies, gave no assistance. He was an extremely religious man and a philanthropist, but his method of administration was 'doing nothing reduced to a system'. In spite of his private virtues he earned the unenviable reputation of being the worst Colonial Secretary of the nineteenth century. Molesworth's attacks in support of his report never flagged. Although the general system of transportation did not long survive its condemnation by the great inquiry, it lingered in Western Australia till 1867. It was continued also in Van Diemen's Land until, in 1852, that island refused at last to act any longer as a cesspool for the home country and three years later marked its aversion to its own past by changing its name to Tasmania.

Popular and even judicial opinion sometimes favours a return to harder penalties for crime; the evidence of Molesworth's Committee may still have some value in demonstrating the ultimate stages which deterrent punishment may attain.

For Molesworth the end of the inquiry was but an incident in the zestful pageant of his life. He was soon at work upon a monumental edition of the works of the philosopher Hobbes, and supporting Lord Durham's mission to Canada, which was to issue in the celebrated Durham Report. In the matter of the reform of colonial government, as in so much else, Molesworth was a generation in advance of his time. It was the work of his life. He never doubted that to be truly loyal the colonies must be truly free, and he strove unceasingly for colonial self-government. He lived to see constitutions granted to the Australian colonies, and, at a time when these dependencies had earned the title of 'the opprobrium of the Empire', to say with far-seeing wisdom, 'I feel convinced that if the Colonies were governed as they ought to be, they would gladly and willingly come to the aid of the mother country in any just and necessary war.'

In 1844 Molesworth married. Having been twice prevented by his reputedly extreme opinions from marrying within his class he chose to marry outside it. Andalusia

Temple West was a widow with 'exceedingly gentle, caressing manners', who had been an actress and was consumed by social ambition. The marriage cost him friends and may have been the cause of a sudden change from a secluded mode of life to one of ceaseless social activity, which, combined with intense intellectual efforts, can but have strained a constitution which hardly knew the meaning of health. It was thus perhaps a double gratification for him when Lord Aberdeen offered him the First Commissionership of Works with a seat in the Cabinet in 1852. With characteristic courage he braved the anger of the Sabbatarians and gratified all subsequent generations of the public by throwing open Kew Gardens on Sundays. In July 1855 he became Secretary of State for the Colonies, thus achieving his life's ambition, a crowning social position for his wife, and an apparent future of unlimited usefulness for himself. Three months later, with every glittering prospect of service and happiness before him, he died of utter exhaustion at the age of forty-five.

Today Molesworth is almost forgotten, yet in the matter of transportation alone, though many others helped, it can be said of him so far as it can be said of any man, that by his own hand he slew a monstrous dragon.

VIII

CASES PENDING

This same truth is a naked and open daylight.
FRANCIS BACON.

FEELINGS OF indignation are easily aroused by the conditions which these reports reveal. But an age in which such cruelties existed was also an age with enough courage to make fearless investigation of them. Parties both of the right and of the left could lay claim to men who achieved reform by unwearying inquiry through the time-honoured method of question and answer. Their success was largely due to the excellence of the parliamentary machine and to the prestige attaching to reports from committees appointed by Parliament.

The clarity with which the evidence of these committees invests the subject of inquiry is remarkable. 'The system of transportation was productive of horrible cruelties and fearful abuses', say the history books, and their words scarcely impress our minds at all. But when we have witnessed Ernest Augustus Slade gloating as his victims writhe under the lash, Marshall selling off his emigrant girls, Pierce standing at last sick with self-disgust upon the shore —then indeed transportation stands naked before us.

At times the clashes between Select Committees of Parliament and some of the witnesses they examined are equal in dramatic interest to the famous trials of British history. The latter were usually concerned with but one victim and one culprit; but Select Committees have often attacked hundreds and defended thousands. Their powers have proved especially valuable in cases where no law has technically been infringed but where fundamental decencies have been disregarded. Again, where questions of fact and questions of principle in some broad problem of general interest seem inextricably confused, a Select Committee has not seldom proved the best of all arbiters. In spite of contemporary criticisms on the ground of partiality, there are few published records which maintain their authority unchallenged from century to century as do the more notable of the reports of Select Committees. Their work is not yet finished. Until humanity is perfect there will always be matters demanding inquiry—cases pending.

FINIS